TULSIDAS

तुलसीदास

# THE EPIC OF RAM

VOLUME 3

Translated by
PHILIP LUTGENDORF

MURTY CLASSICAL LIBRARY OF INDIA

HARVARD UNIVERSITY PRESS

Cambridge, Massachusetts

London, England

2018

SERIES DESIGN BY M9DESIGN

*Library of Congress Cataloging-in-Publication Data*

Tulasidasa, 1532–1623.
The epic of Ram / Tulsidas ; translated by Philip Lutgendorf.
volume cm. — (Murty Classical Library of India ; 15)
In English and Awadhi on facing pages.
Includes bibliographical references and index.
ISBN 978-0-674-42501-9 (cloth : alk. paper) (vol. 1)
ISBN 978-0-674-08861-0 (cloth : alk. paper) (vol. 2)
ISBN 978-0-674-97501-9 (cloth : alk. paper) (vol. 3)
I. Lutgendorf, Philip, translator.
II. Tulasidasa, 1532–1623. Ramacaritamanasa. English.
III. Tulasidasa, 1532–1623. Ramacaritamanasa. IV. Title.
PK1947.9.T83R313 2016
891.4'312—dc23     2015016322

# CONTENTS

# INTRODUCTION

## *The* Rāmcaritmānas *and Tulsidas*

The *Rāmcaritmānas* (Divine lake of Ram's deeds) by Tulsidas is among the most beloved and revered works of Indian literature.[1] An epic poem composed in Hindi in the late sixteenth century, the *Mānas* rapidly acquired the renown and sanctity usually reserved for compositions in Sanskrit, the ancient and elite "language of the gods." Over the next three centuries its fame grew steadily, spread by oral expounders, itinerant singers, and scholarly exegetes, some of whom were patronized by the princely rulers of the Indo-Gangetic Plain. In the colonial era, British scholars and administrators recognized it as "the Bible of Northern India" and "the best and most trustworthy guide to the popular living faith of its people."[2] In the twentieth century it assumed an important place in the emerging Hindi literary canon, inspired major works by modernist poets, and was regularly quoted during India's freedom struggle by Mohandas Gandhi, who wrote that he considered it "the greatest book of all devotional literature."[3] Later its impact was enhanced by the release of millions of inexpensive printed copies, by performances available on records, audiocassettes, and compact discs, and by a television serialization partially based on it that held much of India spellbound in 1987–1989. A comprehensive early twenty-first-century study of the development of Hindi literature assesses the *Mānas* as "a defining work of

Indian culture" and concludes that it "remains the leading vernacular scripture of north India today."[4]

A retelling of the ancient and popular tale of Ram and Sita, which first appeared in literary form in Valmiki's Sanskrit epic *Rāmāyaṇa* (last centuries B.C.E.), the *Mānas* belongs to a long tradition of works that recast the narrative in distinctive ways. Despite the prestige accorded to the Sanskrit archetype, subsequent retellings never favored literal translation. Instead, poets and storytellers working in Sanskrit, various Prakrits, and later regional literary vernaculars of southern and northern India exercised great freedom in crafting original versions that, while preserving the basic characters and outline of the narrative, introduced significant innovations. The result was a multiform oral and literary tradition that, although sometimes encompassed by the generic label "Ramayana," may better be termed *Rāmakathā*, or "Rama storytelling." Tulsidas's own version emerges from an influential current in this vast river of story, imbued with the ideology of "sharing" in or devotion to—*bhakti* is the Indic term—a personal god or goddess and the emotional, public worship of that deity.

A poet of extraordinary versatility and vision, Tulsidas is celebrated as the author of a dozen works, most of which are dedicated to Ram, and which collectively advance a theology in which Ram is adored as the supreme, transcendent God to whom other revered Hindu deities are ultimately subordinate. Through his writings and his legendary biography, Tulsidas has come to exert a profound and perhaps unsurpassed influence on the ideology and practice of popular Hinduism throughout much of northern and central India and beyond, including several communities of the Indian diaspora. Not surprisingly, a figure of such stature is also, in certain contexts, controversial; his works have been subject to vastly differing interpretations, and there are few details of his biography that have not been contested, beginning with his date of birth (variously posited as 1497, 1526, and 1543—the last being favored by the majority of modern scholars); a death date of 1623 is widely accepted. He was evidently literate—a few manuscripts survive that may be in his own hand—and seems to have received a classical Sanskrit education that was, in his day, generally the prerogative of the Brahman caste. Some of his works hint at autobiographical details, and three include dates of composition, indicating that he was active during the reigns of the Mughal emperors Akbar and Jahangir. There is evidence that he spent a good part of his life in Banaras, regularly participated in the public performance of devotional texts, including his own, and was supported in part by the offerings of appreciative listeners. His name means "servant of tulsi," referring to the "holy basil" plant considered especially pleasing to Vishnu, and thus signals the poet's likely initiation into a Vaishnava religious order or guru lineage, -*dās* being a common suffix for initiatory names in several orders. The poet himself often shortens this name to "Tulsi" in his poetic "signature" (*chāp*, or *bhaṇitā*). Yet although he has been proudly claimed by a number of branches of one ascetic order (the Ramanandis), Tulsi's formal affiliation has never been proven to the satisfaction of nonsectarian scholars. He does not seem to have established a sect, yet he came to be revered in his own life-time as a *gosāī,* or "master"; today "Goswami" (in its stan-dard Anglicized spelling) is typically prefixed to his name to indicate his status as preceptor and exemplar to millions.

Tulsi's most celebrated work, the *Rāmcaritmānas,* bears a date of composition corresponding to 1574. It comprises roughly 12,800 lines, divided into 1,073 "stanzas" set within seven sections, which early manuscripts simply denote as numbered "stairs" or "stairways" (*sopāna*)—"first stair," "second stair," and so on—descending into the allegori-cal Manas Lake to which the title alludes (1.36–43). Later tradition has given them additional names as *kāṇḍs,* or sub-books, that reflect the architecture of the *Vālmīki Rāmāyaṇa.* But apart from its basic storyline, the *Mānas* bears only an occasional direct resemblance to Valmiki's poem. Instead, drawing creatively on many sources, Tulsi retells the story of Ram, as he says, "for his own inner joy" (1.0.7), through a set of four interlocking dialogues that ingeniously frame the epic tale. The conversations between the gods Shiva and Parvati, the Vedic sages Yajnavalkya and Bharadvaj, the immortal crow Bhushundi and the divine eagle Garuda, and finally the discourse of Tulsidas to his presumed audience, interwoven throughout much of the text, are announced in the allegory of Lake Manas as its framing banks, or ghats. To traditional commentators, they suggest four distinct "points of view" from which the epic tale may be interpreted, even as they invoke a lineage of transmission that encourages future interpretive performances. A vibrant tradition of such performances— by storytellers and singers, and by amateur and professional actors who mount annual drama cycles collectively known as *Rāmlīlā* ("Ram's play")—has existed for centuries and remains influential in many parts of India today.

### *The* Ayodhyākāṇḍ *in the* Rāmcaritmānas

Although the "second stair" of Tulsi's epic soon acquired, in manuscripts, the same name as the second sub-book of Valmiki's classical poem, the Sanskrit name of Ram's capital city—Ayodhyā ("unassailable")—never appears in *Ayodhyākāṇḍ.* Instead, as in *Bālkāṇḍ,* the city ruled by the Raghu dynasty of kings is always referred to as "Avadh"—the name favored in the premodern Hindi dialect in which the *Mānas* is composed, which is itself known as Avadhi, "the speech of Avadh."

Like *Bālkāṇḍ,* the second sub-book may also be divided thematically into nearly equal halves, and it is similarly offered, in this dual-language edition, in two volumes. The first half, presented here, tells the story of Ram's exile from Avadh. Accompanied by his wife, Sita, and brother Lakshman, Ram is exiled on the very day set for his consecration as heir-apparent to the throne of King Dasarath, his father, owing to the scheming of his stepmother Kaikeyi and her maid, Manthara. The story then follows their journey of exile through the Kosala kingdom (of which Avadh is the capital) and into the wilderness that lies beyond its boundaries, in the course of which they have emotional encounters with villagers, tribal people, and sages. The first half ends with their settling down in a semipermanent hermitage near the beautiful hill of Chitrakut. The second half of the sub-book (presented as volume 4 of this translation) focuses on Ram's younger half-brother Bharat, Kaikeyi's son, who was absent from the kingdom during the events leading to Ram's exile. On his return, Bharat disavows his mother, refuses the kingship that has been secured on his behalf, and undertakes an anguished and penitential pilgrimage to the forest of Chitrakut, accompanied by the entire court and much of the city's population, to plead with Ram to return and assume the throne.

Comprising 326 stanzas (sets of verses primarily in the meters *caupāī* and *dohā*), the *Ayodhyākāṇḍ* nearly equals the length of the first sub-book, *Bālkāṇḍ* (361 stanzas), and between them, these two great "stairs" constitute roughly three-fifths of the total epic.[5] However, they show notable differences in both metrical structure and predominant *rasa,* or emotional mood. The stanzas of *Bālkāṇḍ* vary considerably in their number of *caupāīs,* their concluding *dohās* sometimes come in clusters of two or more, and there are frequent occurrences of *chand* quatrains (which, with their longer lines and complex patterns of internal and end rhyme, are the most lyrical of *Mānas* verse forms), reaching an ecstatic climax in the description of Ram and Sita's wedding festivities with which that sub-book concludes. *Ayodhyākāṇḍ,* in contrast, is as regular in metrical structure as it is, for the most part, somber and poignant in mood. Its repeated alternation of eight lines in *caupāī* meter with a single capping *dohā* is hardly ever varied, and the rare intrusion of *chand* quatrains is similarly regular, occurring every twenty-five stanzas.[6]

Yet if the experience of *darśan*—the beautiful and

auspicious vision of God, embodied as Ram and Sita—offered by the second sub-book is less uniformly happy than that found in the first, it is nonetheless powerfully conveyed. Many lovely and stirring passages muse on the incongruence and theological irony of the avatar or divine incarnation's acceptance of exile from his home and his wandering in the wilderness, or celebrate his unexpected accessibility to rustic villagers and tribal hunters and gatherers, who exult in his compassionate and uplifting presence. Given the prominence of such themes, it is not surprising that the second sub-book of the *Mānas* has been so admired, both by traditional audiences and, in the nineteenth and early twentieth centuries, by British administrators and Christian clergy stationed in India, who saw in Tulsi's Ram a Christlike figure, admirable both in his own right and also as an antidote to what they typically viewed as less noble divine archetypes in the Hindu pantheon.[7]

## Narrative Tradition and Innovation

Scholarship on Tulsidas and on the probable genesis of his epic has emphasized the influence on the poet of a number of Sanskrit-language sources, most prominently the primordial and revered *Rāmāyana* of Valmiki and the *Adhyātmarāmāyana* (Esoteric Ramayana), a fifteenth-century retelling strongly influenced by the Advaita, or nondualist, philosophical tradition. Though these influences are no less apparent in *Ayodhyākāṇḍ*, they are complemented by numerous innovations that highlight Tulsidas's psychological insight, poetic brilliance, and devotional fervor. As in the *Adhyātmarāmāyaṇa*, Tulsi introduces the non-Valmikian plot device of having the gods conspire to "pervert" the mind of Queen Kaikeyi's hunchbacked maidservant, Manthara, to get her to convince her mistress to demand Bharat's enthronement and Ram's banishment. The celestials accomplish this with the reluctant assistance of Sharada (Sarasvati), goddess of speech and intelligence, who "enters" or possesses the maid. Once this deus ex machina is introduced, however, Tulsi's account of the events leading up to Ram's departure preserves, with characteristic economy of language, much of the psychological realism and hints of family tension found in Valmiki's version. His portrayal of the saucy, clinching speech with which the hunchback manipulates Kaikeyi into abandoning her affectionate loyalty to Ram is both deliciously perverse and psychologically plausible (see 2.16). Similarly, King Dasarath's abject infatuation with his junior queen is effectively captured in his wheedling but chilling pledge to execute anyone she happens to dislike: "I can slay even an immortal, if he is your foe / never mind wretched, worm-like men and women!" (2.26.2).

The poignancy of Ram's exile is conveyed with similar poetic power. Among the words that often recur in the first half of this *kāṇḍ* are *byākula* and *bikala,* two variants on a Sanskrit adjective signifying "distraught, anguished"— the mental and emotional state to which Ram's departure reduces the king, royal family, courtiers, citizens, and even the animals and birds of Avadh. However, the mood of tragedy is tempered by both metaphysical reflection and devotional fervor. Another passage that shows the evident influence of the *Adhyātmarāmāyaṇa* occurs on the second night of exile, when Lakshman dispassionately instructs the tribal chief Guha, who is overcome at the sight of Ram and Sita sleeping on the ground, about the illusory nature of worldly life and on Ram's supreme divinity (2.92.2–94.1; compare *Adhyātmarāmāyaṇa* 2.6.4–15). This famous lecture, delivered in "sweet, gentle words, / imbued with wisdom, dispassion, and devotion's nectar," and popularly known as "Lakshman Gita," for its evocation of Krishna's battlefield instruction to Arjuna in the *Mahābhārata,* presents a different side of Ram's devoted younger brother, in contrast to the impulsive and sometimes hotheaded figure portrayed in Valmiki's version.

After the exiles cross the Ganga and move farther away from Avadh city, Tulsidas offers an innovative and touching account of their journey that dwells at length on their emotional interactions with villagers, other wayfarers, and, in one abruptly interpolated stanza (that nevertheless appears in the oldest surviving manuscripts), a mysterious and enraptured young ascetic. This young man, some commentators maintain, may actually be Tulsi himself, and the passage may be an account of a vision granted to the poet when, as a young renouncer, he was wandering through this very region (see 2.110.4–111.3). The great expansion of the section describing the exiles' journey prefigures the similarly emotional pilgrimage of Prince Bharat in the second half of the sub-book, but it also suggests Tulsi's delight in the landscape and folkways of his own native region in the eastern Ganga valley, which he believed Ram, Sita, and Lakshman had sanctified with their footsteps.

## Acknowledgments

I am grateful to Rohan Murty for his generosity and to the production staff of Harvard University Press for the extraordinary care and diligence they have brought to the production of this translation series. I thank general editor Sheldon Pollock and coeditor Francesca Orsini for offering me the opportunity to undertake this translation and for their subsequent guidance. I also thank Eliot Weinberger and Linda Hess for additional helpful suggestions, and Shrinath Mishra, a revered *rāmāyaṇī* (traditional *Mānas* scholar) of Banaras, for his generous help and encouragement, and Pranav Prakash and Justin Ben-Hain for their careful editing and proofreading of the Devanagari text. Among early mentors who guided me toward this work, I gratefully cite Professors Emeritus Kali Charan Bahl and Colin P. Masica of the University of Chicago.

I dedicate this translation to Meher Baba, who inspires me; to the many *Mānas* scholars and devotees who have instructed and encouraged me; and to the memory of three dear mentors and friends—Ramji Pande, A. K. Ramanujan, and Chandradharprasad Narayan Singh ("Bhanuji").

### NOTES

1 For a more detailed general introduction to the *Mānas* and its author, see volume 1 of this translation (Lutgendorf 2016: vol. 1, vii–xxii).
2 Macfie 1930; Growse 1978: xxxviii.
3 Gandhi 1968: 47; on the role of the *Mānas* in the emerging Hindi literary canon, see Orsini 1998.
4 McGregor 2003: 917–939.
5 Additional information about the metrical structure of the

*Mānas* is given in the introduction to volume 1 of this translation (Lutgendorf 2016: vol. 1, xviii–xx). Readers should note that, in citations of specific verses, the poem's stanzas are referenced by the numbers of their sub-book and concluding *dohā*, with any additional number referring to a *caupāī* or *chand* that precedes the numbered *dohā*. Thus "2.25.3" refers to the third *caupāī* preceding *dohā* number 25 in *Ayodhyākāṇḍ*.

6    There occur just thirteen *chands* in the entire *Ayodhyākāṇḍ*, none exceeding a single quatrain in length.

7    George Grierson praised the *Mānas* for having "saved the country from the tantric obscenities of Shaivism," and F. S. Growse, in the introduction to his 1891 translation (the first complete one into English), held that "the purity of its moral sentiments ... render it a singularly unexceptionable text-book for native boys" (Grierson 1977: 2; Growse 1891 [1978]: lv). Growse also observed that, of the epic's sub-books, *Ayodhyākāṇḍ* was the most popular in his day, despite its length, slow pace, and the obscurity of certain passages (Growse 1891 [1978]: lvii); for a discussion of the problem of obscurity, see the introduction to volume 4 of this translation.

# NOTE ON THE TEXT
# AND TRANSLATION

Despite its prestige and popularity, the *Rāmcaritmānas* has not been accorded a truly critical edition, which might yet be assembled from careful comparative study of (reportedly) surviving manuscripts dating to the first hundred years after its composition. Copies of some of these were in the possession of celebrated *Mānas* expounders of the nineteenth century and became the basis for published versions, edited by them and issued by the new vernacular presses of the period. Differences among these were (by the standards of premodern Hindi literature) comparatively minor but of course much debated, and in the twentieth century three more authoritative and scholarly editions attempted to resolve them—though none could claim to have adhered to the standards followed, for example, in the long-term projects to reconstruct the early texts of the Sanskrit *Rāmāyaṇa* and *Mahābhārata*.[1] The first of these, issued by the industrious Gita Press of Gorakhpur and accompanied by a readable gloss in Hindi, has become, by default, the standard edition of the epic, and has been used by every translator since Growse, including me. However, I also constantly consult the most elaborate and celebrated of published commentaries, *Mānaspīyūṣ* (Nectar of the *Mānas*), which incorporates the insights of many traditional scholars of the nineteenth and twentieth centuries. It, too, uses the Gita Press edition as basic text, but it periodically offers variant readings from manuscripts and older published editions. When such variations seem significant, I explain this in an endnote, as I do in the (very rare) instances in which I adopt a variant reading in preference to that found in the Gita Press version.

Readers may note occasional discrepancies between the Avadhi of Tulsidas's Devanagari text and the transliteration scheme adopted for characters' names in the translation, notes, and glossary. Thus, "Shankar," one of the common names of the god Shiva, appears as *sankara* (in its Devanagari equivalent) in the original text and in any notes that quote it directly, but as "Shankar" (the common, modern Hindi pronunciation) in the translation. Standard Sanskritic transliteration (e.g., *śaṅkara*), used in much scholarly writing, is additionally offered in the glossary.

The *Rāmcaritmānas* has already seen nine complete English translations.[2] Although this is not surprising for such an influential scripture—the *Bhagavadgītā* can boast of more than two hundred—it is more than have been accorded any other long premodern vernacular work in the Indian tradition. Why, then, a tenth? The obvious reason, of course, is to try to improve on them. Seven of the translations are into prose, and although two of them have considerable merit (Growse's is spirited and Hill's is admirably accurate), they all produce an effect that is on the whole turgid and "prosaic"—a sad fate for a poem that regularly urges the "singing" of its lines, and whose rhythmic recitation has been moving audiences for more than four centuries. On the other hand, two complete rhyming-verse renditions (by Atkins and Satya Dev), though certainly labors of love and tours de force in their way, take unfortunate liberties with the meaning of the verses in order to produce a metrical effect that often sounds jangling and trite, like a Victorian greeting card.

The challenges inherent in rendering the *Mānas* in English have been noted before.[3] As a devotional work intended for episodic oral performance, the text seems repetitious when set in a linguistic medium that is normally experienced through individual, silent communion with the printed page, and its frequent use of formulaic phrases (though common in epic poetry worldwide) may appear redundant and saccharine—for example, "eyes filling with tears" and "limbs thrilling with love" (the latter, one choice for the nearly untranslatable *pulak*—in plain English, "goose bumps" or the dismally medical "horripilation"; besides "thrilling," I sometimes use "trembling," "quivering," "flushed," or "shivering"), and the poet's often-repeated assertion that some person, place, event, or emotion "cannot be described," which he usually follows with its very apt description. Some of Tulsi's apparent "repetitiveness," however, actually reflects the great asymmetry in lexicons between the two languages. English has more than one verb for "seeing"—the most important and recurrent act in which *Mānas* characters engage, especially "seeing" the unworldly beauty of Ram and Sita—but it does not have (as I have counted in *Bālkāṇḍ* alone) fourteen. Similarly, one can think of several synonyms for the adjective "beautiful"—but not the twenty-two, each slightly different, that Tulsi deploys to convey the overwhelming visual attraction of his divine characters and their world. And, like "camel" in the Arabic lexicon, "lotus" in the *Mānas* is not a single word—rather, it is, by my count, twenty-nine, each nuanced and suited to different contexts of meaning, meter, rhyme, and alliteration. Tulsi's vocabulary is indeed immense, and he is often credited with having expanded the lexicon of what would become modern Hindi through his revival and adaptation of Sanskrit loanwords; no Sanskrit chauvinist, he also used, according to a recent count, more than ninety Arabic and Persian ones.[4] In English, much of this verbal richness (to echo the poet) simply "cannot be expressed."

What, then, is my impetus and aim in this new translation? My own engagement with the epic began more than three decades ago, after several periods of travel in north India made me realize the extent to which the *Mānas* was ingrained in its living culture. In my initial study of the text as a graduate student, I was fortunate to have a teacher who insisted that I learn to chant its verses aloud to simple melodies—a skill that I have since shared with many students, because I know that it enhances both enjoyment and understanding of the work.[5] My first book grew out of that in-class "performance" and examined the many ways in which the *Mānas* "lives" in its cultural context. My first effort at translation of a section of the epic—its beloved "Fifth Stair," *Sundarkāṇḍ*—came much later.[6] Although I was not altogether happy with it, I loved the opportunity it gave me to engage deeply with the poem and (imaginatively) with its author. It was also my first sustained attempt at what, following the commission and editorial guidelines of the Murty Classical Library of India, I am now attempting to do for the complete epic: produce a straightforward, readable, free-verse rendering in contemporary language. I readily concede that most of the enchanting music of Tulsidas—his rhyme, alliteration, and almost hypnotic rhythm—is lost in my version. What I seek to preserve, as much as possible, is clarity, compactness of expression, and a certain momentum. I am especially happy to be contributing to a dual-language version, and I hope that serious readers, even if they do not know Hindi, might at least acquire facility with its easy, phonetic script so that they can begin to sound out the lines of the original—for truly, there is verbal magic in every stanza of the *Mānas*.

NOTES

1   The three scholarly editions are Poddar 1938, Mishra 1962, and Shukla et al. 1973.
2   A list appears in the bibliography.
3   Growse 1978: lvii–lviii; Hill 1952: xx; Lutgendorf 1991: 29–33.
4   McGregor 2003: 938; Stasik 2009.
5   I would like to pay tribute to my University of Chicago mentors, Kali Charan Bahl (who taught me to chant the *Mānas*) and Colin P. Masica (who helped me understand its cultural impact). A. K. Ramanujan and Wendy Doniger were also inspirations, both as scholars and translators.
6   Lutgendorf 1994, 1995, 2001.

# The Epic of Ram

*An Enthronement Thwarted*

# अयोध्याकाण्ड

१ यस्याङ्कें च विभाति भूधरसुता देवापगा मस्तके
भाले बालविधुर्गले च गरलं यस्योरसि व्यालराट् ।
सोऽयं भूतिविभूषणः सुरवरः सर्वाधिपः सर्वदा
शर्वः सर्वगतः शिवः शशिनिभः श्रीशङ्करः पातु माम् ॥

२ प्रसन्नतां या न गताभिषेकतस्तथा न मम्ले
वनवासदुःखतः ।
मुखाम्बुजश्री रघुनन्दनस्य मे सदास्तु सा
मञ्जुलमङ्गलप्रदा ॥

३ नीलाम्बुजश्यामलकोमलाङ्गं
सीतासमारोपितवामभागम् ।
पाणौ महासायकचारुचापं नमामि रामं
रघुवंशनाथम् ॥

० श्रीगुरु चरन सरोज रज निज मनु मुकुरु सुधारि ।
बरनउँ रघुबर बिमल जसु जो दायकु फल चारि ॥

# INVOCATION

May he, at whose left side shines[1]                                      1
the mountain's daughter, on his head, the gods' river,
on his brow, the new moon,
with poison in his throat, serpent on his breast,
who is adorned with ash, foremost of gods
and eternal overlord of all,
destroyer and end of everything—may he,
moon-bright Shiva, Lord Shankar, protect me.

May that countenance, which showed neither delight       2
at royal consecration nor dismay at forest exile,
may that lotus-like face of the Raghus' joy
forever bless me.

To him—of tender limbs dusky as a blue lotus,               3
with Sita radiant at his left side,
with mighty arrows and lovely bow in his hands—
to Ram, lord and master of the Raghu clan, I bow in
      homage.[2]

Having polished the mirror of my heart                            0
with the dust of my guru's holy feet,
I recount the flawless fame of the Raghu lord,
which grants all four of life's fruits.[3]

१ जब तें रामु ब्याहि घर आए ।
नित नव मंगल मोद बधाए ॥
भुवन चारिदस भूधर भारी ।
सुकृत मेघ बरषहिं सुख बारी ॥

२ रिधि सिधि संपति नदीं सुहाई ।
उमगि अवध अंबुधि कहुँ आई ॥
मनिगन पुर नर नारि सुजाती ।
सुचि अमोल सुंदर सब भाँती ॥

३ कहि न जाइ कछु नगर बिभूती ।
जनु एतनिअ बिरंचि करतूती ॥
सब बिधि सब पुर लोग सुखारी ।
रामचंद मुख चंदु निहारी ॥

४ मुदित मातु सब सखीं सहेली ।
फलित बिलोकि मनोरथ बेली ॥
राम रूपु गुन सीलु सुभाऊ ।
प्रमुदित होइ देखि सुनि राऊ ॥


१ सब कें उर अभिलाषु अस कहहिं मनाइ महेसु ।
आप अछत जुबराज पद रामहि देउ नरेसु ॥


१ एक समय सब सहित समाजा ।
राजसभाँ रघुराजु बिराजा ॥
सकल सुकृत मूरति नरनाहू ।
राम सुजसु सुनि अतिहि उछाहू ॥

Ever since Ram came home wedded, his realm     1
enjoyed endless auspiciousness and rejoicing.
On the lofty summits of the fourteen worlds
virtue-clouds rained torrents of happiness
while rivers of prosperity and spiritual attainment     2
streamed in full flood into Avadh's sea.
Its men and women were treasuries of gems,
flawless, priceless, and most beautiful.
The city's splendor, surpassing description,     3
seemed the very apex of Brahma's craft.
Its citizens found all-fulfilling joy
in gazing on the face of the Raghu moon.
With their friends and maids, the royal mothers rejoiced     4
to see the vine of their yearnings bear fruit.
Ram's beauty, nobility, and gracious disposition,
observed and reported, delighted the king.

In everyone's heart was this longing,     1
which they voiced in prayers to Shiva—
"May the ruler of men, while alive and well,
make Ram his heir-apparent."[4]

One day, amid all his courtiers,     1
the Raghu king sat in his assembly hall.
That ruler of men, embodiment of merit,
was thrilled to hear of Ram's renown.

२ नृप सब रहहिं कृपा अभिलाषें।
लोकप करहिं प्रीति रुख राखें॥
तिभुवन तीनि काल जग माहीं।
भूरि भाग दसरथ सम नाहीं॥

३ मंगलमूल रामु सुत जासू।
जो कछु कहिअ थोर सबु तासू॥
रायँ सुभायँ मुकुरु कर लीन्हा।
बदनु बिलोकि मुकुटु सम कीन्हा॥

४ श्रवन समीप भए सित केसा।
मनहुँ जरठपनु अस उपदेसा॥
नृप जुबराजु राम कहुँ देहू।
जीवन जनम लाहु किन लेहू॥


२ यह बिचारु उर आनि नृप सुदिनु सुअवसरु पाइ।
प्रेम पुलकि तन मुदित मन गुरहि सुनायउ जाइ॥


१ कहइ भुआलु सुनिअ मुनिनायक।
भए राम सब बिधि सब लायक॥
सेवक सचिव सकल पुरबासी।
जे हमारे अरि मित्र उदासी॥

२ सबहि रामु प्रिय जेहि बिधि मोही।
प्रभु असीस जनु तनु धरि सोही॥
बिप्र सहित परिवार गोसाईं।
करहिं छोहु सब रौरिहि नाईं॥

All earthly kings yearned for his favor      2
and the world-guardians lovingly awaited his command.[5]
In creation's three worlds, past, present, and future,
none was as fortunate as Dasarath,
whose son was Ram, root of all blessing.      3
Whatever one says of him will fall short!
That king chanced to take a mirror in hand
to adjust his crown, and glanced at his face.
Above his ears, the hair had gone white,      4
as if old age was offering this counsel:
"King, why not make Ram your appointed heir,
and reap the full reward of your birth and long life?"

Keeping this thought in mind,      2
the king awaited a propitious day and time.
With happy heart and body flushed with joy,
he went to inform his guru.

The king said, "Sovereign of sages,      1
Ram has become worthy in every way.
Attendants, ministers, and all citizens,
averse, friendly, or indifferent to me,
all cherish Ram just as I do, and it seems      2
that your blessing, lord, is embodied in him.
The Brahmans and their kin, master,
all love him, too, as much as you do.

7

३ जे गुर चरन रेनु सिर धरहीं ।
ते जनु सकल बिभव बस करहीं ॥
मोहि सम यहु अनुभयउ न दूजें ।
सबु पायउँ रज पावनि पूजें ॥

४ अब अभिलाषु एकु मन मोरें ।
पूजिहि नाथ अनुग्रह तोरें ॥
मुनि प्रसन्न लखि सहज सनेहू ।
कहेउ नरेस रजायसु देहू ॥

३ राजन राउर नामु जसु सब अभिमत दातार ।
फल अनुगामी महिप मनि मन अभिलाषु तुम्हार ॥

१ सब बिधि गुरु प्रसन्न जियँ जानी ।
बोलेउ राउ रहँसि मृदु बानी ॥
नाथ रामु करिअहिं जुबराजू ।
कहिअ कृपा करि करिअ समाजू ॥

२ मोहि अछत यहु होइ उछाहू ।
लहहिं लोग सब लोचन लाहू ॥
प्रभु प्रसाद सिव सबइ निबाहीं ।
यह लालसा एक मन माहीं ॥

३ पुनि न सोच तनु रहउ कि जाऊ ।
जेहिं न होइ पाछें पछिताऊ ॥
सुनि मुनि दसरथ बचन सुहाए ।
मंगल मोद मूल मन भाए ॥

Lowly ones who bear the dust of gurus' feet ⁣ 3
on their brows hold sway over all splendor,
and none knows this better than I,
who, adoring that holy dust, have attained all.
Now but one wish remains in my heart, ⁣ 4
and that, too, by your grace, will be fulfilled."
The sage was pleased by his sincere love,
and said, "Command me, ruler of men.

Your Majesty's very name and renown ⁣ 3
themselves grant all desired boons,
and fulfillment, jewel of kings, but duly follows
any wish of your heart."[6]

Knowing his guru to be entirely pleased, ⁣ 1
the king said happily, in a gentle voice—
"Master, make Ram our young king!
Graciously order me to prepare for
this celebration while I still live, ⁣ 2
to give all my people their eyes' reward.
By your grace, Shiva has granted all my wishes,
yet this one yearning remains in my heart.
Achieving it, I will have no care if this body stays ⁣ 3
or goes, nor have cause for later regret."
When the sage heard Dasarath's welcome words,
blessed and delightful, he was pleased.

४ सुनु नृप जासु बिमुख पछिताहीं ।
जासु भजन बिनु जरनि न जाहीं ॥
भयउ तुम्हार तनय सोइ स्वामी ।
रामु पुनीत प्रेम अनुगामी ॥

४ बेगि बिलंबु न करिअ नृप साजिअ सबुइ समाजु ।
सुदिन सुमंगलु तबहिं जब रामु होहिं जुबराजु ॥

१ मुदित महीपति मंदिर आए ।
सेवक सचिव सुमंत्रु बोलाए ॥
कहि जयजीव सीस तिन्ह नाए ।
भूप सुमंगल बचन सुनाए ॥

२ जौं पाँचहि मत लागै नीका ।
करहु हरषि हियँ रामहि टीका ॥

३ मंत्री मुदित सुनत प्रिय बानी ।
अभिमत बिरवँ परेउ जनु पानी ॥
बिनती सचिव करहिं कर जोरी ।
जिअहु जगतपति बरिस करोरी ॥

४ जग मंगल भल काजु बिचारा ।
बेगिअ नाथ न लाइअ बारा ॥
नृपहि मोदु सुनि सचिव सुभाषा ।
बढ़त बौंड़ जनु लही सुसाखा ॥

"King, he whose foes alone endure regret,         4
and without worshiping whom, anguish never ends—
that very Lord has become your son,
for Ram faithfully follows pure love.

Now, lord of men, quickly and without delay        4
make all necessary preparations.
Auspicious will be that very day
when Ram becomes our young king!"[7]

Returning happily to his palace, the king        1
called his servants and the minister Sumantra.
They bowed, saying, "Live long, be victorious!"
and the lord of earth told them the blessed news.
"If this course pleases my council, then[8]        2
with glad hearts prepare Ram's consecration."
The minister rejoiced to hear these words,        3
like a sapling receiving much-needed water.
With palms joined, he prayed,
"Live for a million years, lord of earth!
You conceive an act to benefit the whole world,        4
so make haste, master, do not delay."
The king was pleased by the minister's speech,
like a reaching vine that finds a sturdy branch.

५ कहेउ भूप मुनिराज कर जोइ जोइ आयसु होइ।
राम राज अभिषेक हित बेगि करहु सोइ सोइ ॥

१ हरषि मुनीस कहेउ मृदु बानी।
आनहु सकल सुतीरथ पानी ॥
औषध मूल फूल फल पाना।
कहे नाम गनि मंगल नाना ॥

२ चामर चरम बसन बहु भाँती।
रोम पाट पट अगनित जाती ॥
मनिगन मंगल बस्तु अनेका।
जो जग जोगु भूप अभिषेका ॥

३ बेद बिदित कहि सकल बिधाना।
कहेउ रचहु पुर बिबिध बिताना ॥
सफल रसाल पूगफल केरा।
रोपहु बीथिन्ह पुर चहुँ फेरा ॥

४ रचहु मंजु मनि चौकें चारू।
कहहु बनावन बेगि बजारू ॥
पूजहु गनपति गुर कुलदेवा।
सब बिधि करहु भूमिसुर सेवा ॥

६ ध्वज पताक तोरन कलस सजहु तुरग रथ नाग।
सिर धरि मुनिबर बचन सबु निज निज काजहिं
लाग ॥

The protector of earth said, "Each and every order     5
of that king of sages, Vasishtha,
for Ram's royal consecration,
carry out promptly and precisely."

Well pleased, the supreme sage said softly,     1
"Bring water from all the holy places."
Healing herbs, roots, flowers, fruits, and leaves
of many auspicious kinds he named, one by one,
and fly whisks, deerskins, diverse garments,     2
and countless woolens, silks, and cottons,
gems, and other sacred substances—
whatever in the world is fit to consecrate a king.
He described all the steps set out in the Veda,     3
saying, "Erect numerous pavilions in the city,
and plant fruit-bearing trees—mango, betel,
and banana—along the lanes in every quarter.
Make lovely square designs of gemstones,[9]     4
and order all the markets quickly decorated.
Worship Ganesh, the guru, the clan deity,
and in every way serve Brahmans, the earthly gods.

Decorate banners, pennants, arches, vessels,     6
horses, chariots, and elephants."
Revering the command of that best of sages,
they all set about their respective tasks.

१	जो मुनीस जेहि आयसु दीन्हा ।
सो तेहिं काजु प्रथम जनु कीन्हा ॥
बिप्र साधु सुर पूजत राजा ।
करत राम हित मंगल काजा ॥

२	सुनत राम अभिषेक सुहावा ।
बाज गहागह अवध बधावा ॥
राम सीय तन सगुन जनाए ।
फरकहिं मंगल अंग सुहाए ॥

३	पुलकि सप्रेम परसपर कहहीं ।
भरत आगमनु सूचक अहहीं ॥
भए बहुत दिन अति अवसेरी ।
सगुन प्रतीति भेंट प्रिय केरी ॥

४	भरत सरिस प्रिय को जग माहीं ।
इहइ सगुन फलु दूसर नाहीं ॥
रामहि बंधु सोच दिन राती ।
अंडन्हि कमठ हृदउ जेहि भाँती ॥

७	एहि अवसर मंगलु परम सुनि रहँसेउ रनिवासु ।
सोभत लखि बिधु बढ़त जनु बारिधि बीचि बिलासु ॥

१	प्रथम जाइ जिन्ह बचन सुनाए ।
भूषन बसन भूरि तिन्ह पाए ॥
प्रेम पुलकि तन मन अनुरागीं ।
मंगल कलस सजन सब लागीं ॥

14

Whatever order the great sage gave to anyone                    1
was as if completed even before it was given!
The king worshiped Brahmans, sadhus, and gods,
doing auspicious deeds for Ram's sake.
Hearing the glad news of Ram's consecration,                    2
the city of Avadh erupted in celebration.
Ram and Sita felt bodily portents
as their auspicious limbs began to throb.[10]
Shivering with love, they told one another,                     3
"This must foretell Bharat's return!
Many days have passed, and we are so anxious,
yet these signs affirm a dear one's coming,
and who in the world is as dear as Bharat?                      4
Nothing else can be the fruit of these omens!"
Ram's concern for his brother, day and night,
was as heartfelt as a mother turtle's for her eggs.

Hearing these supremely good tidings,                           7
the women of the royal household exulted,
as the ocean's wave-play is enhanced
by the sight of the waxing moon.

The first to come bearing the news                              1
received heaps of jewelry and garments.
Trembling with love, their hearts aglow,
the queens prepared auspicious vessels.

२ चौकें चारु सुमित्राँ पूरी ।
मनिमय बिबिध भाँति अति रूरी ॥
आनँद मगन राम महतारी ।
दिए दान बहु बिप्र हँकारी ॥

३ पूजीं ग्रामदेबि सुर नागा ।
कहेउ बहोरि देन बलिभागा ॥
जेहि बिधि होइ राम कल्यानू ।
देहु दया करि सो बरदानू ॥

४ गावहिं मंगल कोकिलबयनीं ।
बिधुबदनीं मृगसावकनयनीं ॥

८ राम राज अभिषेकु सुनि हियँ हरषे नर नारि ।
लगे सुमंगल सजन सब बिधि अनुकूल बिचारि ॥

१ तब नरनाहँ बसिष्ठु बोलाए ।
रामधाम सिख देन पठाए ॥
गुर आगमनु सुनत रघुनाथा ।
द्वार आइ पद नायउ माथा ॥

२ सादर अरघ देइ घर आने ।
सोरह भाँति पूजि सनमाने ॥
गहे चरन सिय सहित बहोरी ।
बोले रामु कमल कर जोरी ॥

16

Sumitra traced lovely sacred squares                2
and filled them with various gemstones.
Ram's mother, Kausalya, lost in bliss,
summoned Brahmans and gave lavish gifts.
Propitiating local goddesses, gods, and serpents,            3
she pledged them future offerings:
"Whatever will ensure Ram's well being,
by your mercy, grant me as a boon."
Songs of blessing were sweetly intoned             4
by fair-faced, doe-eyed women.

When they heard of Ram's royal consecration,            8
the townsmen and women rejoiced,
and all began auspicious preparation,
confident that fate was in their favor.

Then the ruler of men summoned Vasishtha            1
and sent him to Ram's abode to give instruction.
At word of his guru's coming, the Raghu lord
came to the door and bowed at his feet.
Presenting a welcoming drink, he brought him in            2
and honored him with the sixteen courtesies.[11]
With Sita, Ram once more touched the guru's feet,
then spoke, his lovely palms joined in reverence:

३ सेवक सदन स्वामि आगमनू ।
मंगल मूल अमंगल दमनू ॥
तदपि उचित जनु बोलि सप्रीती ।
पठइअ काज नाथ असि नीती ॥

४ प्रभुता तजि प्रभु कीन्ह सनेहू ।
भयउ पुनीत आजु यहु गेहू ॥
आयसु होइ सो करौं गोसाईं ।
सेवकु लहइ स्वामि सेवकाईं ॥

९ सुनि सनेह साने बचन मुनि रघुबरहि प्रसंस ।
राम कस न तुम्ह कहहु अस हंस बंस अवतंस ॥

१ बरनि राम गुन सील सुभाऊ ।
बोले प्रेम पुलकि मुनिराऊ ॥
भूप सजेउ अभिषेक समाजू ।
चाहत देन तुम्हहि जुबराजू ॥

२ राम करहु सब संजम आजू ।
जौं बिधि कुसल निबाहै काजू ॥
गुरु सिख देइ राय पहिं गयऊ ।
राम हृदयँ अस बिसमउ भयऊ ॥

३ जनमे एक संग सब भाई ।
भोजन सयन केलि लरिकाई ॥
करनबेध उपबीत बिआहा ।
संग संग सब भए उछाहा ॥

"The entry of a master into a servant's home                    3
is a source of blessing that destroys evil.
Though it would be right to fondly summon
this humble one, lord, for your work,
you show us affection, relinquishing your high station,         4
and today this house is sanctified.
Whatever you order, master, I will do,
for a servant's good lies in service to his lord."

Hearing these words, imbued with affection,                     9
the sage praised that best of Raghus:
"What wonder, Ram, that you would speak so,
for you are crown jewel of the solar line."

Praising Ram's innate goodness and nobility,                    1
the king of sages spoke, trembling with love:
"The lord of earth has arranged a consecration rite,
for he wishes to designate you as young king.
So today, Ram, observe all obligatory restraints,[12]          2
that Brahma may grant fulfillment of this task."
 Having instructed him, the guru returned to the king,
but Ram felt dismay in his heart, musing,
"We four brothers were all born at one time,                    3
we ate, slept, and played together as boys.
Ear-piercing, thread ceremony, marriage—
we were always together in all joyous rites.

४ बिमल बंस यहु अनुचित एकू ।
बंधु बिहाइ बड़ेहि अभिषेकू ॥
प्रभु सप्रेम पछितानि सुहाई ।
हरउ भगत मन कै कुटिलाई ॥

१० तेहि अवसर आए लखन मगन प्रेम आनंद ।
सनमाने प्रिय बचन कहि रघुकुल कैरव चंद ॥

१ बाजहिं बाजने बिबिध बिधाना ।
पुर प्रमोदु नहिं जाइ बखाना ॥
भरत आगमनु सकल मनावहिं ।
आवहुँ बेगि नयन फलु पावहिं ॥

२ हाट बाट घर गलीं अथाई ।
कहहिं परसपर लोग लोगाई ॥
कालि लगन भलि केतिक बारा ।
पूजिहि बिधि अभिलाषु हमारा ॥

३ कनक सिंघासन सीय समेता ।
बैठहिं रामु होइ चित चेता ॥
सकल कहहिं कब होइहि काली ।
बिघन मनावहिं देव कुचाली ॥

४ तिन्हहि सोहाइ न अवध बधावा ।
चोरहि चंदिनि राति न भावा ॥
सारद बोलि बिनय सुर करहीं ।
बारहिं बार पाय लै परहीं ॥

20

In our noble family, this alone seems wrong—      4
that the eldest is consecrated without his brothers."[13]
May this heartfelt regret, felt by the Lord,
banish suspicion from the minds of devotees.

Just then, Lakshman arrived,      10
delirious with loving joy,
and was fondly greeted
by the moon of the lilies of the Raghu line.

Outside, all kinds of instruments resounded      1
as the city's rejoicing surpassed description.
Everyone prayed for Bharat's arrival:
"May he come soon and gain his eyes' reward."
In markets and streets, in homes and squares,      2
men and women asked one another,
"At what time tomorrow will that moment come
when God fulfills our yearnings,
when, with Sita, on a golden throne,      3
Ram sits, and our hearts are sated?"
Everyone said, "Oh, when will tomorrow come?"
But the devious gods were plotting an obstruction.
They were not charmed by Avadh's festivity,      4
as a burglar does not relish a moonlit night.
They summoned Sharada* and begged of her,
falling again and again at her feet.

---

* Sarasvati, goddess of speech and intelligence.

११  बिपति हमारि बिलोकि बड़ि मातु करिअ सोइ आजु ।
  रामु जाहिं बन राजु तजि होइ सकल सुरकाजु ॥

१  सुनि सुर बिनय ठाढ़ि पछिताती ।
  भइउँ सरोज बिपिन हिमराती ॥
  देखि देव पुनि कहहिं निहोरी ।
  मातु तोहि नहिं थोरिउ खोरी ॥
२  बिसमय हरष रहित रघुराऊ ।
  तुम्ह जानहु सब राम प्रभाऊ ॥
  जीव करम बस सुख दुख भागी ।
  जाइअ अवध देव हित लागी ॥
३  बार बार गहि चरन सँकोची ।
  चली बिचारि बिबुध मति पोची ॥
  ऊँच निवासु नीचि करतूती ।
  देखि न सकहिं पराइ बिभूती ॥
४  आगिल काजु बिचारि बहोरी ।
  करिहहिं चाह कुसल कबि मोरी ॥
  हरषि हृदयँ दसरथ पुर आई ।
  जनु ग्रह दसा दुसह दुखदाई ॥

१२  नामु मंथरा मंदमति चेरी कैकइ केरि ।
  अजस पेटारी ताहि करि गई गिरा मति फेरि ॥

"Behold our awful affliction, mother,                                   11
and take such action today
that Ram will leave the kingdom and go to the forest,
and all the gods' work will be done."

Hearing the gods' plea, she mused ruefully,                            1
"Am I to be night-frost on a lotus-lake?"
Seeing this, the gods again supplicated her:
"Mother, you will not be faulted in the least.
The Raghu lord is beyond grief and happiness,                          2
and you fully understand Ram's greatness.
But souls in karma's grip partake of pleasure and pain,[14]
so go to Avadh for the gods' sake."
They repeatedly clasped her feet. Abashed,                             3
she left, thinking, "The gods are mean-minded.
Lofty in station but lowly in deeds,
they cannot bear to see another's glory."
But thinking again of the task ahead, she mused,                       4
"Great poets will surely commend me for this,"
and arrived, content, in Dasarath's city,
like some woe-giving planetary conjunction.

Queen Kaikeyi had a dull-witted maid                                    12
by the name of Manthara.
Choosing her as a vessel of infamy, Lady Speech
entered her and perverted her wits.

१ दीख मंथरा नगरु बनावा ।
मंजुल मंगल बाज बधावा ॥
पूछेसि लोगन्ह काह उछाहू ।
राम तिलकु सुनि भा उर दाहू ॥

२ करइ बिचारु कुबुद्धि कुजाती ।
होइ अकाजु कवनि बिधि राती ॥
देखि लागि मधु कुटिल किराती ।
जिमि गवँ तकइ लेउँ केहि भाँती ॥

३ भरत मातु पहिं गइ बिलखानी ।
का अनमनि हसि कह हँसि रानी ॥
ऊतरु देइ न लेइ उसासू ।
नारि चरित करि ढारइ आँसू ॥

४ हँसि कह रानि गालु बड़ तोरें ।
दीन्ह लखन सिख अस मन मोरें ॥
तबहुँ न बोल चेरि बड़ि पापिनि ।
छाड़इ स्वास कारि जनु साँपिनि ॥

१३ सभय रानि कह कहसि किन कुसल रामु महिपालु ।
लखनु भरतु रिपुदमनु सुनि भा कुबरी उर सालु ॥

१ कत सिख देइ हमहि कोउ माई ।
गालु करब केहि कर बलु पाई ॥
रामहि छाड़ि कुसल केहि आजू ।
जेहि जनेसु देइ जुबराजू ॥

Manthara marked the city's decorations        1
and the tumult of auspicious, celebratory songs.
She asked, "What's all this excitement?"
and hearing, "Ram's consecration," she flared up.
That wicked-minded, lowborn one pondered        2
how this might be undone that very night,
like a sly tribal woman who spies a honey-hive
and devises a stratagem to bring it down.
She went wailing to Bharat's mother,        3
and the queen asked, laughing, "What's the trouble?"
Without replying, she heaved great sighs
and used female wiles to make her tears flow.
The queen chuckled, "You are very cheeky,        4
and I'll bet Lakshman has taught you a lesson!"
Yet still that sinful servant did not speak,
but only puffed like a black she-cobra.

Alarmed, the queen asked, "Why do you not speak?        13
Is all well with Ram and the king,
with Lakshman, Bharat, and Shatrughna?"
Hearing this tore at the hunchback's heart.

"Why would anyone bother to scold me, mother,        1
and on whose authority could I assume airs?
And who is well today except for Ram,
whom the master of men is making young king?

२ भयउ कौसिलहि बिधि अति दाहिन ।
देखत गरब रहत उर नाहिन ॥
देखहु कस न जाइ सब सोभा ।
जो अवलोकि मोर मनु छोभा ॥

३ पूतु बिदेस न सोचु तुम्हारें ।
जानति हहु बस नाहु हमारें ॥
नीद बहुत प्रिय सेज तुराई ।
लखहु न भूप कपट चतुराई ॥

४ सुनि प्रिय बचन मलिन मनु जानी ।
झुकी रानि अब रहु अरगानी ॥
पुनि अस कबहुँ कहसि घरफोरी ।
तब धरि जीभ कढ़ावउँ तोरी ॥

१४ काने खोरे कूबरे कुटिल कुचाली जानि ।
तिय बिसेषि पुनि चेरि कहि भरतमातु मुसुकानि ॥

१ प्रियबादिनि सिख दीन्हिउँ तोही ।
सपनेहुँ तो पर कोपु न मोही ॥
सुदिनु सुमंगल दायकु सोई ।
तोर कहा फुर जेहि दिन होई ॥

२ जेठ स्वामि सेवक लघु भाई ।
यह दिनकर कुल रीति सुहाई ॥
राम तिलकु जौं साँचेहुँ काली ।
देउँ मागु मन भावत आली ॥

Fate has indeed been kind to Kausalya,       2
and to see this fills her heart with pride.[15]
Just go look at all the decorations
which have so disturbed my mind.
Your son is abroad, yet you are unconcerned,      3
for you suppose your lord to be in your power.
Too fond of sleep on your downy bed,
you don't perceive the king's wily scheming."
Hearing good news and knowing her maid's mean nature,  4
the queen scolded her, "Now, be quiet!
If you ever speak like this again, house-wrecker,
I will have your tongue ripped out.

The one-eyed, lame, and hunchbacked      14
are known to be twisted and perverse,
especially women—and moreover, a serving-maid!"
So Bharat's mother said, but then smiled.

"Sweet-talker, I merely chide you,      1
for I could never be angry with you.
It will be the best and most blessed day
when your words become reality.
Elder brother as lord, junior as servant—      2
this is the noble precedent of the solar line.
If Ram is truly anointed tomorrow,
my dear, I will give you anything you ask!

३ कौसल्या सम सब महतारी ।
रामहि सहज सुभायँ पिआरी ॥
मो पर करहिं सनेहु बिसेषी ।
मैं करि प्रीति परीछा देखी ॥

४ जौं बिधि जनमु देइ करि छोहू ।
होहुँ राम सिय पूत पुतोहू ॥
प्रान तें अधिक रामु प्रिय मोरें ।
तिन्ह कें तिलक छोभु कस तोरें ॥

१५ भरत सपथ तोहि सत्य कहु परिहरि कपट दुराउ ।
हरष समय बिसमउ करसि कारन मोहि सुनाउ ॥

१ एकहिं बार आस सब पूजी ।
अब कछु कहब जीभ करि दूजी ॥
फोरै जोगु कपारु अभागा ।
भलेउ कहत दुख रउरेहि लागा ॥

२ कहहिं झूठि फुरि बात बनाई ।
ते प्रिय तुम्हहि करइ मैं माई ॥
हमहुँ कहबि अब ठकुरसोहाती ।
नाहिं त मौन रहब दिनु राती ॥

३ करि कुरूप बिधि परबस कीन्हा ।
बवा सो लुनिअ लहिअ जो दीन्हा ॥
कोउ नृप होउ हमहि का हानी ।
चेरि छाड़ि अब होब कि रानी ॥

Just like Kausalya, all we mothers 3
are truly and naturally dear to Ram,
but he shows special affection to me,
as I have observed by testing his love.
If the creator is kind, in my next birth, 4
let Ram be my son, Sita, my daughter-in-law!
Ram is dearer to me than my breath,
so why does his consecration disturb you?

I swear on Bharat: renounce your guile 15
and evasion, speak the truth,
and tell me the real reason why
you cast gloom on this happy occasion."

Manthara said, "Just once, I gave vent to all my hopes. 1
Now I had better speak with a different tongue.
My luckless skull deserves to be smashed
if my well-meant words caused you grief.
Those who spin lies to deceive 2
please you, mother, whereas I seem harsh.
Now I, too, will affect fawning speech,
or else just keep silent, day and night.
First fate made me ugly, then dependent— 3
but one reaps as one sows, tit for tat.
Whoever becomes king, what will I lose?
Will I cease to be a maid or be made queen?[16]

४  जारै जोगु सुभाउ हमारा ।
   अनभल देखि न जाइ तुम्हारा ॥
   ताते कछुक बात अनुसारी ।
   छमिअ देबि बड़ि चूक हमारी ॥

१६ गूढ़ कपट प्रिय बचन सुनि तीय अधरबुधि रानि ।
   सुरमाया बस बैरिनिहि सुहृद जानि पतिआनि ॥

१  सादर पुनि पुनि पूँछति ओही ।
   सबरी गान मृगी जनु मोही ॥
   तसि मति फिरी अहइ जसि भाबी ।
   रहसी चेरि घात जनु फाबी ॥

२  तुम्ह पूँछहु मैं कहत डेराऊँ ।
   धरेहु मोर घरफोरी नाऊँ ॥
   सजि प्रतीति बहुबिधि गढ़ि छोली ।
   अवध साढ़साती तब बोली ॥

३  प्रिय सिय रामु कहा तुम्ह रानी ।
   रामहि तुम्ह प्रिय सो फुरि बानी ॥
   रहा प्रथम अब ते दिन बीते ।
   समउ फिरें रिपु होहिं पिरीते ॥

४  भानु कमल कुल पोषनिहारा ।
   बिनु जल जारि करइ सोइ छारा ॥
   जरि तुम्हारि चह सवति उखारी ।
   रूँधहु करि उपाउ बर बारी ॥

30

My nature needs a thorough purging,                              4
for I can't bear to witness your misfortune.
That is why I spoke out a little,
mistress—pardon my great indiscretion!"

At these wily, allusive, and flattering words,                   16
the queen, with a woman's wavering mind
and in the grip of divine maya,
took this foe for a friend, and trusted her.

Humbly, she questioned her time and again,                       1
like a deer entranced by a hunter-woman's call,
for if fate ordains, good sense is overthrown.
Sensing her chance, the maidservant rejoiced.
"You ask, yet I am fearful of speaking,                           2
for you have labeled me a home-wrecker."
Thus whittling away at her, firming her trust,
Avadh's malefic star at last declared,[17]
"Queen, you say you love Sita and Ram,                           3
and Ram loves you—all well and true
once, in the past, but those days are over!
When times change, dear ones become foes.
The very sun that nurtures lotuses,                              4
without water, burns them to ash.
Your co-wife wants to uproot you—
protect yourself with a fence of stratagems.

१७ तुम्हहि न सोचु सोहाग बल निज बस जानहु राउ ।
मन मलीन मुह मीठ नृपु राउर सरल सुभाउ ॥

१ चतुर गँभीर राम महतारी ।
बीचु पाइ निज बात सँवारी ॥
पठए भरतु भूप ननिअउरें ।
राम मातु मत जानब रउरें ॥

२ सेवहिं सकल सवति मोहि नीकें ।
गरबित भरत मातु बल पी कें ॥
सालु तुम्हार कौसिलहि माई ।
कपट चतुर नहिं होइ जनाई ॥

३ राजहि तुम्ह पर प्रेमु बिसेषी ।
सवति सुभाउ सकइ नहिं देखी ॥
रचि प्रपंचु भूपहि अपनाई ।
राम तिलक हित लगन धराई ॥

४ यह कुल उचित राम कहुँ टीका ।
सबहि सोहाइ मोहि सुठि नीका ॥
आगिलि बात समुझि डरु मोही ।
देउ दैउ फिरि सो फलु ओही ॥

१८ रचि पचि कोटिक कुटिलपन कीन्हेसि कपट प्रबोधु ।
कहिसि कथा सत सवति कै जेहि बिधि बाढ़ बिरोधु ॥

Securely wed, you never worried,          17
thinking the king was under your thumb.
The lord of men is sweet-tongued but cruel-hearted,
and you are simply naïve.

Ram's mother is clever and secretive.         1
Gaining a chance, she strengthened her hand.
The king sent Bharat to your father's place,
but know that the idea came from Ram's mother!
She thinks, 'All the other wives serve me well,      2
but Bharat's mother is haughty, by our lord's favor.'
You are Kausalya's sore point, mother,
though through her cunning it goes unperceived.
The king has special love for you         3
that a co-wife naturally cannot bear to see.
Concocting a scheme and winning over the king,
she got the date set for Ram's consecration.
It is rightful clan practice that Ram should be king—    4
this pleases everyone and is fine with me, too.
It is what will come later that frightens me.
Oh God, may fate pay her back in kind!"

Craftily conniving in countless ways,        18
Manthara gave her deceitful instruction
and told hundreds of tales
of vengeful co-wives to feed her enmity.

१     भावी बस प्रतीति उर आई ।
        पूँछ रानि पुनि सपथ देवाई ॥
        का पूँछहु तुम्ह अबहुँ न जाना ।
        निज हित अनहित पसु पहिचाना ॥

२     भयउ पाखु दिन सजत समाजू ।
        तुम्ह पाई सुधि मोहि सन आजू ॥
        खाइअ पहिरिअ राज तुम्हारें ।
        सत्य कहें नहिं दोषु हमारें ॥

३     जौं असत्य कछु कहब बनाई ।
        तौ बिधि देइहि हमहि सजाई ॥
        रामहि तिलक कालि जौं भयऊ ।
        तुम्ह कहुँ बिपति बीजु बिधि बयऊ ॥

४     रेख खँचाइ कहउँ बलु भाषी ।
        भामिनि भइहु दूध कइ माखी ॥
        जौं सुत सहित करहु सेवकाई ।
        तौ घर रहहु न आन उपाई ॥


१९    कहूँ बिनतहि दीन्ह दुखु तुम्हहि कौसिलाँ देब ।
       भरतु बंदिगृह सेइहहिं लखनु राम के नेब ॥


१     कैकयसुता सुनत कटु बानी ।
        कहि न सकइ कछु सहमि सुखानी ॥
        तन पसेउ कदली जिमि काँपी ।
        कुबरीं दसन जीभ तब चाँपी ॥

In destiny's clutches, the queen believed                    1
and questioned again, making her swear an oath.
"Still you ask? Do you not yet understand?
Even a beast knows what's good or bad for it!
Preparations have been on for two weeks,                     2
yet you only got news of it from me today.
Fed and clothed by your royal largesse,
I do not err by speaking the truth.
Were I to fabricate and utter lies,                          3
the creator would punish me.
If Ram is really consecrated tomorrow,
fate will sow disaster's seed for you.
I draw a line and firmly declare:[18]                        4
woman, you have become a fly in the milk!
Only if you grovel along with your son
will you stay in this house, not otherwise.

The misery that Kadru visited on Vinata,                     19
Kausalya will inflict on you.[19]
Bharat will slave in the dungeons
while Lakshman will be Ram's right hand."

When Kaikeya's daughter heard these bitter words             1
she grew pale with fright and could not speak.
She broke out in sweat, trembling like a plantain tree,
and the hunchback briefly held her tongue.

२ कहि कहि कोटिक कपट कहानी ।
धीरजु धरहु प्रबोधिसि रानी ॥
कीन्हेसि कठिन पढ़ाइ कुपाठू ।
जिमि न नवइ फिरि उकठ कुकाठू ॥

३ फिरा करमु प्रिय लागि कुचाली ।
बकिहि सराहइ मानि मराली ॥
सुनु मंथरा बात फुरि तोरी ।
दहिनि आँखि नित फरकइ मोरी ॥

४ दिन प्रति देखउँ राति कुसपने ।
कहउँ न तोहि मोह बस अपने ॥
काह करौं सखि सूध सुभाऊ ।
दाहिन बाम न जानउँ काऊ ॥

२० अपनें चलत न आजु लगि अनभल काहुक कीन्ह ।
केहिं अघ एकहि बार मोहि दैअँ दुसह दुखु दीन्ह ॥

१ नैहर जनमु भरब बरु जाई ।
जिअत न करबि सवति सेवकाई ॥
अरि बस दैउ जिआवत जाही ।
मरनु नीक तेहि जीवन चाही ॥

२ दीन बचन कह बहुबिधि रानी ।
सुनि कुबरीं तियमाया ठानी ॥
अस कस कहहु मानि मन ऊना ।
सुखु सोहागु तुम्ह कहुँ दिन दूना ॥

Then, with a million deceitful tales,      2
she instructed the queen to take courage.
With wicked instruction she hardened her
and made her as unbending as a dead tree trunk.[20]
Her karma reversed, Kaikeyi cherished wicked counsel   3
and praised that wily stork as if she were a *haṃsa*.
"Listen, Manthara, your words must be true,
for my right eye throbs continuously.[21]
I have had nightmares every night,      4
but in my deluded state, did not tell you.
Oh friend, what shall I do? I am so naïve
that I have never known right from left!

When I had the power, I never,      20
till today, mistreated anyone.
For what sin has fate suddenly dealt me
this unbearable sorrow?

I can go back to my parents to pass my days,      1
but will never live as my co-wife's slave.
One fated to subsist under a rival's sway
would be better off dead!"
So the queen spoke wretchedly,      2
and the hunchback reinforced her womanly wiles.
"Why speak so, reckoning yourself worthless?
May your wedded bliss yet double every day!

३ जेहिं राउर अति अनभल ताका ।
सोइ पाइहि यहु फलु परिपाका ॥
जब तें कुमत सुना मैं स्वामिनि ।
भूख न बासर नींद न जामिनि ॥

४ पूँछेउँ गुनिन्ह रेख तिन्ह खाँची ।
भरत भुआल होहिं यह साँची ॥
भामिनि करहु त कहौं उपाऊ ।
है तुम्हरीं सेवा बस राऊ ॥

२१ परउँ कूप तुअ बचन पर सकउँ पूत पति त्यागि ।
कहसि मोर दुखु देखि बड़ कस न करब हित लागि ॥

१ कुबरीं करि कबुली कैकेई ।
कपट छुरी उर पाहन टेई ॥
लखइ न रानि निकट दुखु कैसें ।
चरइ हरित तिन बलिपसु जैसें ॥

२ सुनत बात मृदु अंत कठोरी ।
देति मनहुँ मधु माहुर घोरी ॥
कहइ चेरि सुधि अहइ कि नाहीं ।
स्वामिनि कहिहु कथा मोहि पाहीं ॥

३ दुइ बरदान भूप सन थाती ।
मागहु आजु जुड़ावहु छाती ॥
सुतहि राजु रामहि बनबासू ।
देहु लेहु सब सवति हुलासू ॥

She who has plotted your ruin                                    3
will herself richly harvest that very fruit.
Mistress, ever since I heard of the plot,
I've had no appetite nor sleep at night.
I asked astrologers, who calculated                              4
that Bharat will definitely become king.
If you will act, woman, I will tell you the means,
for the king is still indebted to you."

Kaikeyi said, "At your word, I would jump                       21
into a well, or abandon my son and my lord.
How can I not do what you, who see
my great sorrow, tell me for my own good?"

Making Kaikeyi her willing victim, the hunchback                 1
whet the blade of deceit on the stone of her heart.
The queen no more saw her grief approaching
than does a placidly grazing sacrificial beast.
Her speech, sweet to hear but harsh in effect,                   2
was like a honey-drink laced with poison.
The maid said, "Do you recall or not,
mistress, that you once told me a story?
You hold two boons promised by the king—                        3
demand them today and appease your heart.
Give the kingdom to your son, exile to Ram,
and take back all your co-wife's pleasure!

४ भूपति राम सपथ जब करई ।
तब मागेहु जेहिं बचनु न टरई ॥
होइ अकाजु आजु निसि बीतें ।
बचनु मोर प्रिय मानेहु जी तें ॥

२२ बड़ कुघातु करि पातकिनि कहेसि कोपगृहँ जाहु ।
काजु सँवारेहु सजग सबु सहसा जनि पतिआहु ॥

१ कुबरिहि रानि प्रानप्रिय जानी ।
बार बार बड़ि बुद्धि बखानी ॥
तोहि सम हित न मोर संसारा ।
बहे जात कइ भइसि अधारा ॥

२ जौं बिधि पुरब मनोरथु काली ।
करौं तोहि चख पूतरि आली ॥
बहुबिधि चेरिहि आदरु देई ।
कोपभवन गवनी कैकेई ॥

३ बिपति बीजु बरषा रितु चेरी ।
भुइँ भइ कुमति कैकई केरी ॥
पाइ कपट जलु अंकुर जामा ।
बर दोउ दल दुख फल परिनामा ॥

४ कोप समाजु साजि सबु सोई ।
राजु करत निज कुमति बिगोई ॥
राउर नगर कोलाहलु होई ।
यह कुचालि कछु जान न कोई ॥

When the king swears an oath on Ram,      4
ask then, so he cannot stray from his word.
You will be undone once this night passes,
unless you hold my advice dearer than your life."

Buttressing her wicked stratagem, that sinner said,    22
"Go into the sulking chamber.[22]
Carefully contrive everything,
and do not suddenly start believing him."

The queen thought the hunchback dear as life    1
and effusively praised her great wisdom:
"I have no benefactor like you in this world,
to support me as I was being swept away.
If fate fulfills my wishes tomorrow,    2
I will make you, dear, the light of my eyes!"[23]
Constantly praising that maidservant,
Kaikeyi retired to the sulking room.
In Manthara's monsoon, the seed of calamity    3
lodged in the soil of Kaikeyi's twisted mind.
Watered with guile, it germinated,
to leaf in two boons, with woe their final fruit.
Artfully contriving displeasure, Kaikeyi lay down—    4
a queen ruined by her own delusion.
Yet in palace and city a happy tumult reigned,
for no one even suspected this treachery.

२३ प्रमुदित पुर नर नारि सब सजहिं सुमंगलचार ।
एक प्रबिसहिं एक निर्गमहिं भीर भूप दरबार ॥

१ बाल सखा सुनि हियँ हरषाहीं ।
मिलि दस पाँच राम पहिं जाहीं ॥
प्रभु आदरहिं प्रेमु पहिचानी ।
पूँछहिं कुसल खेम मृदु बानी ॥

२ फिरहिं भवन प्रिय आयसु पाई ।
करत परसपर राम बड़ाई ॥
को रघुबीर सरिस संसारा ।
सीलु सनेहु निबाहनिहारा ॥

३ जेहिं जेहिं जोनि करम बस भ्रमहीं ।
तहँ तहँ ईसु देउ यह हमहीं ॥
सेवक हम स्वामी सियनाहू ।
होउ नात यह ओर निबाहू ॥

४ अस अभिलाषु नगर सब काहू ।
कैकयसुता हृदयँ अति दाहू ॥
को न कुसंगति पाइ नसाई ।
रहइ न नीच मतें चतुराई ॥

२४ साँझ समय सानंद नृपु गयउ कैकई गेहँ ।
गवनु निठुरता निकट किय जनु धरि देह सनेहँ ॥

All the city's men and women, overjoyed,     23
were engaged in auspicious preparation.
People constantly came and went
through the crowded royal gate.

His boyhood friends, delighted at the news,     1
went in small groups to meet Ram.
Marking their love, the Lord respectfully
and sweetly inquired after their welfare.
Returning home with his kind leave,     2
they sang Ram's praise to one another.
"Who in the world is like the Raghu hero,
the epitome of nobility and affection?
Into whatever birth karma impels us,     3
oh God, grant us this favor:
may we be servants, and our master, Sita's lord,
and may this bond endure to the end!"
Such was the yearning of everyone in the city,     4
yet Kaikeyi's heart was aflame with rage,
for who is not ruined by bad company?
With wicked counsel, good sense departs.

At twilight, the lord of men     24
went blissfully to Kaikeyi's apartment,
like the embodiment of affection
approaching the court of cruelty.

१ कोपभवन सुनि सकुचेउ राऊ ।
भय बस अगहुड़ परइ न पाऊ ॥
सुरपति बसइ बाहँबल जाकें ।
नरपति सकल रहहिं रुख ताकें ॥

२ सो सुनि तिय रिस गयउ सुखाई ।
देखहु काम प्रताप बड़ाई ॥
सूल कुलिस असि अँगवनिहारे ।
ते रतिनाथ सुमन सर मारे ॥

३ सभय नरेसु प्रिया पहिं गयऊ ।
देखि दसा दुखु दारुन भयऊ ॥
भूमि सयन पटु मोट पुराना ।
दिए डारि तन भूषन नाना ॥

४ कुमतिहि कसि कुबेषता फाबी ।
अनअहिवातु सूच जनु भाबी ॥
जाइ निकट नृपु कह मृदु बानी ।
प्रानप्रिया केहि हेतु रिसानी ॥

Hearing of her displeasure, the king was alarmed,     1
and, seized by dread, could not go forward.
He by whose arms' might Indra held sway,
and whose glance was warily watched by all kings,
withered at word of a woman's anger—     2
behold the awesome power of desire!
One who endured blows of spear, mace, and sword
was felled by a flower-arrow of Rati's spouse.*
Timidly, the king approached his beloved,     3
deeply grieved at seeing her condition.
She lay on the floor in old, coarse garments,
with all her body's jewelry cast aside.
Yet this grim dress well suited that deluded one,     4
as if announcing her approaching widowhood.
The king came near and spoke sweet words,
"My dearest, why are you annoyed?"

* Kama, the love god.

५ केहि हेतु रानि रिसानि परसत
पानि पतिहि नेवारई ।
मानहुँ सरोष भुअंग भामिनि
बिषम भाँति निहारई ॥
दोउ बासना रसना दसन बर
मरम ठाहरु देखई ।
तुलसी नृपति भवतब्यता बस
काम कौतुक लेखई ॥

२५ बार बार कह राउ सुमुखि सुलोचनि पिकबचनि ।
कारन मोहि सुनाउ गजगामिनि निज कोप कर ॥

१ अनहित तोर प्रिया केइँ कीन्हा ।
केहि दुइ सिर केहि जमु चह लीन्हा ॥
कहु केहि रंकहि करौं नरेसू ।
कहु केहि नृपहि निकासौं देसू ॥
२ सकउँ तोर अरि अमरउ मारी ।
काह कीट बपुरे नर नारी ॥
जानसि मोर सुभाउ बरोरू ।
मनु तव आनन चंद चकोरू ॥
३ प्रिया प्रान सुत सरबसु मोरें ।
परिजन प्रजा सकल बस तोरें ॥
जौं कछु कहौं कपटु करि तोही ।
भामिनि राम सपथ सत मोही ॥

46

"Why are you upset, my queen?"[24]                    5
But at the touch of her husband's hand,
she drew back like an enraged cobra
and gazed at him in fury.
Her wishes were its split tongue, the boons its fangs,
and she searched for a vulnerable spot to strike.
But, Tulsi says, in the grip of fate,
the king supposed it all to be but love-play.

Time and again the king entreated her,                25
"My long-eyed beauty, sweet-voiced one—
tell me, amply endowed woman,[25]
the cause of your pique.

Who has crossed you, my darling?                      1
Who has a head to spare? Who does death long to claim?
Tell me what pauper I should enthrone,
or what king eject from his realm.
I can slay even an immortal, if he is your foe,        2
never mind wretched, worm-like men and women!
Fair-hipped beauty, you know my nature—
my heart is a *cakor* bird to the moon of your face.
Dearest, my very life, my sons, my entire fortune,     3
my kin and subjects—all are under your sway.
If I have said anything to deceive you, woman,
I forswear it a hundred times, on Ram's name!

४   बिहसि मागु मनभावति बाता ।
    भूषन सजहि मनोहर गाता ॥
    घरी कुघरी समुझि जियँ देखू ।
    बेगि प्रिया परिहरहि कुबेषू ॥

२६  यह सुनि मन गुनि सपथ बड़ि बिहसि उठी मतिमंद ।
    भूषन सजति बिलोकि मृगु मनहुँ किरातिनि फंद ॥

१   पुनि कह राउ सुहृद जियँ जानी ।
    प्रेम पुलकि मृदु मंजुल बानी ॥
    भामिनि भयउ तोर मनभावा ।
    घर घर नगर अनंद बधावा ॥

२   रामहि देउँ कालि जुबराजू ।
    सजहि सुलोचनि मंगल साजू ॥
    दलकि उठेउ सुनि हृदउ कठोरू ।
    जनु छुइ गयउ पाक बरतोरू ॥

३   ऐसिउ पीर बिहसि तेहिं गोई ।
    चोर नारि जिमि प्रगटि न रोई ॥
    लखहिं न भूप कपट चतुराई ।
    कोटि कुटिल मनि गुरू पढ़ाई ॥

४   जद्यपि नीति निपुन नरनाहू ।
    नारिचरित जलनिधि अवगाहू ॥
    कपट सनेहु बढ़ाइ बहोरी ।
    बोली बिहसि नयन मुहु मोरी ॥

Now smile, ask for your heart's delight,                                    4
and adorn your lovely body with jewels.
Reflect on what befits the occasion,
dearest, and abandon this cruel garb."

Hearing this and musing on his great oath,                                  26
that deluded one rose with a laugh,
and began to don her jewels,
like a huntress sighting a deer and setting her snare.

Thinking her appeased, the king spoke again,                                1
trembling with love, his voice most tender:
"Woman, your heart's wish has been fulfilled,
and in every home there is festive rejoicing.
Tomorrow, I will give the kingship to Ram,                                  2
my lovely, so don your most auspicious jewels!"
When she heard him, her cruel heart shook
as though a ripe boil had been touched.
Yet even such anguish she hid with a smile,                                 3
as a captured thief's woman suppresses her tears.[26]
The king did not perceive her devious ploy,
for she was schooled by the crown jewel of deceivers.
Though the lord of men was adept at statecraft,                             4
the ways of women are a fathomless sea.
Once more feigning fresh affection,
she averted her gaze, smiled, and said,

२७ मागु मागु पै कहहु पिय कबहुँ न देहु न लेहु ।
देन कहेहु बरदान दुइ तेउ पावत संदेहु ॥

१ जानेउँ मरमु राउ हँसि कहई ।
तुम्हहि कोहाब परम प्रिय अहई ॥
थाती राखि न मागिहु काऊ ।
बिसरि गयउ मोहि भोर सुभाऊ ॥

२ झूठेहुँ हमहि दोषु जनि देहू ।
दुइ कै चारि मागि मकु लेहू ॥
रघुकुल रीति सदा चलि आई ।
प्रान जाहुँ बरु बचनु न जाई ॥

३ नहिं असत्य सम पातक पुंजा ।
गिरि सम होहिं कि कोटिक गुंजा ॥
सत्यमूल सब सुकृत सुहाए ।
बेद पुरान बिदित मनु गाए ॥

४ तेहि पर राम सपथ करि आई ।
सुकृत सनेह अवधि रघुराई ॥
बात दृढ़ाइ कुमति हँसि बोली ।
कुमत कुबिहग कुलह जनु खोली ॥

२८ भूप मनोरथ सुभग बनु सुख सुबिहंग समाजु ।
भिल्लिनि जिमि छाड़न चहति बचनु भयंकरु बाजु ॥

"Darling, you keep on saying 'Ask, ask!'                    27
yet nothing is ever given or taken.
You had promised to grant me two favors,
and I doubt of getting even these."

"Now I know the secret!" the king said, laughing.          1
"You are so very fond of pouting.
Holding my word in trust, you never asked,
and I, absent-minded, simply forgot.
But do not accuse me of falsehood—                         2
instead of two, take four boons!
For this has ever been the way of the Raghus:
we may give up our lives, but not our word.[27]
No mass of sins can compare to one untruth!                3
Can a billion seed-grains equal a mountain?[28]
Truth is the root of all noble acts,
as Veda and *purāṇas* affirm and Manu declares.
Moreover, I have sworn on Ram,                             4
lord of Raghus, the epitome of virtue and love."
Having gained her goal, that deluded one laughed
and spoke as if unhooding the hawk of ill will.

The king's hopes were a lovely forest                      28
full of the gentle fowl of happiness,
on whom, like a savage huntress, she would unleash
the awful prey-bird of her speech.

१ सुनहु प्रानप्रिय भावत जी का ।
देहु एक बर भरतहि टीका ॥
मागउँ दूसर बर कर जोरी ।
पुरवहु नाथ मनोरथ मोरी ॥

२ तापस बेष बिसेषि उदासी ।
चौदह बरिस रामु बनबासी ॥
सुनि मृदु बचन भूप हियँ सोकू ।
ससि कर छुअत बिकल जिमि कोकू ॥

३ गयउ सहमि नहिं कछु कहि आवा ।
जनु सचान बन झपटेउ लावा ॥
बिबरन भयउ निपट नरपालू ।
दामिनि हनेउ मनहुँ तरु तालू ॥

४ माथें हाथ मूदि दोउ लोचन ।
तनु धरि सोचु लाग जनु सोचन ॥
मोर मनोरथु सुरतरु फूला ।
फरत करिनि जिमि हतेउ समूला ॥

५ अवध उजारि कीन्हि कैकेई ।
दीन्हिसि अचल बिपति कै नेई ॥

२९ कवनें अवसर का भयउ गयउँ नारि बिस्वास ।
जोग सिद्धि फल समय जिमि जतिहि अबिद्या नास ॥

"Listen, dearest, to what pleases my heart:     1
give me one boon that Bharat be consecrated king.
And, palms joined in entreaty, I ask
my second boon—husband, fulfill my wish!—
that, renouncing all and garbed as an ascetic,     2
Ram reside in the forest for fourteen years."
Sweetly uttered, her words scorched the king's heart
as the touch of moonbeams afflicts a *kok* bird.[29]
Seized by terror, he could not utter a word,     3
like a quail assailed by a falcon.
The protector of men went utterly pale,
like a palm tree struck by lightning.
His hand on his brow, he shut his eyes     4
and mused, like the very embodiment of gloom:
"The heavenly tree of my hopes, in full flower
and about to fruit, is uprooted by this elephant-cow.
Kaikeyi has devastated Avadh     5
and laid the foundation for calamity.

Oh, when and how has it happened     29
that I am ruined by trusting a woman,
like a yogi on the verge of inner attainment,
destroyed by ignorance?"

१ एहि बिधि राउ मनहिं मन झाँखा ।
देखि कुभाँति कुमति मन माखा ॥
भरतु कि राउर पूत न होंही ।
आनेहु मोल बेसाहि कि मोही ॥

२ जो सुनि सरु अस लाग तुम्हारें ।
काहे न बोलहु बचनु सँभारें ॥
देहु उतरु अनु करहु कि नाहीं ।
सत्यसंध तुम्ह रघुकुल माहीं ॥

३ देन कहेहु अब जनि बरु देहू ।
तजहु सत्य जग अपजसु लेहू ॥
सत्य सराहि कहेहु बरु देना ।
जानेहु लेइहि मागि चबेना ॥

४ सिबि दधीचि बलि जो कछु भाषा ।
तनु धनु तजेउ बचन पनु राखा ॥
अति कटु बचन कहति कैकेई ।
मानहुँ लोन जरे पर देई ॥

३० धरम धुरंधर धीर धरि नयन उघारे रायँ ।
सिरु धुनि लीन्हि उसास असि मारेसि मोहि कुठायँ ॥

१ आगें दीखि जरत रिस भारी ।
मनहुँ रोष तरवारि उघारी ॥
मूठि कुबुद्धि धार निठुराई ।
धरी कूबरीं सान बनाई ॥

54

So the king lamented silently. 1
Seeing his distress, Kaikeyi grew angry.
"Is Bharat not your lawful son,
and did you purchase me for a price?[30]
If hearing my words pains you so, 2
why do you not think before promising?
Answer me: will you do it or not?[31]
Sworn to truth, and in the Raghu lineage,
you said you would give boons. Now, don't give them. 3
Abandon truth and win infamy in the world!
Praising truth, you promised those boons—
did you think I would ask for parched grain?
Whatever Shibi, Dadhichi, and Bali promised 4
they fulfilled, even at cost of life and fortune."[32]
So Kaikeyi spoke, and her cutting words
were like salt rubbed on a burn.

Composing himself, that royal bearer 30
of dharma's burden opened his eyes,
beat his brow, and sighed deeply, musing,
"She has struck my weakest spot."[33]

He saw her before him, aflame with anger, 1
like an unsheathed sword of rage,
its hilt her delusion, its blade of cruelty
honed on the hunchback's whetting stone.

२ लखी महीप कराल कठोरा ।
सत्य कि जीवनु लेइहि मोरा ॥
बोले राउ कठिन करि छाती ।
बानी सबिनय तासु सोहाती ॥

३ प्रिया बचन कस कहसि कुभाँती ।
भीर प्रतीति प्रीति करि हाँती ॥
मोरें भरतु रामु दुइ आँखी ।
सत्य कहउँ करि संकरु साखी ॥

४ अवसि दूतु मैं पठइब प्राता ।
ऐहहिं बेगि सुनत दोउ भराता ॥
सुदिन सोधि सबु साजु सजाई ।
देउँ भरत कहुँ राजु बजाई ॥

३१ लोभु न रामहि राजु कर बहुत भरत पर प्रीति ।
मैं बड़ छोट बिचारि जियँ करत रहेउँ नृपनीति ॥

१ राम सपथ सत कहउँ सुभाऊ ।
राममातु कछु कहेउ न काऊ ॥
मैं सबु कीन्ह तोहि बिनु पूँछें ।
तेहि तें परेउ मनोरथु छूछें ॥

२ रिस परिहरु अब मंगल साजू ।
कछु दिन गएँ भरत जुबराजू ॥
एकहि बात मोहि दुखु लागा ।
बर दूसर असमंजस मागा ॥

Observing her hard ferocity, he wondered,        2
"Is she truly bent on taking my life?"
Then fortifying himself, the king spoke
conciliatory words meant to please her.
"Dear, how can you utter such harsh words     3
that shatter modesty, trust, and love?
Bharat and Ram are my two eyes—
so I swear, with Shiva as my witness.
In the morning, I will definitely send couriers    4
to summon both brothers* home at once.
Then choosing a favorable day and with due planning
I will with full pomp bestow the kingdom on Bharat.

Ram has no craving for the crown,        31
and he loves Bharat very much.
Considering his seniority,
I was but acting on royal precedent.

Sincerely, I swear by Ram a hundred times:    1
Ram's mother never had any say in this!
But I did it all without consulting you,
and so my wish has proven fruitless.
Now quit your anger and adorn yourself.     2
In a few days, Bharat will be heir-apparent.
Just one thing pains me:
that second boon you asked is so disturbing,

* Bharat and Shatrughna.

३ अजहूँ हृदउ जरत तेहि आँचा ।
रिस परिहास कि साँचेहुँ साँचा ॥
कहु तजि रोषु राम अपराधू ।
सबु कोउ कहइ रामु सुठि साधू ॥
४ तुहूँ सराहसि करसि सनेहू ।
अब सुनि मोहि भयउ संदेहू ॥
जासु सुभाउ अरिहि अनुकूला ।
सो किमि करिहि मातु प्रतिकूला ॥

३२ प्रिया हास रिस परिहरहि मागु बिचारि बिबेकु ।
जेहिं देखौं अब नयन भरि भरत राज अभिषेकु ॥

१ जिऐ मीन बरु बारि बिहीना ।
मनि बिनु फनिकु जिऐ दुख दीना ॥
कहउँ सुभाउ न छलु मन माहीं ।
जीवनु मोर राम बिनु नाहीं ॥
२ समुझि देखु जियँ प्रिया प्रबीना ।
जीवनु राम दरस आधीना ॥
सुनि मृदु बचन कुमति अति जरई ।
मनहुँ अनल आहुति घृत परई ॥
३ कहइ करहु किन कोटि उपाया ।
इहाँ न लागिहि राउरि माया ॥
देहु कि लेहु अजसु करि नाहीं ।
मोहि न बहुत प्रपंच सोहाहीं ॥

58

my heart still burns from its excessiveness.                    3
Was it anger or jest, or was it truth?
Forsake your ire, tell me Ram's offense,
for everyone declares him most virtuous.
You too ever praise and cherish him,                            4
so hearing this now bewilders me.
One who by nature is kind even to foes—
how could he act against his mother?

So darling, give up teasing and pouting,                        32
and thoughtfully ask a proper boon,
that I may now wholeheartedly enjoy
the sight of Bharat's royal consecration.

A fish might go on living without water,                         1
and a poor cobra without its forehead-gem,
but I declare truly, with heartfelt sincerity
that I cannot live without Ram!
Consider in your heart, my clever darling,                      2
how my life depends on seeing Ram."
At his gentle speech, that ill-willed one flared up
like a sacred fire on which ghee is poured.
She said, "Try a million stratagems,                            3
but your artifice will not work here.
Give me my boons, or refuse and earn infamy.
I have no taste for all this fabrication.

४ रामु साधु तुम्ह साधु सयाने ।
राममातु भलि सब पहिचाने ॥
जस कौसिलाँ मोर भल ताका ।
तस फलु उन्हहि देउँ करि साका ॥

३३ होत प्रातु मुनिबेष धरि जौं न रामु बन जाहिं ।
मोर मरनु राउर अजस नृप समुझिअ मन माहिं ॥

१ अस कहि कुटिल भई उठि ठाढ़ी ।
मानहुँ रोष तरंगिनि बाढ़ी ॥
पाप पहार प्रगट भइ सोई ।
भरी क्रोध जल जाइ न जोई ॥

२ दोउ बर कूल कठिन हठ धारा ।
भवँर कूबरी बचन प्रचारा ॥
ढाहत भूपरूप तरु मूला ।
चली बिपति बारिधि अनुकूला ॥

३ लखी नरेस बात फुरि साँची ।
तिय मिस मीचु सीस पर नाची ॥
गहि पद बिनय कीन्ह बैठारी ।
जनि दिनकर कुल होसि कुठारी ॥

४ मागु माथ अबहीं देउँ तोही ।
राम बिरहँ जनि मारसि मोही ॥
राखु राम कहुँ जेहि तेहि भाँती ।
नाहिं त जरिहि जनम भरि छाती ॥

Ram is so noble, you too, noble and wise,        4
Ram's mother is good—oh, I know you all.
But just as Kausalya was looking to do to me,
so I will repay her in full measure!

Come morning, should Ram not go        33
to the forest, clad in ascetic garb,
I will take my own life and your good name,
king—know this with certainty."

Saying this, that perverse one stood up,        1
like a river of wrath rising in flood.
Mountains of sin were its source,
and its raging water, awful to behold,
had the boons for banks, her cruel will as current,        2
and eddies driven by the hunchback's speech.
Uprooting the tree of the lord of earth,
it surged toward a sea of suffering.
Then the king saw it was truly so—        3
death, disguised as a woman, danced on his head.
Clutching her feet, he bade her sit, and pleaded,
"Do not be an axe for the solar clan's tree.
Ask for my head—I will give it at once,        4
but do not kill me by separation from Ram.
Keep Ram here on some pretext or other,
or your heart will burn for the rest of your life."

३४ देखी ब्याधि असाध नृपु परेउ धरनि धुनि माथ ।
कहत परम आरत बचन राम राम रघुनाथ ॥

१ ब्याकुल राउ सिथिल सब गाता ।
करिनि कलपतरु मनहुँ निपाता ॥
कंठु सूख मुख आव न बानी ।
जनु पाठीनु दीन बिनु पानी ॥

२ पुनि कह कटु कठोर कैकेई ।
मनहुँ घाय महुँ माहुर देई ॥
जौं अंतहुँ अस करतबु रहेऊ ।
मागु मागु तुम्ह केहिं बल कहेऊ ॥

३ दुइ कि होइ एक समय भुआला ।
हँसब ठठाइ फुलाउब गाला ॥
दानि कहाउब अरु कृपनाई ।
होइ कि खेम कुसल रौताई ॥

४ छाड़हु बचनु कि धीरजु धरहू ।
जनि अबला जिमि करुना करहू ॥
तनु तिय तनय धामु धनु धरनी ।
सत्यसंध कहुँ तृन सम बरनी ॥

३५ मरम बचन सुनि राउ कह कहु कछु दोषु न तोर ।
लागेउ तोहि पिसाच जिमि कालु कहावत मोर ॥

When he saw that her disease was incurable,                    34
the king collapsed, beating his head,
and crying out in a most pitiable voice,
"Oh Ram, Ram, lord of the Raghus!"

The king was in anguish, his body limp,                        1
like a wishing tree felled by a she-elephant.
His throat went dry and he could not speak,
like a huge fish crazed by lack of water.
Kaikeyi again spoke harsh, biting words,                       2
as if pouring bitter poison in a wound:
"If in the end you carry on like this,
what emboldened you to say 'Ask, ask'?
Can one do two things at once, king—                           3
laugh loudly while holding one's breath?[34]
Call oneself generous but act stingily?
Be a war hero yet stay unscathed?
Either break your word or summon your courage,                 4
but don't wail like some wretched woman.
Life, wife, son, home, wealth, and land
are said to be but straw to the oath-bound."

Hearing her piercing words, the king said,                     35
"Rant on, for it is not your fault.
My death, like a demon, possesses you
and makes you speak so.

१  चहत न भरत भूपतिह भोरें ।
   बिधि बस कुमति बसी जिय तोरें ॥
   सो सबु मोर पाप परिनामू ।
   भयउ कुठाहर जेहिं बिधि बामू ॥

२  सुबस बसिहि फिरि अवध सुहाई ।
   सब गुन धाम राम प्रभुताई ॥
   करिहहिं भाइ सकल सेवकाई ।
   होइहि तिहुँ पुर राम बड़ाई ॥

३  तोर कलंकु मोर पछिताऊ ।
   मुएहुँ न मिटिहि न जाइहि काऊ ॥
   अब तोहि नीक लाग करु सोई ।
   लोचन ओट बैठु मुहु गोई ॥

४  जब लगि जिऔं कहउँ कर जोरी ।
   तब लगि जनि कछु कहसि बहोरी ॥
   फिरि पछितैहसि अंत अभागी ।
   मारसि गाइ नहारू लागी ॥

३६  परेउ राउ कहि कोटि बिधि काहे करसि निदानु ।
    कपट सयानि न कहति कछु जागति मनहुँ मसानु ॥

१  राम राम रट बिकल भुआलू ।
   जनु बिनु पंख बिहंग बेहालू ॥
   हृदयँ मनाव भोरु जनि होई ।
   रामहि जाइ कहै जनि कोई ॥

Bharat would not dream of coveting kingship,　　　1
but destiny's grip has perverted your soul.
It is all the result of my sins
that fate turns against me at this evil hour.
Fair Avadh will surely flourish again,　　　2
and Ram, abode of virtues, will reign.
All his brothers will attend on him
and his fame will echo in the three worlds.
But your sin and my remorse　　　3
will endure forever, not effaced even by death.
Now do whatever you please,
but hide your face from my sight.
For as long as I live, I beg you:　　　4
never speak to me again!
Luckless one, you will in the end repent
killing a cow for a scrap of sinew."[35]

The king collapsed, lamenting in countless ways,　　　36
"Why do you ruin us?"
But that wily woman, saying nothing,
sat like a sorceress in a cremation ground.[36]

Repeating "Ram, Ram!" in anguish, the lord of earth　　　1
was like a wingless, demented bird.
His heart pleaded, "Let morning not come,
let no one go and tell Ram of this.

२ उदउ करहु जनि रबि रघुकुल गुर ।
अवध बिलोकि सूल होइहि उर ॥
भूप प्रीति कैकइ कठिनाई ।
उभय अवधि बिधि रची बनाई ॥

३ बिलपत नृपहि भयउ भिनुसारा ।
बीना बेनु संख धुनि द्वारा ॥
पढ़हिं भाट गुन गावहिं गायक ।
सुनत नृपहि जनु लागहिं सायक ॥

४ मंगल सकल सोहाहिं न कैसें ।
सहगामिनिहि बिभूषन जैसें ॥
तेहि निसि नीद परी नहिं काहू ।
राम दरस लालसा उछाहू ॥

३७ द्वार भीर सेवक सचिव कहहिं उदित रबि देखि ।
जागेउ अजहुँ न अवधपति कारनु कवनु बिसेषि ॥

१ पछिले पहर भूपु नित जागा ।
आजु हमहि बड़ अचरजु लागा ॥
जाहु सुमंत्र जगावहु जाई ।
कीजिअ काजु रजायसु पाई ॥

२ गए सुमंत्रु तब राउर माहीं ।
देखि भयावन जात डेराहीं ॥
धाइ खाइ जनु जाइ न हेरा ।
मानहुँ बिपति बिषाद बसेरा ॥

Sun, preceptor of the Raghus—do not rise,       2
for the sight of Avadh will break your heart!"
His tender love and Kaikeyi's virulence—
the creator had crafted each to perfection.
The king wailed on till dawn came,       3
when lute, flute, and conch sounded at the gate.
Bards intoned homage, singers sang praise,
and to hear them struck the king like an arrow.
Auspiciousness was as distasteful to him       4
as adornment to a widow pledged to burn.[37]
No one had slept a wink that night,
in their eagerness to behold Ram.

At the king's door, a crowd of servants       37
and ministers saw the rising sun
and said, "What can be the reason why
the lord of Avadh is not yet awake?

The king always rises in night's last watch,       1
so today we are greatly surprised.
Go, Sumantra, awaken him,
that we may execute our tasks at his command."
Sumantra went to the royal abode,       2
but seeing it grim, grew fearful as he entered.
It seemed too menacing to behold,
as if calamity and grief had moved in.

३ पूछें कोउ न ऊतरु देई ।
गए जेहिं भवन भूप कैकेई ॥
कहि जयजीव बैठ सिरु नाई ।
देखि भूप गति गयउ सुखाई ॥

४ सोच बिकल बिबरन महि परेऊ ।
मानहुँ कमल मूलु परिहरेऊ ॥
सचिउ सभीत सकइ नहिं पूँछी ।
बोली असुभ भरी सुभ छूँछी ॥

३८ परी न राजहि नीद निसि हेतु जान जगदीसु ।
रामु रामु रटि भोरु किय कहइ न मरमु महीसु ॥

१ आनहु रामहि बेगि बोलाई ।
समाचार तब पूँछेहु आई ॥
चलेउ सुमंत्रु राय रुख जानी ।
लखी कुचालि कीन्हि कछु रानी ॥

२ सोच बिकल मग परइ न पाऊ ।
रामहि बोलि कहिहि का राऊ ॥
उर धरि धीरजु गयउ दुआरें ।
पूँछहिं सकल देखि मनु मारें ॥

३ समाधानु करि सो सबही का ।
गयउ जहाँ दिनकर कुल टीका ॥
राम सुमंत्रहि आवत देखा ।
आदरु कीन्ह पिता सम लेखा ॥

He inquired, but no one replied,           3
so he went to where Kaikeyi dwelt with the king.
Wishing long life and victory, he bowed,
but seeing the king's state, was stricken.
Distracted and pale, he lay on the ground     4
like a lotus flower cut off at the root.
The minister was too terrified to question,
but that sinister woman brazenly spoke.

"His majesty did not sleep a wink all night,     38
and God alone knows the reason!
He kept repeating 'Ram, Ram'
till morning, but never said why.

Go quickly and summon Ram,           1
then come back to ask for news."
As Sumantra left, he caught the king's eye
and surmised that the queen had done some ill.
He could not set out, anxiously pondering,     2
"When Ram is sent for, what will the king say?"
Then he composed himself and went to the gate.
Seeing him grave, everyone questioned him,
but somehow he placated them all     3
and went to the crown jewel of the solar line.
Ram saw Sumantra approaching
and paid homage, treating him as his father.

४    निरखि बदनु कहि भूप रजाई ।
रघुकुलदीपहि चलेउ लेवाई ॥
रामु कुभाँति सचिव सँग जाहीं ।
देखि लोग जहँ तहँ बिलखाहीं ॥

३९    जाइ दीख रघुबंसमनि नरपति निपट कुसाजु ।
सहमि परेउ लखि सिंघिनिहि मनहुँ बृद्ध गजराजु ॥

१    सूखहिं अधर जरइ सबु अंगू ।
मनहुँ दीन मनिहीन भुअंगू ॥
सरुष समीप दीखि कैकेई ।
मानहुँ मीचु घरीं गनि लेई ॥

२    करुनामय मृदु राम सुभाऊ ।
प्रथम दीख दुखु सुना न काऊ ॥
तदपि धीर धरि समउ बिचारी ।
पूँछी मधुर बचन महतारी ॥

३    मोहि कहु मातु तात दुख कारन ।
करिअ जतन जेहिं होइ निवारन ॥
सुनहु राम सबु कारन एहू ।
राजहि तुम्ह पर बहुत सनेहू ॥

४    देन कहेन्हि मोहि दुइ बरदाना ।
मागेउँ जो कछु मोहि सोहाना ॥
सो सुनि भयउ भूप उर सोचू ।
छाड़ि न सकहिं तुम्हार सँकोचू ॥

Looking at his face, Sumantra conveyed the royal order          4
and then left with the light of the Raghu clan.
When they saw Ram's untimely departure with the
    courtier
people everywhere were greatly dismayed.

The jewel of the Raghus went there                               39
and beheld the lord of men lying in disarray,
like an old bull elephant who has collapsed
in dread at the sight of a lioness.

His lips were dry and his limbs flushed,                         1
like a cobra bereft of his gemstone.
Nearby he saw a wrathful Kaikeyi,
like vigilant death, tallying his hours.
Ram, tender and compassionate by nature,                         2
now saw, for the first time, unheard-of sorrow.
Yet composing himself, mindful of the moment,
he gently inquired of his royal mother,
"Tell me, mother, the cause of father's grief,                   3
and what may be done to allay it."
She replied, "Hear well, Ram. The whole cause
is simply the king's great affection for you!
He had promised to give me two boons,                            4
and so I asked for whatever I pleased.
Hearing this, the king grew heartsick,
for he cannot shed his attachment to you.

४० सुत सनेहु इत बचनु उत संकट परेउ नरेसु ।
सकहु त आयसु धरहु सिर मेटहु कठिन कलेसु ॥

१ निधरक बैठि कहइ कटु बानी ।
सुनत कठिनता अति अकुलानी ॥
जीभ कमान बचन सर नाना ।
मनहुँ महिप मृदु लच्छ समाना ॥

२ जनु कठोरपनु धरें सरीरू ।
सिखइ धनुषबिद्या बर बीरू ॥
सबु प्रसंगु रघुपतिहि सुनाई ।
बैठि मनहुँ तनु धरि निठुराई ॥

३ मन मुसुकाइ भानुकुल भानू ।
रामु सहज आनंद निधानू ॥
बोले बचन बिगत सब दूषन ।
मृदु मंजुल जनु बाग बिभूषन ॥

४ सुनु जननी सोइ सुतु बड़भागी ।
जो पितु मातु बचन अनुरागी ॥
तनय मातु पितु तोषनिहारा ।
दुर्लभ जननि सकल संसारा ॥

४१ मुनिगन मिलनु बिसेषि बन सबहि भाँति हित मोर ।
तेहि महँ पितु आयसु बहुरि संमत जननी तोर ॥

72

On one side, love for a son, on the other, his word—    40
the king has fallen into a crisis!
If you are able, promise to uphold
his order and ease his terrible anguish."

She sat coolly, uttering these cruel words,    1
that would make harshness itself ashamed.
The bow of her tongue fired many word-arrows,
and the lord of earth was like her soft target.
It was as if cruelty had taken a body    2
as a warrior, to give lessons in archery.
Recounting everything to the Raghu prince,
she sat there like an incarnation of malice.
Smiling inwardly, the sun of the solar line,    3
Ram, the abode of inherent bliss,
spoke utterly flawless words
of a mildness and beauty fit to adorn speech herself.
"Mother, he alone is a fortunate son    4
who cherishes his father's and mother's word.
Yet a son who can satisfy mother and father
is rare in all the world, mother.

Only in the forest can one meet hosts of sages.    41
This will be altogether beneficial for me,
even as I uphold father's command,
moreover, with your approval, mother,

१ भरतु प्रानप्रिय पावहिं राजू ।
बिधि सब बिधि मोहि सनमुख आजू ॥
जौं न जाउँ बन ऐसेहु काजा ।
प्रथम गनिअ मोहि मूढ़ समाजा ॥

२ सेवहिं अरँडु कलपतरु त्यागी ।
परिहरि अमृत लेहिं बिषु मागी ॥
तेउ न पाइ अस समउ चुकाहीं ।
देखु बिचारि मातु मन माहीं ॥

३ अंब एक दुखु मोहि बिसेषी ।
निपट बिकल नरनायकु देखी ॥
थोरिहिं बात पितहि दुख भारी ।
होति प्रतीति न मोहि महतारी ॥

४ राउ धीर गुन उदधि अगाधू ।
भा मोहि तें कछु बड़ अपराधू ॥
जातें मोहि न कहत कछु राऊ ।
मोरि सपथ तोहि कहु सतिभाऊ ॥

४२ सहज सरल रघुबर बचन कुमति कुटिल करि जान ।
चलइ जोंक जल बक्रगति जद्यपि सलिलु समान ॥

१ रहसी रानि राम रुख पाई ।
बोली कपट सनेहु जनाई ॥
सपथ तुम्हार भरत कै आना ।
हेतु न दूसर मैं कछु जाना ॥

while Bharat, dear as my breath, gains kingship— 1
it seems fate favors me in every way today!
If, for such ends, I do not enter the woods,
I should earn first place in the ranks of fools.
One who forsakes heaven's tree for a weed,[38] 2
and spurns nectar to take poison—even he
would not miss such an opportunity!
Reflect on this in your heart, mother.
But, dear mother, one thing troubles me— 3
to see the lord of men in such distress.
That this trifling matter should pain father so—
I cannot believe it, mother,
for the king is an ocean of forbearance and virtue. 4
Surely I have committed some great offense
for which his majesty will not speak to me.
I implore you, on my life: tell me the truth."

The noble Raghu's speech was simple and sincere, 42
yet that wicked woman thought it devious,
for a leech pursues its own crooked course
even in the calmest water.

The queen, pleased by Ram's demeanor, 1
spoke with a false show of affection:
"I swear by you, and on Bharat, too,
that I know no other reason for all this.

२  तुम्ह अपराध जोगु नहिं ताता ।
   जननी जनक बंधु सुखदाता ॥
   राम सत्य सबु जो कछु कहहू ।
   तुम्ह पितु मातु बचन रत अहहू ॥
३  पितहि बुझाइ कहहु बलि सोई ।
   चौथेंपन जेहिं अजसु न होई ॥
   तुम्ह सम सुअन सुकृत जेहिं दीन्हे ।
   उचित न तासु निरादरु कीन्हे ॥
४  लागहिं कुमुख बचन सुभ कैसे ।
   मगहँ गयादिक तीरथ जैसे ॥
   रामहि मातु बचन सब भाए ।
   जिमि सुरसरि गत सलिल सुहाए ॥

४३  गइ मुरुछा रामहि सुमिरि नृप फिरि करवट लीन्ह ।
    सचिव राम आगमन कहि बिनय समय सम कीन्ह ॥

१  अवनिप अकनि रामु पगु धारे ।
   धरि धीरजु तब नयन उघारे ॥
   सचिवँ सँभारि राउ बैठारे ।
   चरन परत नृप रामु निहारे ॥
२  लिए सनेह बिकल उर लाई ।
   गै मनि मनहुँ फनिक फिरि पाई ॥
   रामहि चितइ रहेउ नरनाहू ।
   चला बिलोचन बारि प्रबाहू ॥

Incapable of giving offense, son,                            2
you delight your mother, father, and brothers.
Whatever you say is but truth, Ram;
you are devoted to your parents' command.
I implore you: convince your father                          3
not to incur infamy in his old age.
The merit that gave him a son like you
should not be tarnished—it is not right."
In her foul mouth, these fair words seemed                   4
like the holy sites in sinful Magadh.³⁹
But all his mother's words pleased Ram,
like water when it flows into the Ganga.

Regaining his senses, the lord of men                        43
stirred and uttered Ram's name.
His minister, mindful of the moment,
respectfully informed him of Ram's arrival.

When the king heard that Ram had come                        1
he found courage to open his eyes.
His minister helped the king sit up,
and he saw Ram prostrate at his feet.
Overcome with love, he drew him to his breast,              2
like a snake recovering his lost jewel.
The lord of men kept gazing at Ram
while his eyes shed torrents of tears.

३ सोक बिबस कछु कहै न पारा ।
हृदयँ लगावत बारहिं बारा ॥
बिधिहि मनाव राउ मन माहीं ।
जेहिं रघुनाथ न कानन जाहीं ॥
४ सुमिरि महेसहि कहइ निहोरी ।
बिनती सुनहु सदासिव मोरी ॥
आसुतोष तुम्ह अवढर दानी ।
आरति हरहु दीन जनु जानी ॥

४४ तुम्ह प्रेरक सब के हृदयँ सो मति रामहि देहु ।
बचनु मोर तजि रहहिं घर परिहरि सीलु सनेहु ॥

१ अजसु होउ जग सुजसु नसाऊ ।
नरक परौं बरु सुरपरु जाऊ ॥
सब दुख दुसह सहावहु मोही ।
लोचन ओट रामु जनि होंही ॥
२ अस मन गुनइ राउ नहिं बोला ।
पीपर पात सरिस मनु डोला ॥
रघुपति पितहि प्रेमबस जानी ।
पुनि कछु कहिहि मातु अनुमानी ॥
३ देस काल अवसर अनुसारी ।
बोले बचन बिनीत बिचारी ॥
तात कहउँ कछु करउँ ढिठाई ।
अनुचितु छमब जानि लरिकाई ॥

78

In sorrow's grip, he could not speak,      3
but embraced him again and again.
Inwardly, the king implored the creator
not to let the Raghu lord go to the forest.
Then, invoking mighty Shiva, he prayed,      4
"Eternal one, hear my petition!
Easily pleased, impulsively generous,
you know my wretchedness, so remove my grief.

You who inwardly inspire all,      44
make Ram of a mind
to ignore my promise, discard virtue
and affection, and remain at home!

Let me be disgraced in the world, my fame destroyed,      1
let me fall into hell and lose my place in heaven,
make me suffer every dreaded torment,
but do not take Ram from my sight."
So the king prayed, though silently,      2
his heart trembling like a peepul leaf.
Ram, perceiving his father overcome by love,
and surmising that his mother would again speak out,
as befit the time, occasion, and circumstance,      3
spoke thoughtful and conciliatory words.
"Father, I presume to speak, although improperly,
so pardon me, considering my youth.

४ अति लघु बात लागि दुखु पावा ।
काहुँ न मोहि कहि प्रथम जनावा ॥
देखि गोसाइँहि पूँछिउँ माता ।
सुनि प्रसंगु भए सीतल गाता ॥

४५ मंगल समय सनेह बस सोच परिहरिअ तात ।
आयसु देइअ हरषि हियँ कहि पुलके प्रभु गात ॥

१ धन्य जनमु जगतीतल तासू ।
पितहि प्रमोदु चरित सुनि जासू ॥
चारि पदारथ करतल ताकें ।
प्रिय पितु मातु प्रान सम जाकें ॥

२ आयसु पालि जनम फलु पाई ।
ऐहउँ बेगिहिं होउ रजाई ॥
बिदा मातु सन आवउँ मागी ।
चलिहउँ बनहि बहुरि पग लागी ॥

३ अस कहि राम गवनु तब कीन्हा ।
भूप सोक बस उतरु न दीन्हा ॥
नगर ब्यापि गइ बात सुतीछी ।
छुअत चढ़ी जनु सब तन बीछी ॥

४ सुनि भए बिकल सकल नर नारी ।
बेलि बिटप जिमि देखि दवारी ॥
जो जहँ सुनइ धुनइ सिरु सोई ।
बड़ बिषादु नहिं धीरजु होई ॥

You suffer over a most trifling matter                                            4
of which I had not been told before.
Seeing my lord's distress, I asked mother,
and hearing her account, felt wholly relieved.[40]

At this sacred hour, shed your anxiety                                           45
born of overpowering affection, father,
and give your order with a glad heart."
So the Lord said, his body flushed with emotion.

"He alone is blessed, born on this earth,                                         1
whose deeds, when heard, bring joy to his father,
and life's four goals come readily to one
for whom his parents are dear as breath.
Obeying your order, obtaining my birth's reward,                                  2
I will soon come back—so give your command.
Taking leave of my mother, I will come
touch your feet again, then go to the forest."
So Ram spoke, and departed.                                                       3
The king, overcome by grief, gave no reply.
The shocking news spread through the city
as a scorpion's sting instantly pervades the body.
Hearing it, men and women were distraught,                                       4
like trees and vines that see a forest fire.
Everywhere, whoever heard it beat his brow
in awful grief, losing all composure.

४६ मुख सुखाहिं लोचन स्त्रवहिं सोकु न हृदयँ समाइ ।
मनहुँ करुन रस कटकई उतरी अवध बजाइ ॥

१ मिलेहि माझ बिधि बात बेगारी ।
जहँ तहँ देहिं कैकइहि गारी ॥
एहि पापिनिहि बूझि का परेऊ ।
छाइ भवन पर पावकु धरेऊ ॥

२ निज कर नयन काढ़ि चह दीखा ।
डारि सुधा बिषु चाहत चीखा ॥
कुटिल कठोर कुबुद्धि अभागी ।
भइ रघुबंस बेनु बन आगी ॥

३ पालव बैठि पेड़ एहिं काटा ।
सुख महुँ सोक ठाटु धरि ठाटा ॥
सदा रामु एहि प्रान समाना ।
कारन कवन कुटिलपनु ठाना ॥

४ सत्य कहहिं कबि नारि सुभाऊ ।
सब बिधि अगहु अगाध दुराऊ ॥
निज प्रतिबिंबु बरुकु गहि जाई ।
जानि न जाइ नारि गति भाई ॥

४७ काह न पावकु जारि सक का न समुद्र समाइ ।
का न करै अबला प्रबल केहि जग कालु न खाइ ॥

Their faces were drawn, eyes streaming,                     46
and hearts could not contain their sorrow,
as if the army of pitiful sentiment, drums booming,
had laid siege to Avadh.[41]

When all was perfect, fate had ruined it!                   1
Everywhere, people cursed Kaikeyi:
"Whatever possessed this sinful woman
to set fire to the house that shelters her?
Tearing out her own eyes, she hopes to see,                 2
and discarding nectar, craves poison's savor.
Perverse and cruel, of warped mind and ill fate,
she is a conflagration in the Raghus' bamboo grove.
Seated on a young branch, she hacks down the tree,          3
and in joy's midst, rigs a scaffold for sorrow.[42]
Ram was ever as dear to her as breath,
so why did she become bent on duplicity?
Truly poets say that women's nature                         4
is wholly inscrutable, profoundly secretive.
One might manage to seize his own shadow,
but women's ways are incomprehensible, brother.

What will fire not burn,                                    47
or the sea not submerge?
What power will women, called weak, not wield?
Who in this world will death not devour?

१ का सुनाइ बिधि काह सुनावा ।
  का देखाइ चह काह देखावा ॥
  एक कहहिं भल भूप न कीन्हा ।
  बरु बिचारि नहिं कुमतिहि दीन्हा ॥

२ जो हठि भयउ सकल दुख भाजनु ।
  अबला बिबस ग्यानु गुनु गा जनु ॥
  एक धरम परमिति पहिचाने ।
  नृपहिं दोसु नहिं देहिं सयाने ॥

३ सिबि दधीचि हरिचंद कहानी ।
  एक एक सन कहहिं बखानी ॥
  एक भरत कर संमत कहहीं ।
  एक उदास भायँ सुनि रहहीं ॥

४ कान मूदि कर रद गहि जीहा ।
  एक कहहिं यह बात अलीहा ॥
  सुकृत जाहिं अस कहत तुम्हारे ।
  रामु भरत कहुँ प्रानपिआरे ॥

४८ चंदु चवै बरु अनल कन सुधा होइ बिषतूल ।
  सपनेहुँ कबहुँ न करहिं किछु भरतु राम प्रतिकूल ॥

१ एक बिधातहि दूषनु देहीं ।
  सुधा देखाइ दीन्ह बिषु जेहीं ॥
  खरभरु नगर सोचु सब काहू ।
  दुसह दाहु उर मिटा उछाहू ॥

Fate proclaimed one thing but ordained another,     1
conceived one plan but revealed another!"
Some said, "The lord of earth did not act rightly
or reflect, giving boons to this malicious woman,
which she willfully made a source of all woe,[43]     2
as if, in her power, his wisdom and virtue fled."
Others, discerning dharma's restraints,
wisely refrained from faulting the king.
Tales of Shibi, Dadhichi, and Harishchandra[44]     3
they recounted to each other.
One accused Bharat of complicity;
another, hearing this, grew depressed,
while another covered his ears, bit his tongue,     4
and declared, "That's a lie!
You lose your merit by saying this,
for Ram is dearer than life to Bharat.

The cool moon might shoot forth flaming embers,     48
or nectar turn to venom,
but never, even in a dream,
would Bharat do anything against Ram."

One railed at the divine ordainer,     1
who proffered nectar but produced poison.
There was tumult in the city as all mourned,
their hearts aflame, their festive mood erased.

२ बिप्रबधू कुलमान्य जठेरी ।
जे प्रिय परम कैकई केरी ॥
लगीं देन सिख सीलु सराही ।
बचन बानसम लागहिं ताही ॥

३ भरतु न मोहि प्रिय राम समाना ।
सदा कहहु यहु सबु जगु जाना ॥
करहु राम पर सहज सनेहू ।
केहिं अपराध आजु बनु देहू ॥

४ कबहुँ न कियहु सवति आरेसू ।
प्रीति प्रतीति जान सबु देसू ॥
कौसल्याँ अब काह बिगारा ।
तुम्ह जेहि लागि बज्र पुर पारा ॥

४९ सीय कि पिय सँगु परिहरिहि लखनु कि रहिहहिं धाम ।
राजु कि भूँजब भरत पुर नृपु कि जिइहि बिनु राम ॥

१ अस बिचारि उर छाड़हु कोहू ।
सोक कलंक कोठि जनि होहू ॥
भरतहि अवसि देहु जुबराजू ।
कानन काह राम कर काजू ॥

Brahman wives, elder-women of the clan,                    2
and all who were most dear to Kaikeyi
admonished her, lauding virtue—
but their words were like arrows to her:
"'Even Bharat is not as dear to me as Ram'—            3
so you always said, as everyone knows,
and you loved Ram instinctively.
For what crime do you send him to the woods today?
You were never jealous of your co-wife,                    4
the whole realm knows your love and trust.
Now, how has Kausalya wronged you,
that you would hurl a thunderbolt at the city?

Can Sita part with her beloved?                            49
Can Lakshman remain at home?
Can Bharat relish ruling the realm?
And can the lord of men live without Ram?

Reflecting on this, cast out your anger.                    1
Don't become a vessel of sorrow and disgrace!
Certainly, make Bharat heir-apparent—
but what business has Ram in the forest?

२ नाहिन रामु राज के भूखे ।
धरम धुरीन बिषय रस रूखे ॥
गुर गृह बसहुँ रामु तजि गेहू ।
नृप सन अस बरु दूसर लेहू ॥

३ जौं नहिं लगिहहु कहें हमारे ।
नहिं लागिहि कछु हाथ तुम्हारे ॥
जौं परिहास कीन्हि कछु होई ।
तौ कहि प्रगट जनावहु सोई ॥

४ राम सरिस सुत कानन जोगू ।
काह कहिहि सुनि तुम्ह कहुँ लोगू ॥
उठहु बेगि सोइ करहु उपाई ।
जेहि बिधि सोकु कलंकु नसाई ॥

५ जेहि भाँति सोकु कलंकु जाइ
उपाय करि कुल पालही ।
हठि फेरु रामहि जात बन जनि
बात दूसरि चालही ।
जिमि भानु बिनु दिनु प्रान बिनु तनु
चंद बिनु जिमि जामिनी ।
तिमि अवध तुलसीदास प्रभु बिनु
समुझि धौं जियँ भामिनी ॥

Ram has no craving for the kingdom,      2
he upholds dharma and is indifferent to desire.
Let Ram leave this house to stay with the guru—
ask this of the king as your second boon.
If you do not heed our advice,      3
you will gain nothing at all.
And if you have but made some kind of jest,
then admit it straightaway!
Is a son like Ram fit for forest exile?      4
Hearing this, what will people say of you?
Arise at once and do what is needed
to end this grief and infamy.

Do whatever it takes to dispel grief      5
and disgrace, and to protect the family.
Demand that Ram turn back from going
to the woods—do this and nothing else!
Like a day without sun, a body
without breath, or night without the moon,
so Avadh will be, says Tulsidas, without its lord.[45]
Woman, take this to heart!"

५०	सखिन्ह सिखावनु दीन्ह सुनत मधुर परिनाम हित ।
	तेइँ कछु कान न कीन्ह कुटिल प्रबोधी कूबरी ॥

१	उतरु न देइ दुसह रिस रूखी ।
	मृगिन्ह चितव जनु बाघिनि भूखी ॥
	ब्याधि असाधि जानि तिन्ह त्यागी ।
	चलीं कहत मतिमंद अभागी ॥
२	राजु करत यह दैअँ बिगोई ।
	कीन्हेसि अस जस करइ न कोई ॥
	एहि बिधि बिलपहिं पुर नर नारीं ।
	देहिं कुचालिहि कोटिक गारीं ॥
३	जरहिं बिषम जर लेहिं उसासा ।
	कवनि राम बिनु जीवन आसा ॥
	बिपुल बियोग प्रजा अकुलानी ।
	जनु जलचर गन सूखत पानी ॥
४	अति बिषाद बस लोग लोगाईं ।
	गए मातु पहिं रामु गोसाईं ॥
	मुख प्रसन्न चित चौगुन चाऊ ।
	मिटा सोचु जनि राखै राऊ ॥

५१	नव गयंदु रघुबीर मनु राजु अलान समान ।
	छूट जानि बन गवनु सुनि उर अनंदु अधिकान ॥

Thus her friends instructed her                                    50
with sweet words and beneficial advice,
yet she gave no ear to it,
schooled as she was by the perverse hunchback.


Coarsened by rage, she offered no reply,                           1
like a hungry tigress eyeing a herd of does.
Knowing her sickness was incurable, they left,
declaring her an ill-fated fool.
"Fate has ruined her, even as she reigns,                          2
for she has done what no one would do!"
So the men and women of the city lamented,
hurling heaps of abuse at that wrongdoer.
Feverish with woe, they sighed deeply, asking,                     3
"What hope is there of life, without Ram?"
They were as distraught at their looming loss
as water creatures in a worsening drought—
all men and women, overcome by utter grief.                        4
But Lord Ram went to his mother,
his face cheerful, his mind altogether eager,[46]
freed of worry that the king would hold him back.


The Raghu hero's mind was like a young elephant,                   51
newly snared in the harsh fetter of kingship.[47]
Learning of release and freedom to go
to the forest, his heart was filled with joy.

१ रघुकुलतिलक जोरि दोउ हाथा ।
मुदित मातु पद नायउ माथा ॥
दीन्हि असीस लाइ उर लीन्हे ।
भूषन बसन निछावरि कीन्हे ॥

२ बार बार मुख चुंबति माता ।
नयन नेह जलु पुलकित गाता ॥
गोद राखि पुनि हृदयँ लगाए ।
स्रवत प्रेमरस पयद सुहाए ॥

३ प्रेमु प्रमोदु न कछु कहि जाई ।
रंक धनद पदबी जनु पाई ॥
सादर सुंदर बदनु निहारी ।
बोली मधुर बचन महतारी ॥

४ कहहु तात जननी बलिहारी ।
कबहिं लगन मुद मंगलकारी ॥
सुकृत सील सुख सीवँ सुहाई ।
जनम लाभ कइ अवधि अघाई ॥

५२ जेहि चाहत नर नारि सब अति आरत एहि भाँति ।
जिमि चातक चातकि तृषित बृष्टि सरद रितु स्वाति ॥

१ तात जाउँ बलि बेगि नहाहू ।
जो मन भाव मधुर कछु खाहू ॥
पितु समीप तब जाएहु भैआ ।
भइ बड़ि बार जाइ बलि मैआ ॥

That gem of the Raghus joined his palms                    1
and happily bowed at his mother's feet.
Blessing him and clasping him to her heart,
she made propitiatory gifts of jewels and clothing.
Again and again, his mother kissed his face,                2
shedding tears of love, her body thrilling.
She held him in her lap, hugging him,
and her shapely breasts oozed maternal love's nectar.
Her love and delight cannot be expressed—                  3
like a pauper appointed to be god of riches.[48]
Gazing reverently at his beautiful face,
his mother spoke sweet words.
"By my life, son, tell your mother                          4
when the blessed, joyous moment will come,
fulfilling my good deeds, bringing delight,
and yielding my life's ultimate reward,

the moment for which all men and women                    52
yearn, as ardently as
thirst-crazed *cātaka* and *cātaki* birds
craving the monsoon drops of *svāti*.[49]

But son, I avow—you should go and bathe quickly,          1
eat some sweet dish of your liking,
and then proceed, child, to your father,
for, by your mother's life, it is very late!"[50]

93

२     मातु बचन सुनि अति अनुकूला ।
जनु सनेह सुरतरु के फूला ॥
सुख मकरंद भरे श्रियमूला ।
निरखि राम मनु भवँरु न भूला ॥

३     धरम धुरीन धरम गति जानी ।
कहेउ मातु सन अति मृदु बानी ॥
पिताँ दीन्ह मोहि कानन राजू ।
जहँ सब भाँति मोर बड़ काजू ॥

४     आयसु देहि मुदित मन माता ।
जेहिं मुद मंगल कानन जाता ॥
जनि सनेह बस डरपसि भोरें ।
आनँदु अंब अनुग्रह तोरें ॥

५३     बरष चारिदस बिपिन बसि करि पितु बचन प्रमान ।
आइ पाय पुनि देखिहउँ मनु जनि करसि मलान ॥

१     बचन बिनीत मधुर रघुबर के ।
सर सम लगे मातु उर करके ॥
सहमि सूखि सुनि सीतलि बानी ।
जिमि जवास परें पावस पानी ॥

२     कहि न जाइ कछु हृदय बिषादू ।
मनहुँ मृगी सुनि केहरि नादू ॥
नयन सजल तन थर थर काँपी ।
माझहि खाइ मीन जनु मापी ॥

Hearing his mother's most tender words,                              2
like flowers on the love-tree of heaven,
rooted in fortune and imbued with joy's nectar,
the bee of Ram's mind was undistracted.
That bearer of dharma, knowing dharma's way,                         3
spoke very gently to his mother:
"Father has given me the kingdom of the forest,
where I will fulfill my greatest task.
Give me leave, mother, with a glad heart,                            4
that my journey to the woods be happy and blessed.
Do not, out of love, even dream of fearing for me,
for by your grace, mother, all will be joyful.

When I have lived for fourteen years                                 53
in the forest, fulfilling father's promise,
I will return to again behold your feet.
So do not sully your mind with grief."

The sweet, humble words of the best of Raghus                        1
tore into his mother's heart like an arrow.
At their gentle sound, she grew terrified and pale,
like a *javāsa* shrub feeling the first shower.[51]
She grew as indescribably sad                                        2
as a doe who has heard a lion's roar.
Her eyes filled with tears and her body shook,
like a fish deranged by swallowing rain-foam.[52]

३ धरि धीरजु सुत बदनु निहारी ।
गदगद बचन कहति महतारी ॥
तात पितहि तुम्ह प्रान पिआरे ।
देखि मुदित नित चरित तुम्हारे ॥

४ राजु देन कहुँ सुभ दिन साधा ।
कहेउ जान बन केहिं अपराधा ॥
तात सुनावहु मोहि निदानू ।
को दिनकर कुल भयउ कृसानू ॥

५४ निरखि राम रुख सचिवसुत कारनु कहेउ बुझाइ ।
सुनि प्रसंगु रहि मूक जिमि दसा बरनि नहिं जाइ ॥

१ राखि न सकइ न कहि सक जाहू ।
दुहूँ भाँति उर दारुन दाहू ॥
लिखत सुधाकर गा लिखि राहू ।
बिधि गति बाम सदा सब काहू ॥

२ धरम सनेह उभयँ मति घेरी ।
भइ गति साँप छुछुंदरि केरी ॥
राखउँ सुतहि करउँ अनुरोधू ।
धरमु जाइ अरु बंधु बिरोधू ॥

३ कहउँ जान बन तौ बड़ि हानी ।
संकट सोच बिबस भइ रानी ॥
बहुरि समुझि तिय धरमु सयानी ।
रामु भरतु दोउ सुत सम जानी ॥

Gathering her courage, looking at her son's face,  3
his mother spoke in a quavering voice.
"Son, you are dear as life to your father,
and he has always been pleased by your deeds.
Having set a propitious date to give you the realm,  4
for what crime has he ordered you to the forest?
My child, tell me the real cause:
who became fire to consume our solar lineage?"

At a glance from Ram, the chief minister's son  54
gave a full account of the cause.
Hearing it, she was as if dumbstruck,
and her state cannot be described.

She could neither hold him back nor tell him to go;  1
either way, her heart would burn with anguish.
Musing, "Though he meant 'moon,' he wrote 'Rahu'[53]—
fate's course is forever averse to all,"
her mind bound by both duty and love,  2
she was like a snake who has caught a mole.[54]
"If, by entreaty, I cling to my son,
dharma will be lost and brotherly enmity arise,
but if I tell him, 'Go to the woods,' it will be a terrible loss."  3
The queen grew helpless with worry and distress,
but then, wisely pondering her womanly duty
and knowing Ram and Bharat to be equally her sons,

४ सरल सुभाउ राम महतारी ।
बोली बचन धीर धरि भारी ॥
तात जाउँ बलि कीन्हेहु नीका ।
पितु आयसु सब धरमक टीका ॥

५५ राजु देन कहि दीन्ह बनु मोहि न सो दुख लेसु ।
तुम्ह बिनु भरतहि भूपतिहि प्रजहि प्रचंड कलेसु ॥

१ जौं केवल पितु आयसु ताता ।
तौ जनि जाहु जानि बड़ि माता ॥
जौं पितु मातु कहेउ बन जाना ।
तौ कानन सत अवध समाना ॥

२ पितु बनदेव मातु बनदेवी ।
खग मृग चरन सरोरुह सेवी ॥
अंतहुँ उचित नृपहि बनबासू ।
बय बिलोकि हियँ होइ हराँसू ॥

३ बड़भागी बनु अवध अभागी ।
जो रघुबंसतिलक तुम्ह त्यागी ॥
जौं सुत कहौं संग मोहि लेहू ।
तुम्हरे हृदयँ होइ संदेहू ॥

४ पूत परम प्रिय तुम्ह सबही के ।
प्रान प्रान के जीवन जी के ॥
ते तुम्ह कहहु मातु बन जाऊँ ।
मैं सुनि बचन बैठि पछिताऊँ ॥

that good-natured woman, Ram's birth mother,     4
summoned all her courage and spoke:
"My son, I swear, you have acted rightly,
for a father's order is the crown jewel of dharma.

That he promised the kingdom but gave exile     55
does not cause me the least sorrow,
but, without you, Bharat, the king,
and our people will suffer intense grief.

If it were just your father's command, son,     1
you should not go, considering a mother's primacy.
But if father and mother ordered you to the forest,
then the woods are equal to a hundred Avadhs,
with sylvan gods and goddesses for parents,     2
and birds and beasts to adore your lovely feet.
At life's end, forest dwelling is proper for a king,
but seeing your youth, my heart grieves.
Fortunate is the forest and luckless is Avadh,     3
which you, crown jewel of the Raghus, have left.
If I ask you to take me along, my child,
uncertainty will arise in your heart.
Son, you who are supremely beloved to all,     4
the very breath and soul of our lives,
say, 'Mother, I am going to the forest,'
and hearing these words, I sit and lament.

५६    यह बिचारि नहिं करउँ हठ झूठ सनेहु बढ़ाइ ।
     मानि मातु कर नात बलि सुरति बिसरि जनि जाइ ॥

१    देव पितर सब तुम्हहि गोसाईं ।
     राखहुँ पलक नयन की नाईं ॥
     अवधि अंबु प्रिय परिजन मीना ।
     तुम्ह करुनाकर धरम धुरीना ॥

२    अस बिचारि सोइ करहु उपाई ।
     सबहि जिअत जेहिं भेंटहु आई ॥
     जाहु सुखेन बनहि बलि जाऊँ ।
     करि अनाथ जन परिजन गाऊँ ॥

३    सब कर आजु सुकृत फल बीता ।
     भयउ कराल कालु बिपरीता ॥
     बहुबिधि बिलपि चरन लपटानी ।
     परम अभागिनि आपुहि जानी ॥

४    दारुन दुसह दाहु उर ब्यापा ।
     बरनि न जाहिं बिलाप कलापा ॥
     राम उठाइ मातु उर लाई ।
     कहि मृदु बचन बहुरि समुझाई ॥

५७    समाचार तेहि समय सुनि सीय उठी अकुलाइ ।
     जाइ सासु पद कमल जुग बंदि बैठि सिरु नाइ ॥

MURTY CLASSICAL
LIBRARY OF INDIA

*Sheldon Pollock, General Editor*

# TULSIDAS
# THE EPIC OF RAM
## VOLUME 3

### MCLI 15

Reflecting on this, I will not be stubborn                           56
or make a false show of affection.
Yet I ask, on my life: honor the maternal bond
and do not forget me!

May all the gods and ancestors, lord,[55]                            1
protect you as the eyelids do the eyes.
Your exile's term is water, your dear ones, fish,
and you are a merciful upholder of dharma.
Considering this, contrive it so                                     2
that we all may live to greet you on your return.
Go gladly to the forest, on my life,
orphaning your subjects, clan, and city.
Today, the fruit of all our good deeds is spent,                     3
and time has turned hostile and cruel."
Much lamenting, she clung to his feet,
reckoning herself supremely unlucky.
Unbearable sorrow pervaded her heart                                 4
and her countless laments were indescribable.
Ram lifted his mother into his embrace
and consoled her with many tender words.

At that moment, hearing the news,                                    57
Sita arose in great distress,
went to her mother-in-law, saluted her holy feet,
and sat with her face downcast.

१ दीन्हि असीस सासु मृदु बानी ।
अति सुकुमारि देखि अकुलानी ॥
बैठि नमितमुख सोचति सीता ।
रूप रासि पति प्रेम पुनीता ॥

२ चलन चहत बन जीवन नाथू ।
केहि सुकृती सन होइहि साथू ॥
की तनु प्रान कि केवल प्राना ।
बिधि करतबु कछु जाइ न जाना ॥

३ चारु चरन नख लेखति धरनी ।
नूपुर मुखर मधुर कबि बरनी ॥
मनहुँ प्रेम बस बिनती करहीं ।
हमहि सीय पद जनि परिहरहीं ॥

४ मंजु बिलोचन मोचति बारी ।
बोली देखि राम महतारी ॥
तात सुनहु सिय अति सुकुमारी ।
सासु ससुर परिजनहि पिआरी ॥

५८ पिता जनक भूपाल मनि ससुर भानुकुल भानु ।
पति रबिकुल कैरव बिपिन बिधु गुन रूप निधानु ॥

१ मैं पुनि पुत्रबधू प्रिय पाई ।
रूप रासि गुन सील सुहाई ॥
नयन पुतरि करि प्रीति बढ़ाई ।
राखेउँ प्रान जानकिहिं लाई ॥

102

Ram's mother gently gave her blessing,      1
despairing to see her tender youth.
Sita sat in thought, her head bowed,
epitome of beauty and pure wifely love.
"The lord of my life wants to go to the forest.    2
By what act of merit may I accompany him—
in body and soul, or with life breath alone?
The doings of fate elude all understanding."
Her lovely toenails etched the earth[56]    3
making her anklets tinkle sweetly—poets
would say they were pleading, love-struck,
not to be separated from Sita's feet.
Her lovely eyes shed tears,    4
and seeing her, Ram's mother spoke,
"Listen, my son. Sita is a most tender maiden,
dear to her in-laws and to all the clan.

Her father, Janak, is the jewel of earth's lords,    58
her father-in-law, sun of the solar line,
and you, her husband, are moon to the lilies
of the sun-clan, an abode of beauty and virtue.

As for me, I have found a dear daughter-in-law,    1
of surpassing beauty and amiable qualities.
I have doted on her with ever-growing love
entrusting my very life to Janaki.

२ कलपबेलि जिमि बहुबिधि लाली ।
सींचि सनेह सलिल प्रतिपाली ॥
फूलत फलत भयउ बिधि बामा ।
जानि न जाइ काह परिनामा ॥
३ पलँग पीठ तजि गोद हिंडोरा ।
सियँ न दीन्ह पगु अवनि कठोरा ॥
जिअनमूरि जिमि जोगवत रहउँ ।
दीप बाति नहिं टारन कहउँ ॥
४ सोइ सिय चलन चहति बन साथा ।
आयसु काह होइ रघुनाथा ॥
चंद किरन रस रसिक चकोरी ।
रबि रुख नयन सकइ किमि जोरी ॥

५९ करि केहरि निसिचर चरहिं दुष्ट जंतु बन भूरि ।
बिष बाटिकाँ कि सोह सुत सुभग सजीवनि मूरि ॥

१ बन हित कोल किरात किसोरी ।
रचीं बिरंचि बिषय सुख भोरी ॥
पाहन कृमि जिमि कठिन सुभाऊ ।
तिन्हहि कलेसु न कानन काऊ ॥
२ कै तापस तिय कानन जोगू ।
जिन्ह तप हेतु तजा सब भोगू ॥
सिय बन बसिहि तात केहि भाँती ।
चित्रलिखित कपि देखि डेराती ॥

I have cherished her like a heavenly creeper,       2
nurturing her with the water of love,
but just as she flowers and bears fruit, fate has turned
    hostile,
and none knows what the outcome will be.
Never leaving a soft couch, lap, or swing,       3
Sita has yet to set foot on rough earth.
I have guarded her like the herb of immortality,
and never even asked her to trim a lampwick.
Yet this same Sita wants to go with you to the woods.    4
What is your command, Raghu lord?
How can a partridge, nurtured on moonbeams,
turn her eyes toward the blazing sun?

Elephants, lions, demons, and a host       59
of evil creatures range in the forest.
My son, how can a poisonous garden
befit a sweet ambrosial herb?

For the woods, tribal girls, Kols and Kirats,       1
ignorant of comforts, were made by the creator.
By nature crude as rock-slugs,
they never suffer pain in the forest.
Or else, ascetics' wives merit the woods,       2
who have given up all pleasure for austerity.
But son, how could this Sita live in the forest,
who takes fright at a monkey's mere picture?

३　सुरसर सुभग बनज बन चारी ।
　　डाबर जोगु कि हंसकुमारी ॥
　　अस बिचारि जस आयसु होई ।
　　मैं सिख देउँ जानकिहि सोई ॥

४　जौं सिय भवन रहै कह अंबा ।
　　मोहि कहँ होइ बहुत अवलंबा ॥
　　सुनि रघुबीर मातु प्रिय बानी ।
　　सील सनेह सुधाँ जनु सानी ॥

६०　कहि प्रिय बचन बिबेकमय कीन्हि मातु परितोष ।
　　लगे प्रबोधन जानकिहि प्रगटि बिपिन गुन दोष ॥

१　मातु समीप कहत सकुचाहीं ।
　　बोले समउ समुझि मन माहीं ॥
　　राजकुमारि सिखावनु सुनहू ।
　　आन भाँति जियँ जनि कछु गुनहू ॥

२　आपन मोर नीक जौं चहहू ।
　　बचनु हमार मानि गृह रहहू ॥
　　आयसु मोर सासु सेवकाई ।
　　सब बिधि भामिनि भवन भलाई ॥

३　एहि ते अधिक धरमु नहिं दूजा ।
　　सादर सासु ससुर पद पूजा ॥
　　जब जब मातु करिहि सुधि मोरी ।
　　होइहि प्रेम बिकल मति भोरी ॥

Is a *haṃsa* maiden, who glides among lotuses      3
of heaven's lake, fit for a fetid mudflat?
Having considered this, as you command,
so I will instruct Janak's daughter.
But if," his mother added, "Sita stays at home,      4
she will be a great support to me."
The Raghu hero listened to his mother's advice,
imbued with the nectar of virtue and affection,

and spoke loving words,      60
filled with discernment, to please his mother.
He began to instruct Janaki,
describing the various aspects of forest life.

Hesitant to address her before his mother,      1
yet he spoke up, mindful of the moment.
"Princess, listen to my instruction,
and do not even consider anything else.
If you desire the best for yourself and me,      2
then heed my words and stay at home.
In obedience to me and service to my mother,
your good, woman, lies solely in this house.
For there is no greater dharma than this:      3
adoration of the feet of one's in-laws.
Whenever mother starts recollecting me
and becomes distracted by affection,

४ तब तब तुम्ह कहि कथा पुरानी ।
सुंदरि समुझाएहु मृदु बानी ॥
कहउँ सुभायँ सपथ सत मोही ।
सुमुखि मातु हित राखउँ तोही ॥

६१ गुर श्रुति संमत धरम फलु पाइअ बिनहिं कलेस ।
हठ बस सब संकट सहे गालव नहुष नरेस ॥

१ मैं पुनि करि प्रवान पितु बानी ।
बेगि फिरब सुनु सुमुखि सयानी ॥
दिवस जात नहिं लागिहि बारा ।
सुंदरि सिखवनु सुनहु हमारा ॥

२ जौं हठ करहु प्रेम बस बामा ।
तौ तुम्ह दुखु पाउब परिनामा ॥
काननु कठिन भयंकरु भारी ।
घोर घामु हिम बारि बयारी ॥

३ कुस कंटक मग काँकर नाना ।
चलब पयादेहिं बिनु पदत्राना ॥
चरन कमल मृदु मंजु तुम्हारे ।
मारग अगम भूमिधर भारे ॥

then tell her ancient, edifying tales,      4
my beauty, in a comforting voice.
Honestly, I swear a hundred times—it is only
for mother's sake, lovely one, that I keep you at home.

This dharma is in accord with guru and Veda,      61
and yields its fruit without sorrow.
Due to obstinate willfulness, sage Galav
and King Nahush endured every affliction.[57]

And I, having fulfilled my father's promise,      1
will soon return, wise and beautiful one.
It will not take long for these days to pass,
so heed my instructions, lovely one!
If you are willful, woman, from excess of love,      2
you will find sorrow as the outcome.
The forest is harsh and terrifying,
with extremes of heat and cold, rain and wind.
Its paths have sharp grass, thorns, and rocks,      3
and one must go on foot, without footwear.
Your feet are like fair, delicate lotuses,
and the road impassable, the mountains immense.

४     कंदर खोह नदीं नद नारे ।
अगम अगाध न जाहिं निहारे ॥
भालु बाघ बृक केहरि नागा ।
करहिं नाद सुनि धीरजु भागा ॥

६२     भूमि सयन बलकल बसन असनु कंद फल मूल ।
ते कि सदा सब दिन मिलहिं सबुइ समय अनुकूल ॥

१     नर अहार रजनीचर चरहीं ।
कपट बेष बिधि कोटिक करहीं ॥
लागइ अति पहार कर पानी ।
बिपिन बिपति नहिं जाइ बखानी ॥

२     ब्याल कराल बिहग बन घोरा ।
निसिचर निकर नारि नर चोरा ॥
डरपहिं धीर गहन सुधि आएँ ।
मृगलोचनि तुम्ह भीरु सुभाएँ ॥

३     हंसगवनि तुम्ह नहिं बन जोगू ।
सुनि अपजसु मोहि देइहि लोगू ॥
मानस सलिल सुधाँ प्रतिपाली ।
जिअइ कि लवन पयोधि मराली ॥

४     नव रसाल बन बिहरनसीला ।
सोह कि कोकिल बिपिन करीला ॥
रहहु भवन अस हृदयँ बिचारी ।
चंदबदनि दुखु कानन भारी ॥

Caves and passes, rivers and creek hollows                                  4
are too deep and inaccessible even to behold.
Bears, tigers, wolves, lions, and elephants
make sounds that rob you of all courage.

You sleep on bare earth, wear clothes of bark,                             62
and eat tubers, fruit, and roots—
and these, too, you hardly find every day,
but only in their proper season.

Night-stalkers roam there, who feed on men,                                 1
assuming innumerable cunning guises,
and the water of the hills afflicts the body.
The woes of the woods cannot be described!
There are monstrous snakes, terrifying birds,                               2
hordes of demons who snatch men and women.
Even the resolute take fright at the thought of it,
and you, doe-eyed one, are timid by nature.
With your swaying gait, you are unfit for the woods,[58]                     3
and, if they hear of it, people will slander me.
Reared on the ambrosial water of Lake Manas,
can a *haṃsa*-girl survive on the salt sea?
Flitting about in tender mango groves,                                      4
is a cuckoo suited to thorny scrub land?
Reflecting on this, remain at home,
moon-faced one, for the forest is full of pain.

६३ सहज सुहृद गुर स्वामि सिख जो न करइ सिर मानि ।
सो पछिताइ अघाइ उर अवसि होइ हित हानि ॥

१ सुनि मृदु बचन मनोहर पिय के ।
लोचन ललित भरे जल सिय के ॥
सीतल सिख दाहक भइ कैसें ।
चकइहि सरद चंद निसि जैसें ॥

२ उतरु न आव बिकल बैदेही ।
तजन चहत सुचि स्वामि सनेही ॥
बरबस रोकि बिलोचन बारी ।
धरि धीरजु उर अवनिकुमारी ॥

३ लागि सासु पग कह कर जोरी ।
छमबि देबि बड़ि अबिनय मोरी ॥
दीन्हि प्रानपति मोहि सिख सोई ।
जेहि बिधि मोर परम हित होई ॥

४ मैं पुनि समुझि दीखि मन माहीं ।
पिय बियोग सम दुखु जग नाहीं ॥

६४ प्राननाथ करुनायतन सुंदर सुखद सुजान ।
तुम्ह बिनु रघुकुल कुमुद बिधु सुरपुर नरक समान ॥

One who does not accept the instruction 63
of an innately benevolent teacher or husband,
will wholeheartedly repent later
and come to certain harm."

She heard her beloved's sweet, amiable words, 1
and Sita's lovely eyes filled with tears.
His cool directive inflamed her heart,
as moonlit night torments a wild goose.[59]
Vaidehi* made no reply, but anxiously mused, 2
"My dear, noble lord wants to abandon me."
Tenaciously holding back her tears,
and summoning inner strength, the earth's daughter
fell in supplication at her mother-in-law's feet, 3
saying, "Divine lady, forgive my great audacity.
The lord of my life has given instruction
conducive to my greatest good.
Yet on reflection, I perceive that there is 4
no grief on earth like separation from one's love.

Lord of my breath, abode of mercy, 64
handsome, bliss-giving, and wise—
without you, moon of the Raghu night-lilies,
even the city of the gods would be like hell.

---

* Videha's daughter, Sita.

१ मातु पिता भगिनी प्रिय भाई ।
प्रिय परिवारु सुहृद समुदाई ॥
सासु ससुर गुर सजन सहाई ।
सुत सुंदर सुसील सुखदाई ॥

२ जहँ लगि नाथ नेह अरु नाते ।
पिय बिनु तियहि तरनिहु ते ताते ॥
तनु धनु धामु धरनि पुर राजू ।
पति बिहीन सबु सोक समाजू ॥

३ भोग रोगसम भूषन भारू ।
जम जातना सरिस संसारू ॥
प्राननाथ तुम्ह बिनु जग माहीं ।
मो कहुँ सुखद कतहुँ कछु नाहीं ॥

४ जिय बिनु देह नदी बिनु बारी ।
तैसिअ नाथ पुरुष बिनु नारी ॥
नाथ सकल सुख साथ तुम्हारें ।
सरद बिमल बिधु बदनु निहारें ॥

६५ खग मृग परिजन नगरु बनु बलकल बिमल दुकूल ।
नाथ साथ सुरसदन सम परनसाल सुख मूल ॥

१ बनदेबीं बनदेव उदारा ।
करिहहिं सासु ससुर सम सारा ॥
कुस किसलय साथरी सुहाई ।
प्रभु सँग मंजु मनोज तुराई ॥

114

Mother and father, sister and dear brother,     1
loving family and numerous friends,
parents-in-law, guru, helpful well-wishers,
even a handsome, pleasing, well-mannered son—
whatever bonds of affection exist, my lord,     2
scorch like sun a woman without her love.
Body, wealth, home, land, city, and kingdom,
without a husband, are but a horde of sorrows.
Delights are like disease, adornments a burden,     3
and worldly life like the torments of Yama.[60]
Lord of my life's breath, without you
there is nothing, anywhere, to give me joy.
Like body without soul or river without water,     4
just so, my lord, is a woman without a man.
Master, for me all joy is in your companionship
and the sight of your face, radiant like autumn's moon.

Birds and animals will be kin, the forest my city,     65
and bark of trees my sheer muslins,
and lord, by your side, a hut of leaves will be
a source of joy equal to a heavenly mansion.

Benevolent goddesses and gods of the woods     1
will watch over me like doting in-laws,
and a mat of grass and leaf buds,
with my lord, will be Kama's* own coverlet.

—————

* The god of love.

२  कंद मूल फल अमिअ अहारू ।
    अवध सौध सत सरिस पहारू ॥
    छिनु छिनु प्रभु पद कमल बिलोकी ।
    रहिहउँ मुदित दिवस जिमि कोकी ॥

३  बन दुख नाथ कहे बहुतेरे ।
    भय बिषाद परिताप घनेरे ॥
    प्रभु बियोग लवलेस समाना ।
    सब मिलि होहिं न कृपानिधाना ॥

४  अस जियँ जानि सुजान सिरोमनि ।
    लेइअ संग मोहि छाड़िअ जनि ॥
    बिनती बहुत करौं का स्वामी ।
    करुनामय उर अंतरजामी ॥

६६  राखिअ अवध जो अवधि लगि रहत न जनिअहिं प्रान ।
     दीनबंधु सुंदर सुखद सील सनेह निधान ॥

१  मोहि मग चलत न होइहि हारी ।
    छिनु छिनु चरन सरोज निहारी ॥
    सबहि भाँति पिय सेवा करिहौं ।
    मारग जनित सकल श्रम हरिहौं ॥

Bulbs, roots, and fruit will be ambrosial food,                    2
and hilltops like a hundred Avadh mansions.
Constantly gazing on my lord's lovely feet,
I will live as happily as a wild goose in daylight.
My husband spoke much of the forest's woes,                    3
of its great terrors, miseries, and afflictions,
yet compared to one instant apart from my lord,
altogether they are as nothing, merciful one.
Knowing this well, crown jewel of discernment,                    4
take me with you and do not abandon me!
But why should I beg so fervently, lord?
You are the all-compassionate inner knower.[61]

Know this: if you keep me in Avadh                    66
till exile's end, my life's breath will leave,
friend of the humble, and beautiful,
bliss-giving treasury of kindness and love!

Treading the path will not tire me,                    1
when at every instant I see your lotus feet.
I will render every service to my beloved
and ease all the fatigue of your wayfaring.

२ पाय पखारि बैठि तरु छाहीं ।
करिहउँ बाउ मुदित मन माहीं ॥
श्रम कन सहित स्याम तनु देखें ।
कहँ दुख समउ प्रानपति पेखें ॥

३ सम महि तृन तरुपल्लव डासी ।
पाय पलोटिहि सब निसि दासी ॥
बार बार मृदु मूरति जोही ।
लागिहि तात बयारि न मोही ॥

४ को प्रभु सँग मोहि चितवनिहारा ।
सिंघबधुहि जिमि ससक सिआरा ॥
मैं सुकुमारि नाथ बन जोगू ।
तुम्हहि उचित तप मो कहुँ भोगू ॥

६७ ऐसेउ बचन कठोर सुनि जौं न हृदउ बिलगान ।
तौ प्रभु बिषम बियोग दुख सहिहहिं पावँर प्रान ॥

१ अस कहि सीय बिकल भइ भारी ।
बचन बियोगु न सकी सँभारी ॥
देखि दसा रघुपति जियँ जाना ।
हठि राखें नहिं राखिहि प्राना ॥

२ कहेउ कृपाल भानुकुलनाथा ।
परिहरि सोचु चलहु बन साथा ॥
नहिं बिषाद कर अवसरु आजू ।
बेगि करहु बन गवन समाजू ॥

In the shade of a tree, I will wash your feet                    2
and fan you, rejoicing in my heart.
Beholding the dark, sweat-beaded limbs
of my life's lord, when will I ever grieve?
Spreading a bed of grass and shoots on even ground,              3
your maidservant will massage your feet all night.
As I constantly gaze at your soothing form,
hot summer winds will not afflict me.
And who, when I am with my lord, would dare cast his eye         4
    on me,
as a rabbit or jackal on a lion's mate?
Am I a frail maid, and you, husband, fit for the wilds?
Were you bred for austerity and I for indulgence?

But I suppose, since my heart did not burst                     67
on hearing your harsh sentence,
lord, this wretched creature can endure
even awful separation from you."

As she said this, Sita became most distraught,                   1
unable to manage the word "separation."
Perceiving her state, the Raghu lord realized,
"If I compel her to stay, she will not survive."
So the merciful master of the sun clan said,                     2
"Cease worrying and come to the woods with me.
Today there is no occasion for gloom.
Get ready quickly to leave for the forest."

३ कहि प्रिय बचन प्रिया समुझाई ।
लगे मातु पद आसिष पाई ॥
बेगि प्रजा दुख मेटब आई ।
जननी निठुर बिसरि जनि जाई ॥

४ फिरिहि दसा बिधि बहुरि कि मोरी ।
देखिहउँ नयन मनोहर जोरी ॥
सुदिन सुघरी तात कब होइहि ।
जननी जिअत बदन बिधु जोइहि ॥

६८ बहुरि बच्छ कहि लालु कहि रघुपति रघुबर तात ।
कबहिं बोलाइ लगाइ हियँ हरषि निरखिहउँ गात ॥

१ लखि सनेह कातरि महतारी ।
बचनु न आव बिकल भइ भारी ॥
राम प्रबोधु कीन्ह बिधि नाना ।
समउ सनेहु न जाइ बखाना ॥

२ तब जानकी सासु पग लागी ।
सुनिअ माय मैं परम अभागी ॥
सेवा समय दैअँ बनु दीन्हा ।
मोर मनोरथु सफल न कीन्हा ॥

३ तजब छोभु जनि छाड़िअ छोहू ।
करमु कठिन कछु दोसु न मोहू ॥
सुनि सिय बचन सासु अकुलानी ।
दसा कवनि बिधि कहौं बखानी ॥

Instructing his love with these loving words,          3
he bowed at his mother's feet for her blessing.
"Come back soon to assuage your subjects' sorrow,
and do not forget this hard-hearted mother.[62]
Oh fate, will my luck ever turn, that I may again     4
behold this lovely pair before my eyes?
When will that blessed day and hour come, my son,
when your mother, yet alive, sees the moon of your face?

When may I say 'darling son,' and 'dearest boy,'     68
and 'my little Raghu prince,'
call you once again into my arms,
and gaze with delight upon your form?"

When he saw his mother so agitated by love       1
that in awful distress she could not speak,
Ram consoled her in various ways—
the tenderness of that moment is indescribable.
Then Janaki fell at her mother-in-law's feet.     2
"Mother, I am supremely unlucky,
for, instead of serving you, I am fated for exile
and cannot fulfill my own wishes.
Forsake anguish, though not your affection.     3
Karma is cruel, but I am not at fault."
At Sita's words, her mother-in-law grew distraught.
How can I fully describe her condition?

४   बारहिं बार लाइ उर लीन्ही ।
    धरि धीरजु सिख आसिष दीन्ही ॥
    अचल होउ अहिवातु तुम्हारा ।
    जब लगि गंग जमुन जल धारा ॥

६९  सीतहि सासु असीस सिख दीन्हि अनेक प्रकार ।
    चली नाइ पद पदुम सिरु अति हित बारहिं बार ॥

१   समाचार जब लछिमन पाए ।
    ब्याकुल बिलख बदन उठि धाए ॥
    कंप पुलक तन नयन सनीरा ।
    गहे चरन अति प्रेम अधीरा ॥

२   कहि न सकत कछु चितवत ठाढ़े ।
    मीनु दीन जनु जल तें काढ़े ॥
    सोचु हृदयँ बिधि का होनिहारा ।
    सबु सुखु सुकृतु सिरान हमारा ॥

३   मो कहुँ काह कहब रघुनाथा ।
    राखिहहिं भवन कि लेहहिं साथा ॥
    राम बिलोकि बंधु कर जोरें ।
    देह गेह सब सन तृनु तोरें ॥

४   बोले बचनु राम नय नागर ।
    सील सनेह सरल सुख सागर ॥
    तात प्रेम बस जनि कदराहू ।
    समुझि हृदयँ परिनाम उछाहू ॥

122

She hugged Sita again and again,                                    4
and composing herself, instructed and blessed her.
"May your auspicious married state endure
as long as Ganga and Yamuna flow!"

Thus did her mother-in-law, in countless ways,                     69
bless and admonish Sita, and she,
with great affection, bowed repeatedly
at her lovely feet and took her leave.

When Lakshman received the news,                                    1
he came running, his face grief stricken,
his body flushed and trembling, eyes tear filled.
Undone by love, he clasped his brother's feet
but could not speak. He stood up and stared,                        2
like a poor fish taken from the water,
his heart anxious—"Fate! What will happen now?
Are all my happiness and merit exhausted?
What will the Raghu lord say to me?                                  3
Will he keep me at home, or take me along?"
Ram saw his brother standing in supplication,
ready to sever all bodily and domestic ties.[63]
Then Ram, prudent in policy, noble                                  4
and innately loving, ocean of joy, spoke:
"Dear one, do not be overcome by love,
but reflect on our destined final happiness.

123

७० मातु पिता गुरु स्वामि सिख सिर धरि करहिं सुभायँ ।
लहेउ लाभु तिन्ह जनम कर नतरु जनमु जग जायँ ॥

१ अस जियँ जानि सुनहु सिख भाई ।
करहु मातु पितु पद सेवकाई ॥
भवन भरतु रिपुसूदनु नाहीं ।
राउ बृद्ध मम दुखु मन माहीं ॥

२ मैं बन जाउँ तुम्हहि लेइ साथा ।
होइ सबहि बिधि अवध अनाथा ॥
गुरु पितु मातु प्रजा परिवारू ।
सब कहुँ परइ दुसह दुख भारू ॥

३ रहहु करहु सब कर परितोषू ।
नतरु तात होइहि बड़ दोषू ॥
जासु राज प्रिय प्रजा दुखारी ।
सो नृपु अवसि नरक अधिकारी ॥

४ रहहु तात असि नीति बिचारी ।
सुनत लखनु भए ब्याकुल भारी ॥
सिअरें बचन सूखि गए कैसें ।
परसत तुहिन तामरसु जैसें ॥

७१ उतरु न आवत प्रेम बस गहे चरन अकुलाइ ।
नाथ दासु मैं स्वामि तुम्ह तजहु त काह बसाइ ॥

124

Simply honoring and executing the orders 70
of mother, father, teacher, and lord,
we earn the full fruit of our birth.
Otherwise, we are born in this world in vain.

Knowing this, hear my instruction, brother: 1
serve the feet of our mother and father.
Bharat and Shatrughna are away from home,
and the king is aged and grieving over me.
Were I to take you with me to the woods, 2
Avadh would be utterly orphaned.
Our teacher, parents, subjects, and kin
would be burdened with insufferable woe.
So stay and comfort them all, 3
otherwise, child, it will be a great sin.
He in whose realm dear subjects suffer,
that king, surely, is worthy of hell.
So stay, brother, mindful of this principle." 4
Hearing this, Lakshman was greatly upset,
and withered, at these coolly uttered words,
like a lotus touched by frost.

Overcome by love, he could not reply 71
but clung in anguish to his brother's feet.
"Lord, I am a servant; you, my master.
Abandon me, and where is my recourse?

१ दीन्हि मोहि सिख नीकि गोसाईं।
लागि अगम अपनी कदराईं॥
नरबर धीर धरम धुर धारी।
निगम नीति कहुँ ते अधिकारी॥

२ मैं सिसु प्रभु सनेहँ प्रतिपाला।
मंदरु मेरु कि लेहिं मराला॥
गुर पितु मातु न जानउँ काहू।
कहउँ सुभाउ नाथ पतिआहू॥

३ जहँ लगि जगत सनेह सगाई।
प्रीति प्रतीति निगम निजु गाई॥
मोरें सबइ एक तुम्ह स्वामी।
दीनबंधु उर अंतरजामी॥

४ धरम नीति उपदेसिअ ताही।
कीरति भूति सुगति प्रिय जाही॥
मन क्रम बचन चरन रत होई।
कृपासिंधु परिहरिअ कि सोई॥

७२ करुनासिंधु सुबंधु के सुनि मृदु बचन बिनीत।
समुझाए उर लाइ प्रभु जानि सनेहँ सभीत॥

१ मागहु बिदा मातु सन जाई।
आवहु बेगि चलहु बन भाई॥
मुदित भए सुनि रघुबर बानी।
भयउ लाभ बड़ गइ बड़ि हानि॥

126

You have given me apt instructions, lord,                     1
yet, in my timidity, they seem onerous.
Ideal men, who resolutely bear dharma's burden
are entitled to sacred lore and ethical teaching.
I am but a child nurtured by your love.                       2
Can a gosling lift Mount Mandar or Meru?
I know no other guru, father, or mother—
I declare this sincerely, lord, believe me.
Whatever be worldly ties of affection,                        3
love, and trust, of which the Veda itself has spoken,
to me, master, they all are only you,
comforter of the humble, dweller in the heart.
Ethical instruction is given to one                           4
who cherishes fame, glory, and salvation.
But one who, in heart, deed, and word, adores your feet—
ocean of compassion!—will he be abandoned?"

That sea of mercy heard the sweet words                       72
of his dear brother's entreaty,
and knowing his anxiety born of love,
the Lord embraced and instructed him.

"Go, ask leave of your mother,                                1
and return soon, brother, to go to the forest."
Overjoyed at the Raghu lord's words,
Lakshman's looming loss became great gain.

२ हरषित हृदयँ मातु पहिं आए ।
मनहुँ अंध फिरि लोचन पाए ॥
जाइ जननि पग नायउ माथा ।
मनु रघुनंदन जानकि साथा ॥

३ पूँछे मातु मलिन मन देखी ।
लखन कही सब कथा बिसेषी ॥
गई सहमि सुनि बचन कठोरा ।
मृगी देखि दव जनु चहु ओरा ॥

४ लखन लखेउ भा अनरथ आजू ।
एहिं सनेह बस करब अकाजू ॥
मागत बिदा सभय सकुचाहीं ।
जाइ संग बिधि कहिहि कि नाहीं ॥

७३ समुझि सुमित्राँ राम सिय रूपु सुसीलु सुभाउ ।
नृप सनेहु लखि धुनेउ सिरु पापिनि दीन्ह कुदाउ ॥

१ धीरजु धरेउ कुअवसर जानी ।
सहज सुह्रद बोली मृदु बानी ॥
तात तुम्हारी मातु बैदेही ।
पिता रामु सब भाँति सनेही ॥

२ अवध तहाँ जहँ राम निवासू ।
तहँइँ दिवसु जहँ भानु प्रकासू ॥
जौं पै सीय रामु बन जाहीं ।
अवध तुम्हार काजु कछु नाहीं ॥

With glad heart, he approached his mother,    2
like a blind man who has regained his eyes.
He went and bowed at his mother's feet,
though his heart was with Janaki and the Raghus' joy.
Seeing his somber mood, his mother inquired    3
and Lakshman recounted the story in detail.
Sumitra was as stricken by the cruel words
as a doe who sees an engulfing wildfire.
Lakshman thought, "This may go badly now,    4
if, undone by affection, she obstructs me."
So he timidly hesitated to take her leave, thinking,
"Oh God, will she let me go with them, or not?"

Sumitra thought of Ram and Sita's beauty    73
and innate goodness,
and of the king's love, and beat her brow
at that sinful woman's awful stratagem.

Yet, mindful of the crisis and drawing courage,    1
the good-hearted woman spoke gentle words:
"Son, Vaidehi is your mother now,
and your wholly loving father is Ram.
Avadh is that place where Ram resides,    2
just as, wherever sun shines, it is day.
If Sita and Ram truly go to the forest,
you have nothing to do here in Avadh.

३ गुर पितु मातु बंधु सुर साईं ।
सेइअहिं सकल प्रान की नाईं ॥
रामु प्रानप्रिय जीवन जी के ।
स्वारथ रहित सखा सबही के ॥

४ पूजनीय प्रिय परम जहाँ तें ।
सब मानिअहिं राम के नातें ॥
अस जियँ जानि संग बन जाहू ।
लेहु तात जग जीवन लाहू ॥

७४ भूरि भाग भाजनु भयहु मोहि समेत बलि जाउँ ।
जौं तुम्हरें मन छाड़ि छलु कीन्ह राम पद ठाउँ ॥

१ पुत्रवती जुबती जग सोई ।
रघुपति भगतु जासु सुतु होई ॥
नतरु बाँझ भलि बादि बिआनी ।
राम बिमुख सुत तें हित जानी ॥

२ तुम्हरेहिं भाग रामु बन जाहीं ।
दूसर हेतु तात कछु नाहीं ॥
सकल सुकृत कर बड़ फलु एहू ।
राम सीय पद सहज सनेहू ॥

Guru, parents, brother, gods, and master    3
should all be served like life's very breath,
and Ram is dearer than breath, life of every soul,
utterly unselfish and a friend to everyone.
Whoever seems most worthy of praise and love    4
is actually revered by association with Ram.
Knowing this, go with him to the forest,
and reap, my son, the reward of earthly life.

You will earn supreme good fortune,    74
I avow, and I along with you,
if your heart abandons all hypocrisy
and abides at Ram's feet.

In this world, that mother alone is blessed    1
whose son is devoted to the Raghu lord.
Better she were barren, who vainly spawns[64]
and cherishes a son hostile to Ram!
Ram goes to the forest solely for your sake—    2
there is no other purpose, my boy.
For the supreme fruit of all good works
is simple love for Ram and Sita's feet.

३ रागु रोषु इरिषा मदु मोहू ।
जनि सपनेहुँ इन्ह के बस होहू ॥
सकल प्रकार बिकार बिहाई ।
मन क्रम बचन करेहु सेवकाई ॥

४ तुम्ह कहुँ बन सब भाँति सुपासू ।
सँग पितु मातु रामु सिय जासू ॥
जेहिं न रामु बन लहहिं कलेसू ।
सुत सोइ करेहु इहइ उपदेसू ॥

५ उपदेसु यहु जेहिं जात तुम्हरे
राम सिय सुख पावहीं ।
पितु मातु प्रिय परिवार पुर सुख
सुरति बन बिसरावहीं ॥
तुलसी प्रभुहि सिख देइ आयसु
दीन्ह पुनि आसिष दई ।
रति होउ अबिरल अमल सिय
रघुबीर पद नित नित नई ॥

७५ मातु चरन सिरु नाइ चले तुरत संकित हृदयँ ।
बागुर बिषम तोराइ मनहुँ भाग मृगु भाग बस ॥

132

Desire, anger, jealousy, pride, and delusion—  3
do not dream of surrendering to them.
Entirely shedding all imperfections,
offer service in thought, act, and word.
You will be perfectly at ease in the forest,  4
with Ram and Sita as father and mother.
And strive, son, so that Ram may not suffer
in the wilderness. This is my counsel.

My counsel is this: that in going with you,[65]  5
Ram and Sita may find happiness
and be able to forget, in the forest, the joys
of father, mother, dear family, and city."
Tulsi says, having instructed Lakshman,[66]
she gave him leave and blessed him again:
"May your love for the feet of Sita and the Raghu hero
be fervent, pure, and ever renewed!"

Bowing at his mother's feet, he left quickly  75
but with a wary heart,[67]
like a lucky deer, breaking free
from a deadly trap and taking flight.

१ गए लखनु जहँ जानकिनाथू ।
भे मन मुदित पाइ प्रिय साथू ॥
बंदि राम सिय चरन सुहाए ।
चले संग नृपमंदिर आए ॥

२ कहहिं परसपर पुर नर नारी ।
भलि बनाइ बिधि बात बिगारी ॥
तन कृस मन दुखु बदन मलीने ।
बिकल मनहुँ माखी मधु छीने ॥

३ कर मीजहिं सिरु धुनि पछिताहीं ।
जनु बिनु पंख बिहग अकुलाहीं ॥
भइ बड़ि भीर भूप दरबारा ।
बरनि न जाइ बिषादु अपारा ॥

४ सचिवँ उठाइ राउ बैठारे ।
कहि प्रिय बचन रामु पगु धारे ॥
सिय समेत दोउ तनय निहारी ।
ब्याकुल भयउ भूमिपति भारी ॥

७६ सीय सहित सुत सुभग दोउ देखि देखि अकुलाइ ।
बारहिं बार सनेह बस राउ लेइ उर लाइ ॥

१ सकइ न बोलि बिकल नरनाहू ।
सोक जनित उर दारुन दाहू ॥
नाइ सीसु पद अति अनुरागा ।
उठि रघुबीर बिदा तब मागा ॥

Lakshman went straight to Janaki's lord,                        1
his heart glad at regaining his company.
Saluting Ram and Sita's lovely feet,
he went with them to the king's palace.
The townsmen and women said to each other,                      2
"Fate made a splendid plan, then ruined it!"
Wan and sorrowful, their faces downcast,
they were distraught, like bees robbed of their honey.
They wrung their hands, beat their brows,                       3
and lamented, agitated as wingless birds.
A huge crowd had gathered at the royal gate,
and their grief was beyond description.
Lifting the king and seating him, a minister                    4
spoke soothing words: "Ram has entered."
Seeing his two sons along with Sita,
the lord of the earth was confounded.

For a long time, he gazed anxiously                             76
at his two handsome sons, together with Sita,
and, overwhelmed by emotion,
pressed them again and again to his breast.

The lord of men was too distressed to speak                     1
as the awful fire of grief seared his heart.
Bowing at his feet with profound love,
the Raghu hero rose and asked leave to depart.

135

२ पितु असीस आयसु मोहि दीजै ।
हरष समय बिसमउ कत कीजै ॥
तात किएँ प्रिय प्रेम प्रमादू ।
जसु जग जाइ होइ अपबादू ॥

३ सुनि सनेह बस उठि नरनाहाँ ।
बैठारे रघुपति गहि बाहाँ ॥
सुनहु तात तुम्ह कहुँ मुनि कहहीं ।
रामु चराचर नायक अहहीं ॥

४ सुभ अरु असुभ करम अनुहारी ।
ईसु देइ फलु हृदयँ बिचारी ॥
करइ जो करम पाव फल सोई ।
निगम नीति असि कह सबु कोई ॥

७७ औरु करै अपराधु कोउ और पाव फलु भोगु ।
अति बिचित्र भगवंत गति को जग जानै जोगु ॥

१ राँय राम राखन हित लागी ।
बहुत उपाय किए छलु त्यागी ॥
लखी राम रुख रहत न जाने ।
धरम धुरंधर धीर सयाने ॥

२ तब नृप सीय लाइ उर लीन्ही ।
अति हित बहुत भाँति सिख दीन्ही ॥
कहि बन के दुख दुसह सुनाए ।
सासु ससुर पितु सुख समुझाए ॥

136

"Father, bless me and give me your order.                    2
Why do you grieve at this happy time?
To err in duty out of love for a dear one
destroys worldly fame and invites censure."
Hearing this, the king rose, unsteadied by love,           3
clutched at Ram's arm and seated him.
"Listen, my son: of you, sages declare,
'Ram is master of all created beings.'
In accord with virtuous and wicked deeds,                   4
God, on due deliberation, assigns the fruits.
One reaps the harvest of one's own actions—
this is sacred law, affirmed by everyone.

But now, one person commits the sin,                        77
and someone else suffers the consequences.
The blessed Lord's ways are strange indeed.
Who in the world can comprehend them?"

Seeking to hold on to Ram, the king tried                    1
many means, abandoning all pretense.
But he saw from Ram's demeanor that he would not stay,
for he was bent on dharma, steadfast and wise.
Then the lord of men drew Sita to his breast                 2
and tenderly admonished her in various ways.
He spoke of unbearable woes in the woods,
and of the joys of life with in-laws or father.

३ सिय मनु राम चरन अनुरागा ।
घरु न सुगमु बनु बिषमु न लागा ॥
औरउ सबहिं सीय समुझाई ।
कहि कहि बिपिन बिपति अधिकाई ॥

४ सचिव नारि गुर नारि सयानी ।
सहित सनेह कहहिं मृदु बानी ॥
तुम्ह कहुँ तौ न दीन्ह बनबासू ।
करहु जो कहहिं ससुर गुर सासू ॥

७८ सिख सीतलि हित मधुर मृदु सुनि सीतहि न सोहानि ।
सरद चंद चंदिनि लगत जनु चकई अकुलानि ॥

१ सीय सकुच बस उतरु न देई ।
सो सुनि तमकि उठी कैकेई ॥
मुनि पट भूषन भाजन आनी ।
आगें धरि बोली मृदु बानी ॥

२ नृपहि प्रानप्रिय तुम्ह रघुबीरा ।
सील सनेह न छाड़िहि भीरा ॥
सुकृतु सुजसु परलोकु नसाऊ ।
तुम्हहि जान बन कहिहि न काऊ ॥

138

But Sita's heart was enamored of Ram's feet,                    3
and home did not seem easy, nor forest harsh.
Then everyone else, too, warned Sita,
repeatedly telling of the forest's hardships.
The wives of the minister and guru, wise women,                 4
spoke lovingly to her in gentle tones,
"You, after all, were not given exile,
so do as your teacher and in-laws say."

The instruction was calm, sweet,                                78
and well-intended—yet it did not please Sita,
just as the touch of autumn moonlight
only makes the lovelorn *cakvī* bird desperate.[68]

Overcome by modesty, Sita gave no reply,                        1
but hearing all this, Kaikeyi flared up.
She brought ascetics' clothing and gear,
and, placing them before Ram, said coolly,
"Hero, you are dear as life to the king,                        2
and the timid man cannot forsake love and virtue.
He will ruin his good works, name, and hope of heaven,
but he will never tell you to go to the forest.

३ अस बिचारि सोइ करहु जो भावा ।
राम जननि सिख सुनि सुखु पावा ॥
भूपहि बचन बान सम लागे ।
करहिं न प्रान पयान अभागे ॥

४ लोग बिकल मुरुछित नरनाहू ।
काह करिअ कछु सूझ न काहू ॥
रामु तुरत मुनि बेषु बनाई ।
चले जनक जननिहि सिरु नाई ॥

७९ सजि बन साजु समाजु सबु बनिता बंधु समेत ।
बंदि बिप्र गुर चरन प्रभु चले करि सबहि अचेत ॥

१ निकसि बसिष्ठ द्वार भए ठाढ़े ।
देखे लोग बिरह दव दाढ़े ॥
कहि प्रिय बचन सकल समुझाए ।
बिप्र बृंद रघुबीर बोलाए ॥

२ गुर सन कहि बरषासन दीन्हे ।
आदर दान बिनय बस कीन्हे ॥
जाचक दान मान संतोषे ।
मीत पुनीत प्रेम परितोषे ॥

३ दासीं दास बोलाइ बहोरी ।
गुरहि सौंपि बोले कर जोरि ॥
सब कै सार सँभार गोसाईं ।
करबि जनक जननी की नाईं ॥

So reflect on this and do as you please."                           3
Ram was happy with his mother's instruction,
but it pierced the king like an arrow
and he mused, "Why doesn't my wretched soul depart?"
The people were frantic, the king in a faint,              4
and no one could think of what to do.
Ram quickly donned ascetic garb,
bowed to his parents, and departed.

Fully outfitted for forest life,                           79
with his wife and brother, the Lord
saluted the Brahmans and his guru,
and set out, leaving everyone senseless.

As he left, he stood at Vasishtha's door                   1
and saw everyone consumed by separation's fire.
He spoke sweet words, counseling them,
and then the Raghu hero summoned the Brahmans.
Instructing the guru to arrange for their provisions,[69]  2
he won their goodwill with humility and reverent gifts.
He satisfied beggars with respectful charity,
and delighted his friends with pure love.
Then, assembling male and female servants,                 3
he entrusted them to the guru with this plea:
"Master, nurture and look after them all
as a mother or father would do."

४ बारहिं बार जोरि जुग पानी ।
कहत रामु सब सन मृदु बानी ॥
सोइ सब भाँति मोर हितकारी ।
जेहि तें रहै भुआल सुखारी ॥

८० मातु सकल मोरे बिरहँ जेहिं न होहिं दुख दीन ।
सोइ उपाउ तुम्ह करेहु सब पुर जन परम प्रबीन ॥

Then, repeatedly and with palms joined,                    4
Ram entreated them all, in a gentle voice,
"That one will be my true well-wisher
who ensures that the king remains happy,

and that my mothers, enduring                             80
separation from me, are not disconsolate.
I ask you all, supremely wise citizens,
to act toward this end."

*Journey to the Forest*

१ एहि बिधि राम सबहि समुझावा ।
गुर पद पदुम हरषि सिरु नावा ॥
गनपति गौरि गिरीसु मनाई ।
चले असीस पाइ रघुराई ॥

२ राम चलत अति भयउ बिषादू ।
सुनि न जाइ पुर आरत नादू ॥
कुसगुन लंक अवध अति सोकू ।
हरष बिषाद बिबस सुरलोकू ॥

३ गइ मुरुछा तब भूपति जागे ।
बोलि सुमंत्रु कहन अस लागे ॥
रामु चले बन प्रान न जाहीं ।
केहि सुख लागि रहत तन माहीं ॥

४ एहि तें कवन ब्यथा बलवाना ।
जो दुखु पाइ तजहिं तनु प्राना ॥
पुनि धरि धीर कहइ नरनाहू ।
लै रथु संग सखा तुम्ह जाहू ॥

८१ सुठि सुकुमार कुमार दोउ जनकसुता सुकुमारि ।
रथ चढ़ाइ देखराइ बनु फिरेहु गएँ दिन चारि ॥

१ जौं नहिं फिरहिं धीर दोउ भाई ।
सत्यसंध दृढ़ब्रत रघुराई ॥
तौ तुम्ह बिनय करेहु कर जोरी ।
फेरिअ प्रभु मिथिलेसकिसोरी ॥

So Ram counseled everyone,                                   1
and happily laid his head at his teacher's feet.
Then, having worshiped Ganesh, Gauri, and Shiva,
and received blessings, the Raghu lord departed.
As soon as Ram left, lamentation erupted;                    2
the sound of the city's grief was unbearable.
Bad omens arose in Lanka, deep gloom in Avadh,
and the gods' realm was torn between joy and sorrow.[1]
When the king awoke from his faint,                          3
he summoned Sumantra and said,
"Ram went to the forest, yet life's breath
lingers in this body—for what possible joy?
What pain could ever be greater than this,                   4
to cause my grieving soul to quit this body?"
Then composing himself, the king spoke again,
"Take a chariot, dear friend, and go with them.

Those two most tender princes,                               81
and that delicate princess, Janak's daughter—
place them on the chariot, show them the woods
for a few days, and then bring them back.

If the two stalwart brothers will not return,               1
for Ram is pledged to truth, firm in his vow,
then earnestly entreat him thus,
'Lord, just send back Mithila's daughter.'

२ जब सिय कानन देखि डेराई ।
कहेहु मोरि सिख अवसरु पाई ॥
सासु ससुर अस कहेउ सँदेसू ।
पुत्रि फिरिअ बन बहुत कलेसू ॥

३ पितुगृह कबहुँ कबहुँ ससुरारी ।
रहेहु जहाँ रुचि होइ तुम्हारी ॥
एहि बिधि करेहु उपाय कदंबा ।
फिरइ त होइ प्रान अवलंबा ॥

४ नाहिं त मोर मरनु परिनामा ।
कछु न बसाइ भएँ बिधि बामा ॥
अस कहि मुरुछि परा महि राऊ ।
रामु लखनु सिय आनि देखाऊ ॥

८२ पाइ रजायसु नाइ सिरु रथु अति बेग बनाइ ।
गयउ जहाँ बाहेर नगर सीय सहित दोउ भाइ ॥

१ तब सुमंत्र नृप बचन सुनाए ।
करि बिनती रथ रामु चढ़ाए ॥
चढ़ि रथ सीय सहित दोउ भाई ।
चले हृदयँ अवधहि सिरु नाई ॥

२ चलत रामु लखि अवध अनाथा ।
बिकल लोग सब लागे साथा ॥
कृपासिंधु बहुबिधि समुझावहिं ।
फिरहिं प्रेम बस पुनि फिरि आवहिं ॥

When Sita, seeing the forest, takes fright,        2
seize the moment to convey my admonition,
'Your in-laws have sent this message:
Come back, child! The forest is full of pain.
Stay sometimes in your father's house,       3
sometimes at your in-laws'—as you please.'
Thus try every argument, for if she returns
my life will have some firm support.
Otherwise, my death is certain.       4
But nothing can succeed once fate turns hostile."
As he collapsed, senseless, the king cried,
"Bring me Ram, Lakshman, and Sita!"

Receiving the royal order, the minister bowed,     82
then readied a swift chariot,
and went to that place, outside the city,
where Sita and the two brothers had gone.

Sumantra reported the king's words     1
and entreated Ram to mount the chariot.
Both brothers ascended it, with Sita,
and set out, bowing their heads to Avadh.
Seeing Ram go, leaving Avadh orphaned,     2
the desperate townsfolk followed after him.
That ocean of mercy entreated them
and they went back—then came again, impelled by love.

३ लागति अवध भयावनि भारी ।
मानहुँ कालराति अँधिआरी ॥
घोर जंतु सम पुर नर नारी ।
डरपहिं एकहि एक निहारी ॥

४ घर मसान परिजन जनु भूता ।
सुत हित मीत मनहुँ जमदूता ॥
बागन्ह बिटप बेलि कुम्हिलाहीं ।
सरित सरोबर देखि न जाहीं ॥

८३ हय गय कोटिन्ह केलिमृग पुरपसु चातक मोर ।
पिक रथांग सुक सारिका सारस हंस चकोर ॥

१ राम बियोग बिकल सब ठाढ़े ।
जहँ तहँ मनहुँ चित्र लिखि काढ़े ॥
नगरु सफल बनु गहबर भारी ।
खग मृग बिपुल सकल नर नारी ॥

२ बिधि कैकई किरातिनि कीन्ही ।
जेहिं दव दुसह दसहुँ दिसि दीन्ही ॥
सहि न सके रघुबर बिरहागी ।
चले लोग सब ब्याकुल भागी ॥

३ सबहिं बिचारु कीन्ह मन माहीं ।
राम लखन सिय बिनु सुखु नाहीं ॥
जहाँ रामु तहँ सबुइ समाजू ।
बिनु रघुबीर अवध निहं काजू ॥

Avadh appeared most terrifying,                                          3
as though in the dark night of doom.
Its men and women were like gruesome creatures,
fearful at the very sight of each other.
Homes were like cremation grounds, relations like ghosts,    4
sons and well-wishers seemed to be Yama's* envoys.
In gardens, trees and vines withered
and rivers and ponds were too woeful to behold.

Tens of millions of horses and elephants,                        83
game deer and domestic animals,
as well as cuckoos, peacocks, parrots,
geese, starlings, herons, and *haṃsas*

stood motionless everywhere—all stricken               1
by separation from Ram—like painted images.
The city had been a lush, fruit-laden grove,
and all its people, contented birds and beasts.
But Brahma made Kaikeyi a savage huntress[2]           2
who set it ablaze from every side.
Unable to bear the fire of separation from Ram,
the townsfolk all came running in distress.
They thought to themselves, "There is               3
no happiness without Ram, Lakshman, and Sita.
Wherever Ram is, there we should settle,
for what use is Avadh without the Raghu hero?"

***

* The god of death.

४     चले साथ अस मंत्रु दृढ़ाई ।
सुर दुर्लभ सुख सदन बिहाई ॥
राम चरन पंकज प्रिय जिन्हही ।
बिषय भोग बस करहिं कि तिन्हही ॥

८४     बालक बृद्ध बिहाइ गृहँ लगे लोग सब साथ ।
तमसा तीर निवासु किय प्रथम दिवस रघुनाथ ॥

१     रघुपति प्रजा प्रेमबस देखी ।
सदय हृदयँ दुखु भयउ बिसेषी ॥
करुनामय रघुनाथ गोसाँई ।
बेगि पाइअहिं पीर पराई ॥

२     कहि सप्रेम मृदु बचन सुहाए ।
बहुबिधि राम लोग समुझाए ॥
किए धरम उपदेस घनेरे ।
लोग प्रेम बस फिरहिं न फेरे ॥

३     सीलु सनेहु छाड़ि नहिं जाई ।
असमंजस बस भे रघुराई ॥
लोग सोग श्रम बस गए सोई ।
कछुक देवमायाँ मति मोई ॥

४     जबहिं जाम जुग जामिनि बीती ।
राम सचिव सन कहेउ सप्रीती ॥
खोज मारि रथु हाँकहु ताता ।
आन उपायँ बनिहि नहिं बाता ॥

Firm in this judgment, they went with him,       4
leaving rich homes that even gods would envy.
For how can they who love Ram's lotus feet
be overpowered by sensual pleasures?

Leaving infants and the elderly at home,       84
they all went with the exiles.[3]
On that first day, the Raghu lord
made camp on the bank of River Tamasa.

When Ram saw his subjects overcome by love,       1
his compassionate heart was deeply grieved.
Our master, Lord Raghu, is wholly merciful
and quick to feel the pain of others.
With loving and gentle speech,       2
Ram repeatedly instructed the people,
giving innumerable lessons in dharma,
yet those lovesick ones refused to turn back.
Virtuous affection cannot be ignored,       3
and so Ram was caught in a dilemma.
Grieving and exhausted, the people fell asleep,
dazed, too, by some heavenly maya.
When two watches of the night had passed,       4
Ram spoke lovingly to the minister.
"Drive the chariot, friend, so as to hide its tracks,
for there is no other recourse."

८५ राम लखन सिय जान चढ़ि संभु चरन सिरु नाइ ।
सचिवँ चलायउ तुरत रथु इत उत खोज दुराइ ॥

१ जागे सकल लोग भएँ भोरू ।
गे रघुनाथ भयउ अति सोरू ॥
रथ कर खोज कतहुँ नहिं पावहिं ।
राम राम कहि चहुँ दिसि धावहिं ॥

२ मनहुँ बारिनिधि बूड़ जहाजू ।
भयउ बिकल बड़ बनिक समाजू ॥
एकहि एक देहिं उपदेसू ।
तजे राम हम जानि कलेसू ॥

३ निंदहिं आपु सराहहिं मीना ।
धिग जीवनु रघुबीर बिहीना ॥
जौं पै प्रिय बियोगु बिधि कीन्हा ।
तौ कस मरनु न मागें दीन्हा ॥

४ एहि बिधि करत प्रलाप कलापा ।
आए अवध भरे परितापा ॥
बिषम बियोगु न जाइ बखाना ।
अवधि आस सब राखहिं प्राना ॥

८६ राम दरस हित नेम ब्रत लगे करन नर नारि ।
मनहुँ कोक कोकी कमल दीन बिहीन तमारि ॥

Bowing their heads to Lord Shambhu's feet,                     85
Ram, Lakshman, and Sita mounted the chariot,
and the minister swiftly steered it
this way and that, concealing its traces.

When dawn broke, the people awoke                              1
and made an uproar: "Ram is gone!"
They could find no sign of the chariot,
and ran in all directions, crying "Ram, Ram!"
just as, when a ship goes down at sea,                         2
the merchant guild falls into despair.
They consoled one another:
"Understanding our pain, Ram left us."
Damning themselves, envying unsleeping fish,[4]               3
they cried, "A curse on life without Ram!
If the creator parts us from our beloved,
why does he not grant our wish to die?"
So with endless lamentation                                    4
and seared by grief, they returned to Avadh.
Their terrible loss cannot be described—
all clung to life only in hope of the exile's end.

In hope of seeing Ram again,                                   86
men and women undertook strict vows,
wretched as lotuses, or as the cuckoo
and his mate, deprived of sunlight.

१  सीता सचिव सहित दोउ भाई ।
   सृंगबेरपुर पहुँचे जाई ॥
   उतरे राम देवसरि देखी ।
   कीन्ह दंडवत हरषु बिसेषी ॥

२  लखन सचिवँ सियँ किए प्रनामा ।
   सबहि सहित सुखु पायउ रामा ॥
   गंग सकल मुद मंगल मूला ।
   सब सुख करनि हरनि सब सूला ॥

३  कहि कहि कोटिक कथा प्रसंगा ।
   रामु बिलोकहिं गंग तरंगा ॥
   सचिवहि अनुजहि प्रियहि सुनाई ।
   बिबुध नदी महिमा अधिकाई ॥

४  मज्जनु कीन्ह पंथ श्रम गयऊ ।
   सुचि जलु पिअत मुदित मन भयऊ ॥
   सुमिरत जाहि मिटइ श्रम भारू ।
   तेहि श्रम यह लौकिक ब्यवहारू ॥

८७  सुद्ध सच्चिदानंदमय कंद भानुकुल केतु ।
    चरित करत नर अनुहरत संसृति सागर सेतु ॥

१  यह सुधि गुहँ निषाद जब पाई ।
   मुदित लिए प्रिय बंधु बोलाई ॥
   लिए फल मूल भेंट भरि भारा ।
   मिलन चलेउ हियँ हरषु अपारा ॥

The two brothers, with Sita and Sumantra,                    1
arrived at Shringaberapur, on Ganga's bank.
When he saw the sacred river, Ram got down
and joyfully prostrated himself.
Lakshman, the minister, and Sita paid homage,                2
and, with Ram, were filled with gladness.
Ganga is the root of all joy and blessing,
the cause of delight and remover of pain.
Recounting countless holy tales,                             3
Ram gazed at the play of Ganga's waves,
and expounded to Sumantra, his brother,
and his beloved, the glory of the gods' river.
Bathing, they shed the weariness of the road,               4
and drinking the pure water, became joyful.
For him whose mere recollection banishes profound
    fatigue,[5]
such weariness was but concession to worldly conduct.

He—root source of being, consciousness, and bliss,[6]       87
and pure banner of the solar line—
performed deeds like an ordinary man,
as a causeway over the sea of illusory life.

When Guha of the Nishad tribe heard of this,[7]              1
he was delighted and summoned his dear kinsmen.
With great loads of fruit and tubers as gifts,
he went to meet Ram, his heart overjoyed.

२ करि दंडवत भेंट धरि आगें ।
प्रभुहि बिलोकत अति अनुरागें ॥
सहज सनेह बिबस रघुराई ।
पूँछी कुसल निकट बैठाई ॥

३ नाथ कुसल पद पंकज देखें ।
भयउँ भागभाजन जन लेखें ॥
देव धरनि धनु धामु तुम्हारा ।
मैं जनु नीचु सहित परिवारा ॥

४ कृपा करिअ पुर धारिअ पाऊ ।
थापिय जनु सबु लोगु सिहाऊ ॥
कहेहु सत्य सबु सखा सुजाना ।
मोहि दीन्ह पितु आयसु आना ॥

८८ बरष चारिदस बासु बन मुनि ब्रत बेषु अहारु ।
ग्राम बासु नहिं उचित सुनि गुहहि भयउ दुखु भारु ॥

१ राम लखन सिय रूप निहारी ।
कहहिं सप्रेम ग्राम नर नारी ॥
ते पितु मातु कहहु सखि कैसे ।
जिन्ह पठए बन बालक ऐसे ॥

२ एक कहहिं भल भूपति कीन्हा ।
लोयन लाहु हमहि बिधि दीन्हा ॥
तब निषादपति उर अनुमाना ।
तरु सिंसुपा मनोहर जाना ॥

Laying down his gifts, he fell at Ram's feet,                                    2
and gazed with adoration at the Lord.
The Raghu lord, who is won over by simple love,
seated him nearby and inquired of his well-being.
"Master, having seen your lotus feet, I am so well                               3
as to be reckoned among the truly fortunate.
My land, wealth, and home are yours, lord,
and my family and I, your lowly servants.
Now by deigning to set foot in our village,                                      4
magnify this servant, and make all envious."
Ram said: "Wise friend, you speak truly,
but my father commanded me otherwise.

For fourteen years, I must dwell in the woods,                                  88
with ascetic vows, garb, and food,
and it is not right for me to stay in a settlement."
Hearing this, Guha was deeply grieved.

Seeing the beauty of Ram, Lakshman, and Sita,                                    1
village men and women fondly mused,
"Tell me, friend, what sort of father and mother
would send such children to the forest?"
But one said, "The king did well,                                                2
for now God has rewarded our sight."
Then the Nishad chief pondered
and thought of a beautiful rosewood tree.[8]

३ लै रघुनाथहि ठाउँ देखावा ।
कहेउ राम सब भाँति सुहावा ॥
पुरजन करि जोहारु घर आए ।
रघुबर संध्या करन सिधाए ॥

४ गुहँ सँवारि साँथरी डसाई ।
कुस किसलयमय मृदुल सुहाई ॥
सुचि फल मूल मधुर मृदु जानी ।
दोना भरि भरि राखेसि पानी ॥

८९ सिय सुमंत्र भ्राता सहित कंद मूल फल खाइ ।
सयन कीन्ह रघुबंसमनि पाय पलोटत भाइ ॥

१ उठे लखनु प्रभु सोवत जानी ।
कहि सचिवहि सोवन मृदु बानी ॥
कछुक दूरि सजि बान सरासन ।
जागन लगे बैठि बीरासन ॥

२ गुहँ बोलाइ पाहरू प्रतीती ।
ठावँ ठावँ राखे अति प्रीती ॥
आपु लखन पहिं बैठेउ जाई ।
कटि भाथी सर चाप चढ़ाई ॥

३ सोवत प्रभुहि निहारि निषादू ।
भयउ प्रेम बस हृदयँ बिषादू ॥
तनु पुलकित जलु लोचन बहई ।
बचन सप्रेम लखन सन कहई ॥

He showed that place to the Raghu lord,                    3
and Ram said, "This is altogether lovely!"
Saluting him, the villagers returned home,
and the Raghu prince went to perform evening rites.
Guha carefully laid down a bed                             4
of grasses and soft, new leaves,
and selected pure and sweet fruits and bulbs
to set out, with his own hand, in brimful leaf cups.[9]

Having dined on fruits, roots, and tubers,                89
with Sita, Sumantra, and Lakshman,
the jewel of the Raghus lay down to rest
as his brother massaged his feet.

Knowing the Lord was asleep, Lakshman rose                 1
and gently told the minister to take rest.
At a little distance, he readied bow and arrows
and then sat alert to begin his vigil.[10]
Guha summoned his trusted watchmen                         2
and carefully placed them all about,
while he himself went to sit by Lakshman,
with quiver at his waist and arrow set.
When the Nishad saw the Lord sleeping,                     3
his heart grieved, overcome by love.
His body flushed, tears flowing from his eyes,
he spoke loving words to Lakshman.

४ भूपति भवन सुभायँ सुहावा ।
सुरपति सदनु न पटतर पावा ॥
मनिमय रचित चारु चौबारे ।
जनु रतिपति निज हाथ सँवारे ॥

१० सुचि सुबिचित्र सुभोगमय सुमन सुगंध सुबास ।
पलँग मंजु मनि दीप जहँ सब बिधि सकल सुपास ॥

१ बिबिध बसन उपधान तुराई ।
छीर फेन मृदु बिसद सुहाई ॥
तहँ सिय रामु सयन निसि करहीं ।
निज छबि रति मनोज मदु हरहीं ॥

२ ते सिय रामु साथरीं सोए ।
श्रमित बसन बिनु जाहिं न जोए ॥
मातु पिता परिजन पुरबासी ।
सखा सुसील दास अरु दासी ॥

३ जोगवहिं जिन्हहि प्रान की नाईं ।
महि सोवत तेइ राम गोसाईं ॥
पिता जनक जग बिदित प्रभाऊ ।
ससुर सुरेस सखा रघुराऊ ॥

४ रामचंदु पति सो बैदेही ।
सोवत महि बिधि बाम न केही ॥
सिय रघुबीर कि कानन जोगू ।
करम प्रधान सत्य कह लोगू ॥

162

"The house of the king is splendid indeed.                4
Even Indra's abode cannot compare to it.
Its gorgeous, gem-covered pavilions
seem decorated by Kama's own hand.

Immaculate and beautiful, they are filled               90
with comforts and scented by flowers.
With fine beds and jeweled lamps,
they abound in every kind of luxury,

plentiful covers, cushions, and quilts,                   1
as soft and spotless as foam on milk.
There Sita and Ram would lie at night,
their beauty robbing Rati and her spouse* of pride.
That same Sita and Ram now sleep on grass,                2
exhausted, uncovered—unbearable to behold!
He whom parents, relatives, and subjects,
devoted friends, servants, and handmaids,
would guard and cherish like their own breath—           3
that same Ram, our master, sleeps on the ground!
And she whose father is the mighty, world-famed Janak,
whose father-in-law is Indra's friend and Raghu monarch,
whose husband is Ramchandra—if that Vaidehi              4
sleeps on the earth, to whom is fate not cruel?
Are Sita and the Raghu hero fit for forest exile?
Truly people say that destiny is all powerful!

* Kama, god of love.

163

११ कैकयनंदिनि मंदमति कठिन कुटिलपनु कीन्ह ।
जेहिं रघुनंदन जानकिहि सुख अवसर दुखु दीन्ह ॥

१ भइ दिनकर कुल बिटप कुठारी ।
कुमति कीन्ह सब बिस्व दुखारी ॥
भयउ बिषादु निषादहि भारी ।
राम सीय महि सयन निहारी ॥

२ बोले लखन मधुर मृदु बानी ।
ग्यान बिराग भगति रस सानी ॥
काहु न कोउ सुख दुख कर दाता ।
निज कृत करम भोग सबु भ्राता ॥

३ जोग बियोग भोग भल मंदा ।
हित अनहित मध्यम भ्रम फंदा ॥
जनमु मरनु जहँ लगि जग जालू ।
संपति बिपति करमु अरु कालू ॥

४ धरनि धामु धनु पुर परिवारू ।
सरगु नरकु जहँ लगि ब्यवहारू ॥
देखिअ सुनिअ गुनिअ मन माहीं ।
मोह मूल परमारथु नाहीं ॥

१२ सपनें होइ भिखारि नृपु रंकु नाकपति होइ ।
जागें लाभु न हानि कछु तिमि प्रपंच जियँ जोइ ॥

164

It was King Kaikeya's dull-witted daughter      91
who, by devious stratagem
and at a time of happiness, gave grief
to the joy of the Raghus and Janaki.

Becoming an axe to the tree of the solar dynasty,      1
that deluded one has saddened the whole world."
The Nishad was profoundly grieved
to see Ram and Sita lying on the ground.
Then Lakshman spoke sweet, gentle words,      2
imbued with wisdom, dispassion, and devotion's nectar.[11]
"No one gives anyone joy or grief, brother.
All experience the results of their own acts.
Union and separation, the savor of good and bad,      3
friend, foe, and neutral—all are snares of delusion.
Birth and death, anywhere in this cosmic web,
fortune and calamity, action and inexorable time,
land, home, wealth, kingdom, and lineage,      4
heaven and hell, and every sort of activity,
seen or heard or mentally conceived—
are rooted in illusion, and not the supreme goal.

As when a king, in a dream, becomes a beggar,      92
or a pauper, the lord of heaven,[12]
but awakes to neither gain nor loss—
so view, in your soul, the artifice of this world.

१ अस बिचारि नहिं कीजिअ रोसू।
काहुहि बादि न देइअ दोसू॥
मोह निसाँ सबु सोवनिहारा।
देखिअ सपन अनेक प्रकारा॥

२ एहिं जग जामिनि जागहिं जोगी।
परमारथी प्रपंच बियोगी॥
जानिअ तबहिं जीव जग जागा।
जब सब बिषय बिलास बिरागा॥

३ होइ बिबेकु मोह भ्रम भागा।
तब रघुनाथ चरन अनुरागा॥
सखा परम परमारथु एहू।
मन क्रम बचन राम पद नेहू॥

४ राम ब्रह्म परमारथ रूपा।
अबिगत अलख अनादि अनूपा॥
सकल बिकार रहित गतभेदा।
कहि नित नेति निरूपहिं बेदा॥

९३ भगत भूमि भूसुर सुरभि सुर हित लागि कृपाल।
करत चरित धरि मनुज तनु सुनत मिटहिं जग जाल॥

१ सखा समुझि अस परिहरि मोहू।
सिय रघुबीर चरन रत होहू॥
कहत राम गुन भा भिनुसारा।
जागे जग मंगल सुखदारा॥

Reasoning thus, do not yield to anger 1
or vainly fault anyone.
All are sleepers in delusion's night,
watching dreams of countless kinds.
In this cosmic darkness, yogis are awake— 2
seekers of the ultimate, freed of illusion.
Know a soul to be truly awake in this world
only when it renounces all sensual pleasure.
When discrimination dawns, delusion flees, 3
and then comes love for the Raghu lord's feet.
This, friend, is truly the ultimate goal:
to adore Ram's feet in thought, word, and deed.
Ram is *brahma,* embodiment of the supreme, 4
inconceivable, imperceptible, incomparable,
beginningless, utterly flawless, and indivisible,
of whom the Vedas eternally say, "Not this."

That merciful one, for the sake of devotees, 93
the earth, Brahmans, cows, and gods,
takes human form and does noble deeds,
merely hearing of which cuts worldly snares.

Grasping this, friend, renounce delusion 1
and be devoted to Sita and the Raghu hero's feet."
As they spoke of Ram's virtues, dawn broke,
and he who blesses and delights the world awoke.[13]

167

२ सकल सौच करि राम नहावा ।
सुचि सुजान बट छीर मगावा ॥
अनुज सहित सिर जटा बनाए ।
देखि सुमंत्र नयन जल छाए ॥

३ हृदयँ दाहु अति बदन मलीना ।
कह कर जोरि बचन अति दीना ॥
नाथ कहेउ अस कोसलनाथा ।
लै रथु जाहु राम कें साथा ॥

४ बनु देखाइ सुरसरि अन्हवाई ।
आनेहु फेरि बेगि दोउ भाई ॥
लखनु रामु सिय आनेहु फेरी ।
संसय सकल सँकोच निबेरी ॥

९४ नृप अस कहेउ गोसाइँ जस कहइ करौं बलि सोइ ।
करि बिनती पायन्ह परेउ दीन्ह बाल जिमि रोइ ॥

१ तात कृपा करि कीजिअ सोई ।
जातें अवध अनाथ न होई ॥
मंत्रिहि राम उठाइ प्रबोधा ।
तात धरम मतु तुम्ह सबु सोधा ॥

२ सिबि दधीच हरिचंद नरेसा ।
सहे धरम हित कोटि कलेसा ॥
रंतिदेव बलि भूप सुजाना ।
धरमु धरेउ सहि संकट नाना ॥

Ram bathed, emerging fully cleansed;                          2
then that pure, wise one called for banyan sap,
and he and his brother matted their hair.[14]
Watching, Sumantra's eyes filled with tears.
His heart burning and face grave, he spoke                    3
in utter supplication, his palms joined—
"Lord, the king of Kosala commanded me thus:
'Take a chariot and go with Ram.
Show them the woods, let them bathe in Ganga,                 4
then quickly bring the two brothers back!
Bring home Lakshman, Ram, and Sita,
resolving all doubt and hesitation.'

So the king told me. Now, master,                            94
whatever you say, I swear I will do."
Having delivered this plea, he fell
at Ram's feet, sobbing like a child.

"Dear lord, in your mercy, act                                 1
so that Avadh is not left orphaned."
Raising up the minister, Ram consoled him:
"Sir, you have thoroughly studied dharma.
Shibi, Dadhich, and Harishchandra, rulers of men,            2
endured, for dharma's sake, endless sorrows,
and Rantidev and Bali, wise lords of earth,
upheld dharma, bearing many afflictions.[15]

३ धरमु न दूसर सत्य समाना ।
आगम निगम पुरान बखाना ॥
मैं सोइ धरमु सुलभ करि पावा ।
तजें तिहूँ पुर अपजसु छावा ॥

४ संभावित कहुँ अपजस लाहू ।
मरन कोटि सम दारुन दाहू ॥
तुम्ह सन तात बहुत का कहऊँ ।
दिएँ उतरु फिरि पातकु लहऊँ ॥

९५ पितु पद गहि कहि कोटि नति बिनय करब कर जोरि ।
चिंता कवनिहु बात कै तात करिअ जनि मोरि ॥

१ तुम्ह पुनि पितु सम अति हित मोरें ।
बिनती करउँ तात कर जोरें ॥
सब बिधि सोइ करतब्य तुम्हारें ।
दुख न पाव पितु सोच हमारें ॥

२ सुनि रघुनाथ सचिव संबादू ।
भयउ सपरिजन बिकल निषादू ॥
पुनि कछु लखन कही कटु बानी ।
प्रभु बरजे बड़ अनुचित जानी ॥

No other dharma can equal truth—                                    3
so scripture and holy legend expound,
and I have achieved that dharma easily.
Abandoning it, I will be defamed in the three worlds,
and to men of stature, gaining infamy                               4
burns like a billion deaths.
But why tell you all this, revered sir?
I sin by even answering you.

Clasp my father's feet, offer countless salutations,                95
and humbly petition him:
'Father, do not in the least
be worried on my account.'

You, too, cherish me even as Father does,                           1
and so, sir, with palms joined, I beseech you
to make it your duty to ensure
that Father suffers no anxiety over us."
Hearing Ram and the minister's dialogue,                            2
the Nishad and his kin were anguished.
Then Lakshman spoke some bitter words,
but the Lord checked him, thinking them most unseemly.

३ सकुचि राम निज सपथ देवाई ।
  लखन सँदेसु कहिअ जनि जाई ॥
  कह सुमंत्रु पुनि भूप सँदेसू ।
  सहि न सकिहि सिय बिपिन कलेसू ॥
४ जेहि बिधि अवध आव फिरि सीया ।
  सोइ रघुबरहि तुम्हहि करनीया ॥
  नतरु निपट अवलंब बिहीना ।
  मैं न जिअब जिमि जल बिनु मीना ॥

९६ मइकें ससुरें सकल सुख जबहिं जहाँ मनु मान ।
  तहँ तब रहिहि सुखेन सिय जब लगि बिपति बिहान ॥

१ बिनती भूप कीन्ह जेहि भाँती ।
  आरति प्रीति न सो कहि जाती ॥
  पितु सँदेसु सुनि कृपानिधाना ।
  सियहि दीन्ह सिख कोटि बिधाना ॥
२ सासु ससुर गुर प्रिय परिवारू ।
  फिरहु त सब कर मिटै खभारू ॥
  सुनि पति बचन कहति बैदेही ।
  सुनहु प्रानपति परम सनेही ॥
३ प्रभु करुनामय परम बिबेकी ।
  तनु तजि रहित छाँह किमि छेंकी ॥
  प्रभा जाइ कहँ भानु बिहाई ।
  कहँ चंद्रिका चंदु तजि जाई ॥

172

Ashamed, he made Sumantra swear, by Ram's own life,                    3
not to repeat Lakshman's speech.[16]
Sumantra then conveyed the king's message:
"Sita cannot bear the hardships of the forest.
Whatever it takes to bring Sita back to Avadh,                         4
you and the Raghu prince must contrive,
or else, utterly deprived of consolation
and like a fish without water, I will not survive.

In her mother and father's home,                                      96
and at her in-laws', there is every comfort.
Sita can live happily, wherever she pleases,
until this calamity has passed.

The protector of earth made this plea                                  1
with indescribable anguish and love."
Hearing his father's message, the abode of mercy
exhorted Sita in countless ways:
"Think of your in-laws, our guru, and dear kin—                        2
if you would just go back, their woes would cease."
Hearing her husband's speech, Vaidehi said,
"Listen, supremely beloved master of my life,
for you are merciful, lord, and most discerning—                       3
apart from its body, how can a shadow be held fast?
Abandoning the sun, where will its brilliance go,
or moonlight, if it quits the moon?"

४ पतिहि प्रेममय बिनय सुनाई ।
कहति सचिव सन गिरा सुहाई ॥
तुम्ह पितु ससुर सरिस हितकारी ।
उतरु देउँ फिरि अनुचित भारी ॥

९७ आरति बस सनमुख भइउँ बिलगु न मानब तात ।
आरजसुत पद कमल बिनु बादि जहाँ लगि नात ॥

१ पितु बैभव बिलास मैं डीठा ।
नृप मनि मुकुट मिलित पद पीठा ॥
सुखनिधान अस पितु गृह मोरें ।
पिय बिहीन मन भाव न भोरें ॥

२ ससुर चक्रवइ कोसलराऊ ।
भुवन चारिदस प्रगट प्रभाऊ ॥
आगें होइ जेहि सुरपति लेई ।
अरध सिंघासन आसनु देई ॥

३ ससुर एताद्दस अवध निवासू ।
प्रिय परिवारु मातु सम सासू ॥
बिनु रघुपति पद पदुम परागा ।
मोहि केउ सपनेहुँ सुखद न लागा ॥

४ अगम पंथ बनभूमि पहारा ।
करि केहरि सर सरित अपारा ॥
कोल किरात कुरंग बिहंगा ।
मोहि सब सुखद प्रानपति संगा ॥

Having made this loving plea to her husband,    4
she addressed gentle words to the minister:
"You are well-meaning, like father and father-in-law,
so it is most unseemly that I answer you.

Yet affliction compels me to speak;    97
please do not think me presumptuous.
Apart from the holy feet of this noble man,
all relationships are worthless to me.

I have seen my father's radiant grandeur,    1
his footstool brushed by the diadems of kings.
Yet even such a father's pleasure-palace,
without my beloved, could never suit my heart.
My father-in-law is emperor of Kosala,    2
renowned throughout the fourteen worlds,
whom Indra himself comes forward to greet,
seating him on half of his own throne.
With such a father-in-law, Avadh to dwell in,    3
cherished family, and loving mothers-in-law,
but without the pollen-dust of Ram's lotus feet,
I could not even dream of happiness.
Difficult paths, woodlands and mountains,    4
elephants, lions, impassable lakes and rivers,
savage tribes, tawny deer, and wild birds—
with the lord of my life, all will delight me.

175

९८ सासु ससुर सन मोरि हुँति बिनय करबि परि पायँ ।
मोर सोचु जनि करिअ कछु मैं बन सुखी सुभायँ ॥

१ प्राननाथ प्रिय देवर साथा ।
बीर धुरीन धरें धनु भाथा ॥
नहिं मग श्रमु भ्रमु दुख मन मोरें ।
मोहि लगि सोचु करिअ जनि भोरें ॥

२ सुनि सुमंत्रु सिय सीतलि बानी ।
भयउ बिकल जनु फनि मनि हानी ॥
नयन सूझ नहिं सुनइ न काना ।
कहि न सकइ कछु अति अकुलाना ॥

३ राम प्रबोधु कीन्ह बहु भाँती ।
तदपि होति नहिं सीतलि छाती ॥
जतन अनेक साथ हित कीन्हे ।
उचित उतर रघुनंदन दीन्हे ॥

४ मेटि जाइ नहिं राम रजाई ।
कठिन करम गति कछु न बसाई ॥
राम लखन सिय पद सिरु नाई ।
फिरेउ बनिक जिमि मूर गवाँई ॥

९९ रथु हाँकेउ हय राम तन हेरि हेरि हिहिनाहिं ।
देखि निषाद बिषादबस धुनहिं सीस पछिताहिं ॥

Bow at the feet of my mother and father-in-law,       98
and make this plea on my behalf:
'Do not worry about me in the least,
for I will be naturally content in the forest.

With the lord of my life and dear brother-in-law,[17]     1
eminent heroes, bearing bows and quivers,
I will know no fatigue, confusion, or sorrow on the road.
So do not for a moment be anxious for me.'"
When Sumantra heard Sita's calm words,       2
he grew distraught, like a cobra bereft of its jewel,
and his eyes could not see, nor his ears hear.
Profoundly disturbed, he could not speak.
Ram made many attempts to console him,       3
yet his anguished heart was not soothed.
He pleaded time and again to go with them,
but the joy of the Raghus rightly answered him.
Ram's command could not be evaded,       4
and, faced by harsh duty, he was powerless.
He bowed at the feet of Ram, Lakshman, and Sita,
and turned back, like a trader who has lost his goods.

He tried to drive the chariot, but the horses       99
kept looking back at Ram and whinnying.
Seeing this, the Nishad folk were grief stricken,
beat their brows, and lamented—

१ जासु बियोग बिकल पसु ऐसें ।
  प्रजा मातु पितु जिइहहिं कैसें ॥
  बरबस राम सुमंत्रु पठाए ।
  सुरसरि तीर आपु तब आए ॥

२ मागी नाव न केवटु आना ।
  कहइ तुम्हार मरमु मैं जाना ॥
  चरन कमल रज कहुँ सबु कहई ।
  मानुष करनि मूरि कछु अहई ॥

३ छुअत सिला भइ नारि सुहाई ।
  पाहन तें न काठ कठिनाई ॥
  तरनिउ मुनि घरिनी होइ जाई ।
  बाट परइ मोरि नाव उड़ाई ॥

४ एहिं प्रतिपालउँ सबु परिवारू ।
  नहिं जानउँ कछु अउर कबारू ॥
  जौं प्रभु पार अवसि गा चहहू ।
  मोहि पद पदुम पखारन कहहू ॥

"If beasts are so anguished at parting from him,  1
how will his people and parents survive?"
Resolutely, Ram dispatched Sumantra,
then approached the sacred river's shore.
He called for a boat, but the boatman would not bring it,[18]  2
saying, "I know all about you!
Everyone says the dust on your pretty feet
is some magic person-making potion.
At its mere touch, a rock became a lovely lady![19]  3
And wood, after all, is not as hard as stone.
If my boat, too, should turn into a sage's wife
and fly off, I would be ruined.
I support my whole family with this boat,  4
and know no other trade.
If you really want to go across, lord,
give me leave to wash your lovely feet.

५    पद कमल धोइ चढ़ाइ नाव
न नाथ उतराई चहौं ।
मोहि राम राउरि आन दसरथ
सपथ सब साची कहौं ॥
बरु तीर मारहुँ लखनु पै
जब लगि न पाय पखारिहौं ।
तब लगि न तुलसीदास नाथ
कृपाल पारु उतारिहौं ॥

१००   सुनि केवट के बैन प्रेम लपेटे अटपटे ।
बिहसे करुनाऐन चितइ जानकी लखन तन ॥

१    कृपासिंधु बोले मुसुकाई ।
सोइ करु जेहिं तव नाव न जाई ॥
बेगि आनु जल पाय पखारू ।
होत बिलंबु उतारहि पारू ॥

२    जासु नाम सुमिरत एक बारा ।
उतरहिं नर भवसिंधु अपारा ॥
सोइ कृपालु केवटहि निहोरा ।
जेहिं जगु किय तिहु पगहु ते थोरा ॥

३    पद नख निरखि देवसरि हरषी ।
सुनि प्रभु बचन मोहँ मति करषी ॥
केवट राम रजायसु पावा ।
पानि कठवता भरि लेइ आवा ॥

I'll wash your lotus feet, then let you board,        5
master, for I desire no other fare.
I swear by you, Ram, by Dasarath, too,
that I'm telling the whole truth.
Let Lakshman fire arrows at me;
even so, until I wash those feet of yours—
merciful lord of Tulsidas—till then
I will not ferry you across!"

When he heard Kevat the boatman's speech—        100
suffused with love and charmingly devious[20]—
the abode of compassion laughed,
glancing at Janaki and Lakshman.

With a smile, the sea of mercy said,        1
"Act, then, so your boat is not lost.
Quickly bring water and wash my feet,
for it is getting late. Take us across!"[21]
He whose name, recalled just once,        2
carries one over rebirth's boundless sea,
that merciful one—whose three steps
outstrode the universe—obliged a boatman.
Seeing the Lord's toenails, the gods' river rejoiced,        3
and hearing his words, became entranced.[22]
At Ram's command, the ferryman
brought a wooden tub brimming with water.

४ अति आनंद उमगि अनुरागा ।
चरन सरोज पखारन लागा ॥
बरषि सुमन सुर सकल सिहाहीं ।
एहि सम पुन्यपुंज कोउ नाहीं ॥

१०१ पद पखारि जलु पान करि आपु सहित परिवार ।
पितर पारु करि प्रभुहि पुनि मुदित गयउ लेइ पार ॥

१ उतरि ठाढ़ भए सुरसरि रेता ।
सीय रामु गुह लखन समेता ॥
केवट उतरि दंडवत कीन्हा ।
प्रभुहि सकुच एहि नहिं कछु दीन्हा ॥

२ पिय हिय की सिय जाननिहारी ।
मनि मुदरी मन मुदित उतारी ॥
कहेउ कृपाल लेहि उतराई ।
केवट चरन गहे अकुलाई ॥

३ नाथ आजु मैं काह न पावा ।
मिटे दोष दुख दारिद दावा ॥
बहुत काल मैं कीन्हि मजूरी ।
आजु दीन्ह बिधि बनि भलि भूरी ॥

४ अब कछु नाथ न चाहिअ मोरें ।
दीनदयाल अनुग्रह तोरें ॥
फिरती बार मोहि जो देबा ।
सो प्रसादु मैं सिर धरि लेबा ॥

Himself brimful of fervent love and bliss,                                4
he began to wash those pure and holy feet.
The gods, showering blossoms, were all envious—
"None can match this man's treasury of merit!"

He washed Ram's feet and sipped that water,                              101
together with his whole family,
thus ferrying his ancestors to salvation,[23]
and then gladly took the Lord across.

They disembarked and stood on the holy river's sand,                      1
Sita and Ram, with Guha* and Lakshman.
The boatman followed and prostrated himself,
and the Lord felt ashamed to offer him nothing.
Sita, who always knew her husband's heart,                                2
happily removed a jeweled ring,
and the merciful one said, "Here, take your fare."
Greatly upset, the boatman clung to his feet.
"Master! What have I not gained today?                                    3
The fire of sin, sorrow, and want is put out.
I have been toiling like this for so long,
and today God has paid me in full!
Now I want for nothing, master,                                           4
by your kindness, merciful to the meek.
But when you return, whatever you give
I will humbly accept as your grace."

---

* The Nishad chief.

१०२ बहुत कीन्ह प्रभु लखन सियँ नहिं कछु केवटु लेइ ।
बिदा कीन्ह करुनायतन भगति बिमल बरु देइ ॥

१ तब मज्जनु करि रघुकुलनाथा ।
पूजि पारथिव नायउ माथा ॥
सियँ सुरसरिहि कहेउ कर जोरी ।
मातु मनोरथ पुरउबि मोरी ॥

२ पति देवर सँग कुसल बहोरी ।
आइ करौं जेहिं पूजा तोरी ॥
सुनि सिय बिनय प्रेम रस सानी ।
भइ तब बिमल बारि बर बानी ॥

३ सुनु रघुबीर प्रिया बैदेही ।
तव प्रभाउ जग बिदित न केही ॥
लोकप होहिं बिलोकत तोरें ।
तोहि सेवहिं सब सिधि कर जोरें ॥

४ तुम्ह जो हमहि बड़ि बिनय सुनाई ।
कृपा कीन्हि मोहि दीन्हि बड़ाई ॥
तदपि देबि मैं देबि असीसा ।
सफल होन हित निज बागीसा ॥

१०३ प्राननाथ देवर सहित कुसल कोसला आइ ।
पूजिहि सब मनकामना सुजसु रहिहि जग छाइ ॥

Despite all efforts by the Lord, Lakshman, 102
and Sita, the boatman would take nothing,
so the abode of mercy took his leave,
granting him the boon of purest devotion.

Then the lord of the Raghus bathed 1
and, head bowed, worshiped Shiva in earthen form.[24]
Her palms joined, Sita addressed the holy river,
"Mother, fulfill this wish of mine,
that, with my husband and his brother, 2
I may safely return to worship you again."
Hearing Sita's humble petition, imbued with love,
a wondrous voice came from the clear water.
"Vaidehi, beloved of the Raghu hero, listen— 3
who in creation does not know your power?
Your mere glance gives cosmic sovereignty,[25]
and all occult powers reverently serve you.
By your humble petitioning 4
you bless and greatly magnify me.
Yet, divine one, I will offer a blessing
to affirm the truth of my own prophecy.

With the lord of your life and brother-in-law, 103
you will come back happily to Kosala,
all your wishes will be fulfilled,
and your fame will spread through the world."

१ गंग बचन सुनि मंगल मूला ।
मुदित सीय सुरसरि अनुकूला ॥
तब प्रभु गुहहि कहेउ घर जाहू ।
सुनत सूख मुखु भा उर दाहू ॥

२ दीन बचन गुह कह कर जोरी ।
बिनय सुनहु रघुकुलमनि मोरी ॥
नाथ साथ रहि पंथु देखाई ।
करि दिन चारि चरन सेवकाई ॥

३ जेहिं बन जाइ रहब रघुराई ।
परनकुटी मैं करबि सुहाई ॥
तब मोहि कहँ जसि देब रजाई ।
सोइ करिहउँ रघुबीर दोहाई ॥

४ सहज सनेह राम लखि तासू ।
संग लीन्ह गुह हृदयँ हुलासू ॥
पुनि गुहँ ग्याति बोलि सब लीन्हे ।
करि परितोषु बिदा तब कीन्हे ॥

१०४ तब गनपति सिव सुमिरि प्रभु नाइ सुरसरिहि माथ ।
सखा अनुज सिय सहित बन गवनु कीन्ह रघुनाथ ॥

१ तेहि दिन भयउ बिटप तर बासू ।
लखन सखाँ सब कीन्ह सुपासू ॥
प्रात प्रातकृत करि रघुराई ।
तीरथराजु दीख प्रभु जाई ॥

Hearing the words of Ganga, wellspring of grace,                1
Sita rejoiced at the holy river's favor.
Then the Lord told Guha to go home.
Stricken at hearing this, his heart aflame,
Guha spoke humbly, with palms joined—                2
"Jewel of the Raghu line, hear my plea:
Let me stay with you, master, to show the way
and for a few days, serve at your feet.
In whatever forest you settle, Raghu prince,                3
I will build you a fine house of leaves,
and then, whatever you command me,
I swear by you, Raghu hero, I will do."
Seeing his pure and simple love, Ram                4
took him along. With ecstatic heart, Guha
summoned his clan folk,
reassured them, and bade them farewell.[26]

Then, invoking Ganesh and Shiva                104
and bowing his head to the holy river,
accompanied by Sita, his brother, and his friend,
the lord of the Raghus entered the forest.

That day they camped beneath a tree,                1
and Lakshman and Guha saw to their comfort.
After performing morning rites, the ruler of Raghus
went to behold the king of pilgrimage places.[27]

२ सचिव सत्य श्रद्धा प्रिय नारी ।
माधव सरिस मीतु हितकारी ॥
चारि पदारथ भरा भँडारू ।
पुन्य प्रदेस देस अति चारू ॥

३ छेत्रु अगम गढु गाढ़ सुहावा ।
सपनेहुँ नहिं प्रतिपच्छिन्ह पावा ॥
सेन सकल तीरथ बर बीरा ।
कलुष अनीक दलन रनधीरा ॥

४ संगमु सिंहासनु सुठि सोहा ।
छत्रु अखयबटु मुनि मनु मोहा ॥
चवँर जमुन अरु गंग तरंगा ।
देखि होहिं दुख दारिद भंगा ॥

१०५ सेवहिं सुकृती साधु सुचि पावहिं सब मनकाम ।
बंदी बेद पुरान गन कहहिं बिमल गुन ग्राम ॥

१ को कहि सकइ प्रयाग प्रभाऊ ।
कलुष पुंज कुंजर मृगराऊ ॥
अस तीरथपति देखि सुहावा ।
सुख सागर रघुबर सुखु पावा ॥

२ कहि सिय लखनहि सखहि सुनाई ।
श्रीमुख तीरथराज बड़ाई ॥
करि प्रनामु देखत बन बागा ।
कहत महातम अति अनुरागा ॥

This king's minister is truth, his beloved wife faith,                2
and he has a kindly friend in Madhav.[28]
His treasury is filled with life's four goals,
and his lovely country is the realm of merit.
His precincts are a glorious, impregnable fort            3
that foes can never dream of breaching,
and all holy places are his brave soldiers,
steadfast in annihilating the army of sins.
The sacred confluence is his splendid throne,            4
its umbrella, the immortal banyan that enchants sages.
The waves of Yamuna and Ganga are his fly whisks[29]—
just glimpsing them ends sorrow and poverty.

He is served by pure and virtuous sadhus,                105
who gain all that their hearts desire,
and his bards are the Vedas and *purāṇas,*
reciting the litany of his spotless fame.

But who can express the greatness of Prayag,            1
a lion against the elephant of amassed sin?
To behold this glorious monarch of shrines
gave joy to joy's own ocean, the Raghu lord,
who recounted to Sita, Lakshman, and his friend,        2
with his own blessed lips, the greatness of Prayag.
Bowing reverently, gazing at the woods and gardens,
and fervently voicing its praise,

३     एहि बिधि आइ बिलोकी बेनी ।
सुमिरत सकल सुमंगल देनी ॥
मुदित नहाइ कीन्हि सिव सेवा ।
पूजि जथाबिधि तीरथ देवा ॥

४     तब प्रभु भरद्वाज पहिं आए ।
करत दंडवत मुनि उर लाए ॥
मुनि मन मोद न कछु कहि जाई ।
ब्रह्मानंद रासि जनु पाई ॥

१०६    दीन्हि असीस मुनीस उर अति अनंदु अस जानि ।
लोचन गोचर सुकृत फल मनहुँ किए बिधि आनि ॥

१     कुसल प्रस्न करि आसन दीन्हे ।
पूजि प्रेम परिपूरन कीन्हे ॥
कंद मूल फल अंकुर नीके ।
दिए आनि मुनि मनहुँ अमी के ॥

२     सीय लखन जन सहित सुहाए ।
अति रुचि राम मूल फल खाए ॥
भए बिगतश्रम रामु सुखारे ।
भरद्वाज मृदु बचन उचारे ॥

३     आजु सुफल तपु तीरथ त्यागू ।
आजु सुफल जप जोग बिरागू ॥
सफल सकल सुभ साधन साजू ।
राम तुम्हहि अवलोकत आजू ॥

he came in sight of the triple confluence,[30]                    3
mere recollection of which gives all blessings.
Bathing with delight, he worshiped Shiva
and propitiated local gods according to custom.
Then the Lord approached Bharadvaj, bowing           4
in full prostration, but the sage drew him to his breast.
The joy in the sage's heart was beyond expression,
as though he had gained a treasury of divine bliss.

Blissfully, that king of sages gave a blessing,          106
knowing well in his heart
that it was as though God had brought visibly
before him the fruit of all his merit.

Asking their welfare, he offered them seats,           1
delighting them with loving homage
and excellent fare of roots, fruits, and sprouts,
of nectar-like flavor, served by the sage.
With Sita, Lakshman, and their devoted friend,       2
Ram partook with pleasure of the wild forest fare.
When Ram was well rested and happy,
Bharadvaj addressed him with sweet words.
"Today, my austerities, pilgrimage, and renunciation,     3
today, my worship, yogic discipline, detachment,
and all my spiritual practices yield their fruit—
today—in the sight of you, Ram!

४ लाभ अवधि सुख अवधि न दूजी ।
तुम्हरें दरस आस सब पूजी ॥
अब करि कृपा देहु बर एहू ।
निज पद सरसिज सहज सनेहू ॥

१०७ करम बचन मन छाड़ि छलु जब लगि जनु न तुम्हार ।
तब लगि सुखु सपनेहुँ नहीं किएँ कोटि उपचार ॥

१ सुनि मुनि बचन रामु सकुचाने ।
भाव भगति आनंद अघाने ॥
तब रघुबर मुनि सुजसु सुहावा ।
कोटि भाँति कहि सबहि सुनावा ॥

२ सो बड़ सो सब गुन गन गेहू ।
जेहि मुनीस तुम्ह आदर देहू ॥
मुनि रघुबीर परसपर नवहीं ।
बचन अगोचर सुखु अनुभवहीं ॥

३ यह सुधि पाइ प्रयाग निवासी ।
बटु तापस मुनि सिद्ध उदासी ॥
भरद्वाज आश्रम सब आए ।
देखन दसरथ सुअन सुहाए ॥

४ राम प्रनाम कीन्ह सब काहू ।
मुदित भए लहि लोयन लाहू ॥
देहिं असीस परम सुखु पाई ।
फिरे सराहत सुंदरताई ॥

No worldly gain or joy can equal this,                    4
and seeing you, all my yearnings are fulfilled.
Now graciously grant me the boon
of spontaneous love for your holy feet.

Until one abandons guile in act, speech, and mind        107
and becomes wholly devoted to you,
one can never dream of finding happiness
even with a billion efforts."

Though embarrassed by the sage's speech, Ram            1
was blissfully sated by its mood of devotion.
Then the best of Raghus expounded the fame
of that seer to all present, in countless ways.
"Real greatness and abundance of virtues              2
belongs, lord of sages, to one who reveres you."
So sage and Raghu hero honored each other
and experienced unutterable joy.
When the dwellers in Prayag heard the news,           3
they all came—young initiates, ascetics, sages,
adepts, and hermits—to Bharadvaj's ashram
to see the handsome sons of Dasarath.
Ram reverently honored them all,                      4
and they rejoiced, gaining their eyes' reward.
Supremely happy, they gave their blessings
and went back praising his beauty.

१०८ राम कीन्ह बिश्राम निसि प्रात प्रयाग नहाइ ।
चले सहित सिय लखन जन मुदित मुनिहि सिरु नाइ ॥

१ राम सप्रेम कहेउ मुनि पाहीं ।
नाथ कहिअ हम केहि मग जाहीं ॥
मुनि मन बिहसि राम सन कहहीं ।
सुगम सकल मग तुम्ह कहुँ अहहीं ॥

२ साथ लागि मुनि सिष्य बोलाए ।
सुनि मन मुदित पचासक आए ॥
सबन्हि राम पर प्रेम अपारा ।
सकल कहहिं मगु दीख हमारा ॥

३ मुनि बटु चारि संग तब दीन्हे ।
जिन्ह बहु जनम सुकृत सब कीन्हे ॥
करि प्रनामु रिषि आयसु पाई ।
प्रमुदित हृदयँ चले रघुराई ॥

४ ग्राम निकट जब निकसहिं जाई ।
देखहिं दरसु नारि नर धाई ॥
होहिं सनाथ जनम फलु पाई ।
फिरहिं दुखित मनु संग पठाई ॥

१०९ बिदा किए बटु बिनय करि फिरे पाइ मन काम ।
उतरि नहाए जमुन जल जो सरीर सम स्याम ॥

Ram rested there for the night,          108
and in the morning, after bathing at Prayag,
set out with Sita, Lakshman, and their friend,
saluting the sage with joy.

Ram inquired lovingly of the seer,          1
"Master, tell us which way to go."
Smiling to himself, the sage told Ram,
"All paths are easy for you."
Then he called for pupils to go with them,      2
and half a hundred eagerly came forth.
They all felt boundless love for Ram,
and all declared, "We know the way!"
The sage picked four young initiates to go along,  3
who had earned merit through many births.
Then, bowing again and with the sage's leave,
the Raghu lord left with a happy heart.
Whenever they passed near a village        4
all the women and men rushed out to see them.
Comforted, gaining the fruit of their birth, [31]
they went home sadly, sending their hearts with the
    wayfarers.

The Lord humbly bade the pupils farewell,     109
and they returned, their hearts' desire achieved.
Then he went down to bathe in the Yamuna's water,
dark like his own body.

१ सुनत तीरबासी नर नारी ।
धाए निज निज काज बिसारी ॥
लखन राम सिय सुंदरताई ।
देखि करहिं निज भाग्य बड़ाई ॥

२ अति लालसा बसहिं मन माहीं ।
नाउँ गाउँ बूझत सकुचाहीं ॥
जे तिन्ह महुँ बयबिरिध सयाने ।
तिन्ह करि जुगुति रामु पहिचाने ॥

३ सकल कथा तिन्ह सबहि सुनाई ।
बनहि चले पितु आयसु पाई ॥
सुनि सबिषाद सकल पछिताहीं ।
रानी रायँ कीन्ह भल नाहीं ॥

४ तेहि अवसर एक तापसु आवा ।
तेज पुंज लघुबयस सुहावा ॥
कबि अलखित गति बेषु बिरागी ।
मन क्रम बचन राम अनुरागी ॥

११० सजल नयन तन पुलकि निज इष्टदेउ पहिचानि ।
परेउ दंड जिमि धरनितल दसा न जाइ बखानि ॥

१ राम सप्रेम पुलकि उर लावा ।
परम रंक जनु पारसु पावा ॥
मनहुँ प्रेमु परमारथु दोऊ ।
मिलत धरें तन कह सबु कोऊ ॥

When they heard this, people living by the shore        1
came running, forgetting all their chores.
Seeing the beauty of Lakshman, Ram, and Sita,
they praised their own good fortune.
Though inwardly excited to ask        2
their names and village, they held back shyly.
But wise elders among them
were able to discern Ram's identity,
and recounted to all the full story        3
of his going to the forest at his father's order.
Pained to hear this, they all lamented,
"The queen and king have not acted rightly!"
Just then, an ascetic arrived,[32]        4
ardent, very young, and handsome,
a poet, yet unknown, in renouncer's garb,
and wholly, passionately devoted to Ram.

With tearful eyes and body thrilling with love,        110
he recognized his own chosen god
and fell to the ground prostrate, like a stick,
in a state beyond description.

Flushed with love, Ram clasped him to his heart,        1
like a pauper who has found the alchemical stone.
It was as if love and supreme reality had both
taken form and met—so onlookers said.

२ बहुरि लखन पायन्ह सोइ लागा ।
लीन्ह उठाइ उमगि अनुरागा ॥
पुनि सिय चरन धूरि धरि सीसा ।
जननि जानि सिसु दीन्हि असीसा ॥

३ कीन्ह निषाद दंडवत तेही ।
मिलेउ मुदित लखि राम सनेही ॥
पिअत नयन पुट रूपु पियूषा ।
मुदित सुअसनु पाइ जिमि भूखा ॥

४ ते पितु मातु कहहु सखि कैसे ।
जिन्ह पठए बन बालक ऐसे ॥
राम लखन सिय रूपु निहारी ।
होहिं सनेह बिकल नर नारी ॥

१११ तब रघुबीर अनेक बिधि सखहि सिखावनु दीन्ह ।
राम रजायसु सीस धरि भवन गवनु तेइँ कीन्ह ॥

१ पुनि सियँ राम लखन कर जोरी ।
जमुनहि कीन्ह प्रनामु बहोरी ॥
चले ससीय मुदित दोउ भाई ।
रबितनुजा कइ करत बड़ाई ॥

२ पथिक अनेक मिलहिं मग जाता ।
कहहिं सप्रेम देखि दोउ भ्राता ॥
राज लखन सब अंग तुम्हारें ।
देखि सोचु अति हृदय हमारें ॥

Then he bowed at Lakshman's feet,                                    2
and he too drew him up, ecstatic with love.
That ascetic placed the dust of Sita's feet on his head,
and the mother blessed him as her child.[33]
The Nishad prostrated fully at his feet, but the youth              3
embraced him gladly, knowing he was dear to Ram.
Drinking beauty's nectar with the cups of his eyes,
he was as happy as a starving one who gets fine food.
The women said, "Friends, what sort of father and                  4
    mother[34]
would send such children to the woods?"
Seeing the beauty of Ram, Lakshman, and Sita,
all the men and women grew restless with love.


Then the Raghu hero instructed his friend,                         111
and after much persuasion,
Guha resigned himself to Ram's royal decree
and made his way homeward.


Their palms joined, Sita, Ram, and Lakshman                          1
paid repeated homage to holy Yamuna,
and the two brothers, along with Sita, set out
joyously, praising that daughter of the sun.[35]
They met many travelers on the road                                  2
who lovingly addressed the two brothers.
"Your limbs bear the marks of royal birth.
Seeing this, our hearts are much perturbed,

३ मारग चलहु पयादेहि पाएँ ।
ज्योतिषु झूठ हमारें भाएँ ॥
अगमु पंथु गिरि कानन भारी ।
तेहि महँ साथ नारि सुकुमारी ॥
४ करि केहरि बन जाइ न जोई ।
हम सँग चलहिं जो आयसु होई ॥
जाब जहाँ लगि तहँ पहुँचाई ।
फिरब बहोरि तुम्हहि सिरु नाई ॥

११२ एहि बिधि पूँछहिं प्रेम बस पुलक गात जलु नैन ।
कृपासिंधु फेरहिं तिन्हहि कहि बिनीत मृदु बैन ॥

१ जे पुर गाँव बसहिं मग माहीं ।
तिन्हहि नाग सुर नगर सिहाहीं ॥
केहि सुकृतीं केहि घरीं बसाए ।
धन्य पुन्यमय परम सुहाए ॥
२ जहँ जहँ राम चरन चलि जाहीं ।
तिन्ह समान अमरावति नाहीं ॥
पुन्यपुंज मग निकट निवासी ।
तिन्हहि सराहहिं सुरपुरबासी ॥
३ जे भरि नयन बिलोकहिं रामहि ।
सीता लखन सहित घनस्यामहि ॥
जे सर सरित राम अवगाहहिं ।
तिन्हहि देव सर सरित सराहहिं ॥

for since you walk the road on foot,                                    3
we feel that horoscopes must lie.[36]
This arduous path has great peaks and forests.
Moreover, you are with a young woman,
and these woods have elephants and lions, awful to behold.   4
But if you permit us, we will escort you,
make sure you reach your destination,
then salute you and return."

So they implored, spellbound by love,                                 112
with trembling limbs and tear-filled eyes,
but the sea of mercy sent them away
with courteous and gentle words.

Towns and villages that lay along their road                          1
became the envy of gods' and divine serpents' cities—
"What virtuous one, in what blessed hour, settled them,
that they are now so favored, meritorious, and lovely?"
Wherever Ram's feet trod was holy ground                              2
to which Indra's immortal city could not compare,
and the folk dwelling nearby were treasuries of merit
who won praise from the denizens of heaven,
for they could feast their eyes on Ram,                               3
dark as a raincloud, with Sita and Lakshman.
The ponds and rivers where Ram bathed
were lauded by the waterways of the gods,

४ जेहि तरु तर प्रभु बैठहिं जाई ।
करहिं कलपतरु तासु बड़ाई ॥
परसि राम पद पदुम परागा ।
मानति भूमि भूरि निज भागा ॥

११३ छाँह करहिं घन बिबुधगन बरषहिं सुमन सिहाहिं ।
देखत गिरि बन बिहग मृग रामु चले मग जाहिं ॥

१ सीता लखन सहित रघुराई ।
गाँव निकट जब निकसहिं जाई ॥
सुनि सब बाल बृद्ध नर नारी ।
चलहिं तुरत गृह काजु बिसारी ॥

२ राम लखन सिय रूप निहारी ।
पाइ नयन फलु होहिं सुखारी ॥
सजल बिलोचन पुलक सरीरा ।
सब भए मगन देखि दोउ बीरा ॥

३ बरनि न जाइ दसा तिन्ह केरी ।
लहि जनु रंकन्ह सुरमनि ढेरी ॥
एकन्ह एक बोलि सिख देहीं ।
लोचन लाहु लेहु छन एहीं ॥

४ रामहि देखि एक अनुरागे ।
चितवत चले जाहिं सँग लागे ॥
एक नयन मग छबि उर आनी ।
होहिं सिथिल तन मन बर बानी ॥

and any tree under which the Lord sat down                    4
drew praise from heaven's wish-granting tree.
Touched by the pollen-dust of Ram's lotus feet,
Earth reckoned herself supremely fortunate.

The clouds shaded him, and throngs                          113
of envious gods showered blossoms,
as Ram, observing hill and forest,
birds and beasts, walked on that road.

Whenever the Raghu lord, with Sita                           1
and Lakshman, passed near a village,
the news reached young and old, men and women,
and they came at once, forgetting household chores.
Seeing the beauty of Ram, Lakshman, and Sita,               2
they gained their eyes' reward and were happy.
With tear-filled eyes and bodies flushed with joy,
all were stunned at the sight of the two heroes.
Their state was as indescribable as that                     3
of paupers who find a heap of wishing stones.[37]
Calling out, they urged one another
to seize, right now, their eyes' reward.
Some, seeing Ram, grew so infatuated                         4
that they walked beside him, gazing,
or took in his beauty through their eyes' paths
and became silent and motionless, minds stilled.

११४ एक देखि बट छाँह भलि डासि मृदुल तृन पात ।
कहहिं गवाँइअ छिनुकु श्रमु गवनब अबहिं कि प्रात ॥

१ एक कलस भरि आनहिं पानी ।
अँचइअ नाथ कहहिं मृदु बानी ॥
सुनि प्रिय बचन प्रीति अति देखी ।
राम कृपाल सुसील बिसेषी ॥

२ जानी श्रमित सीय मन माहीं ।
घरिक बिलंबु कीन्ह बट छाहीं ॥
मुदित नारी नर देखहिं सोभा ।
रूप अनूप नयन मनु लोभा ॥

३ एकटक सब सोहहिं चहुँ ओरा ।
रामचंद्र मुख चंद चकोरा ॥
तरुन तमाल बरन तनु सोहा ।
देखत कोटि मदन मनु मोहा ॥

४ दामिनि बरन लखन सुठि नीके ।
नख सिख सुभग भावते जी के ॥
मुनिपट कटिन्ह कसें तूनीरा ।
सोहहिं कर कमलनि धनु तीरा ॥

११५ जटा मुकुट सीसनि सुभग उर भुज नयन बिसाल ।
सरद परब बिधु बदन बर लसत स्वेद कन जाल ॥

204

Some, seeing the shade of a great banyan,                                114
spread tender grass and leaves
and said, "Please rest for a moment
and then move on—or stay, perhaps, till morning?"

Some brought vessels filled with water                                   1
and said gently, "Please refresh yourself, master."
Hearing their kind words, seeing their great love,
Ram, compassionate and most courteous,
and knowing that Sita was tired,                                         2
lingered for a time in the banyan's shade.
Overjoyed, men and women took in the beauty
of their incomparable forms, eyes and hearts entranced.
From every side, they gazed unblinking,                                  3
like pretty *cakor* birds, at the face of the Raghu moon,
his body the color of a young bay leaf tree[38]—
a mere glimpse steals the minds of a million Kamas!
Bright as lightning, Lakshman looked handsome                            4
from head to toe, delighting the heart.
Clad as ascetics, quivers cinched at their waists,
they held bows and arrows in their lovely hands.

Heads crowned with matted locks,                                         115
they had broad chests, long arms, and large eyes,
and on the autumn full moons of their faces
gleamed tiny beads of sweat.

१ बरनि न जाइ मनोहर जोरी ।
सोभा बहुत थोरि मति मोरी ॥
राम लखन सिय सुंदरताई ।
सब चितवहिं चित मन मति लाई ॥

२ थके नारि नर प्रेम पिआसे ।
मनहुँ मृगी मृग देखि दिआ से ॥
सीय समीप ग्रामतिय जाहीं ।
पूँछत अति सनेहँ सकुचाहीं ॥

३ बार बार सब लागहिं पाएँ ।
कहहिं बचन मृदु सरल सुभाएँ ॥
राजकुमारि बिनय हम करहीं ।
तिय सुभाएँ कछु पूँछत डरहीं ॥

४ स्वामिनि अबिनय छमबि हमारी ।
बिलगु न मानब जानि गवाँरी ॥
राजकुअँर दोउ सहज सलोने ।
इन्ह तें लही दुति मरकत सोने ॥

११६ स्यामल गौर किसोर बर सुंदर सुषमा ऐन ।
सरद सर्बरीनाथ मुखु सरद सरोरुह नैन ॥

१ कोटि मनोज लजावनिहारे ।
सुमुखि कहहु को आहिं तुम्हारे ॥
सुनि सनेहमय मंजुल बानी ।
सकुची सिय मन महुँ मुसुकानी ॥

The charm of that pair surpasses description,     1
for their glory is great and my intellect meager.
All gazed at the beauty of Ram, Lakshman, and Sita,
focusing their awareness, hearts, and minds.
Thirsty for love, those women and men were as helpless    2
as does and bucks entranced by lamplight.
The village women went to Sita
full of affection, yet too shy to address her.
They bowed repeatedly at her feet    3
and spoke sweet and innocent words.
"Princess, we would question you,
yet women's nature makes us shy to ask.
Pardon our uncouthness, mistress,    4
and knowing we are rustics, do not take offense.
But these two princes, so naturally charming
that emerald and gold must draw luster from them,

these handsome young men, dark and fair,    116
treasuries of good looks,
with faces like the autumn moon
and eyes like that season's lotuses,

who put to shame millions of mind-born gods*—    1
tell us, lovely lady—who are they to you?"
Hearing their gentle, affectionate words,
Sita was embarrassed and smiled to herself.

—————

* Kama, god of love.

२ तिन्हहि बिलोकि बिलोकति धरनी ।
दुहुँ सकोच सकुचति बरबरनी ॥
सकुचि सप्रेम बाल मृग नयनी ।
बोली मधुर बचन पिकबयनी ॥

३ सहज सुभाय सुभग तन गोरे ।
नामु लखनु लघु देवर मोरे ॥
बहुरि बदनु बिधु अंचल ढाँकी ।
पिय तन चितइ भौंह करि बाँकी ॥

४ खंजन मंजु तिरीछे नयननि ।
निज पति कहेउ तिन्हहि सियँ सयननि ॥
भईं मुदित सब ग्रामबधूटीं ।
रंकन्ह राय रासि जनु लूटीं ॥

११७ अति सप्रेम सिय पायँ परि बहुबिधि देहिं असीस ।
सदा सोहागिनि होहु तुम्ह जब लगि महि अहि सीस ॥

१ पारबती सम पतिप्रिय होहू ।
देबि न हम पर छाड़ब छोहू ॥
पुनि पुनि बिनय करिअ कर जोरी ।
जौं एहि मारग फिरिअ बहोरी ॥

२ दरसनु देब जानि निज दासी ।
लखीं सीयँ सब प्रेम पिआसी ॥
मधुर बचन कहि कहि परितोषीं ।
जनु कुमुदिनीं कौमुदीं पोषीं ॥

Glancing at them, then at the ground,      2
the fair woman felt doubly hesitant.[39]
Shyly, that fawn-eyed one
spoke in a voice sweet as a cuckoo's.
"That good-natured, handsome, fair-bodied one—    3
his name is Lakshman, my young brother-in-law."
Then, holding her garment's hem over her moon-like face,
she glanced, with arched brow, toward her beloved,
and with a sidelong look of her lovely eyes,    4
Sita signaled to them that he was her husband.
The village women all became as merry
as paupers who have looted a king's treasury.

Overcome with love, they fell at Sita's feet,    117
pronouncing innumerable blessings—
"May you remain blessed in wedlock for as long
as earth rests on the cosmic serpent's hood,[40]

and may you be, like Parvati, dear to your lord!    1
Divine woman, always look kindly on us.
Hands joined in supplication, we beg you—
if you come back along this same road,
let us see you, considering us your servants."    2
Sita saw that they were all thirsty for love,
and satisfied them with gentle words,
as moonlight gives nurture to night lilies.

३ तबहिं लखन रघुबर रुख जानी ।
पूँछेउ मगु लोगन्हि मृदु बानी ॥
सुनत नारि नर भए दुखारी ।
पुलकित गात बिलोचन बारी ॥

४ मिटा मोदु मन भए मलीने ।
बिधि निधि दीन्ह लेत जनु छीने ॥
समुझि करम गति धीरजु कीन्हा ।
सोधि सुगम मगु तिन्ह कहि दीन्हा ॥

११८ लखन जानकी सहित तब गवनु कीन्ह रघुनाथ ।
फेरे सब प्रिय बचन कहि लिए लाइ मन साथ ॥

१ फिरत नारि नर अति पछिताहीं ।
दैअहिं दोषु देहिं मन माहीं ॥
सहित बिषाद परसपर कहहीं ।
बिधि करतब उलटे सब अहहीं ॥

२ निपट निरंकुस निठुर निसंकू ।
जेहिं ससि कीन्ह सरुज सकलंकू ॥
रूख कलपतरु सागरु खारा ।
तेहिं पठए बन राजकुमारा ॥

३ जौं पै इन्हहि दीन्ह बनबासू ।
कीन्ह बादि बिधि भोग बिलासू ॥
ए बिचरहिं मग बिनु पदत्राना ।
रचे बादि बिधि बाहन नाना ॥

210

Then Lakshman, discerning the Raghu lord's wish,      3
politely asked the folk for onward directions.
As soon as they heard, they all were grief stricken,
with trembling limbs and tear-filled eyes.
Their joy erased, they grew disheartened,      4
as if a God-given treasure was snatched away.
But, musing on their fate, they took courage
and settled on the best route to tell them.

Then the lord of the Raghus went on,      118
together with Lakshman and Janaki,
sending the people back with tender words,
but taking their hearts with him.

As they returned, women and men lamented      1
and inwardly decried the ways of fate.
In anguish, they said to one another,
"All the creator's designs are contrary.
Utterly capricious, cruel, and brazen,      2
he who made the moon sickly and stained,
dried up the wishing tree, and turned the sea salty,
has sent these princes to the woods!
If he decreed forest exile for such as these,      3
then God made pleasure and luxury in vain.
If they must wander the roads barefoot,
then in vain did he craft all sorts of vehicles.

४ ए महि परहिं डासि कुस पाता ।
सुभग सेज कत सृजत बिधाता ॥
तरुबर बास इन्हहि बिधि दीन्हा ।
धवल धाम रचि रचि श्रमु कीन्हा ॥

११९ जौं ए मुनि पट धर जटिल सुंदर सुठि सुकुमार ।
बिबिध भाँति भूषन बसन बादि किए करतार ॥

१ जौं ए कंद मूल फल खाहीं ।
बादि सुधादि असन जग माहीं ॥
एक कहहिं ए सहज सुहाए ।
आपु प्रगट भए बिधि न बनाए ॥

२ जहँ लगि बेद कही बिधि करनी ।
श्रवन नयन मन गोचर बरनी ॥
देखहु खोजि भुअन दस चारी ।
कहँ अस पुरुष कहाँ असि नारी ॥

३ इन्हहि देखि बिधि मनु अनुरागा ।
पटतर जोग बनावै लागा ॥
कीन्ह बहुत श्रम ऐक न आए ।
तेहिं इरिषा बन आनि दुराए ॥

४ एक कहहिं हम बहुत न जानहिं ।
आपुहि परम धन्य करि मानहिं ॥
ते पुनि पुन्यपुंज हम लेखे ।
जे देखहिं देखिहहिं जिन्ह देखे ॥

If they must spread grass and leaves to lie on,                4
then why did he fashion beautiful beds?
If the creator decreed that they dwell under trees,
he wasted his efforts to make splendid mansions.

If these most handsome youths                                  119
wear bark cloth and matted locks,
then in vain did the all-maker
make all kinds of finery and jewelry.

If they eat wild roots and fruit,                              1
delectable foods have no use in this world!"
Someone said, "They are so inherently lovely
they must be self-manifest, not made by Brahma.
In all that the Veda says of the creator's works,             2
perceptible to our ears, eyes, and minds,
and in the fourteen worlds—scour them all—
where is such a man, where such a woman?
Seeing them, Brahma's heart was so taken                       3
that he tried to make others like them,
but all his efforts produced no match,
so in jealous spite, he hid them in the forest."
Another said, "We don't understand much,                       4
but just consider ourselves supremely blessed
and we reckon as most meritorious
all who have seen, or see, or will yet see them."

१२०   एहि बिधि कहि कहि बचन प्रिय लेहिं नयन भरि नीर ।
      किमि चलिहहिं मारग अगम सुठि सुकुमार सरीर ॥

१     नारि सनेह बिकल बस होहीं ।
      चकई साँझ समय जनु सोहीं ॥
      मृदु पद कमल कठिन मगु जानी ।
      गहबरि हृदयँ कहहिं बर बानी ॥

२     परसत मृदुल चरन अरुनारे ।
      सकुचति महि जिमि हृदय हमारे ॥
      जौं जगदीस इन्हहि बनु दीन्हा ।
      कस न सुमनमय मारगु कीन्हा ॥

३     जौं मागा पाइअ बिधि पाहीं ।
      ए रखिअहिं सखि आँखिन्ह माहीं ॥
      जे नर नारि न अवसर आए ।
      तिन्ह सिय रामु न देखन पाए ॥

४     सुनि सुरूपु बूझहिं अकुलाई ।
      अब लगि गए कहाँ लगि भाई ॥
      समरथ धाइ बिलोकहिं जाई ।
      प्रमुदित फिरहिं जनमफलु पाई ॥

१२१   अबला बालक बृद्ध जन कर मीजहिं पछिताहिं ।
      होहिं प्रेमबस लोग इमि रामु जहाँ जहँ जाहिं ॥

Thus they all engaged in loving talk,                    120
while their eyes overflowed with tears.
"How will these most delicate youths
walk on the rough roads?"

Overcome by affection, the women were distraught,        1
like lovely red geese at evening time.[41]
Thinking of their tender feet and that harsh path,
they spoke eloquently from anxious hearts.
"Touched by the rosy soles of those delicate feet,       2
Earth must be as abashed as our own hearts.
If the world creator had to give them exile,
why didn't he strew their path with flowers?
If one can truly get a wish from God,                    3
friends, may he just keep them before our eyes."
Some men and women who had not come in time
had missed the chance to see Sita and Ram.
Hearing of their beauty, they anxiously asked,           4
"Brothers, where must they have reached by now?"
Those who could, went at a run to see them
and returned delighted, their lives fulfilled.

Frail women, children, and the aged                      121
could only wring their hands and lament.
So it was that, wherever Ram went,
the people were overcome by love.

१	गावँ गावँ अस होइ अनंदू।
	देखि भानुकुल कैरव चंदू॥
	जे कछु समाचार सुनि पावहिं।
	ते नृप रानिहि दोसु लगावहिं॥

२	कहहिं एक अति भल नरनाहू।
	दीन्ह हमहि जोइ लोचन लाहू॥
	कहहिं परसपर लोग लोगाईं।
	बातें सरल सनेह सुहाईं॥

३	ते पितु मातु धन्य जिन्ह जाए।
	धन्य सो नगरु जहाँ तें आए॥
	धन्य सो देसु सैलु बनु गाऊँ।
	जहँ जहँ जाहिं धन्य सोइ ठाऊँ॥

४	सुखु पायउ बिरंचि रचि तेही।
	ए जेहि के सब भाँति सनेही॥
	राम लखन पथि कथा सुहाई।
	रही सकल मग कानन छाई॥

१२२	एहि बिधि रघुकुल कमल रबि मग लोगन्ह सुख देत।
	जाहिं चले देखत बिपिन सिय सौमित्रि समेत॥

१	आगें रामु लखनु बने पाछें।
	तापस बेष बिराजत काछें॥
	उभय बीच सिय सोहति कैसें।
	ब्रह्म जीव बिच माया जैसें॥

216

In village after village, this ecstasy spread,                     1
seeing that moon of the lilies of the solar line.
Those who had heard some news
heaped blame on the king and queen.
But one said, "No, the king was very good                          2
to have given us our eyes' reward!"
So men and women spoke among themselves
in simple, affectionate, lovely words.
"Blessed are the parents who gave them birth,                      3
and blessed is the city from which they came.
Blessed is the country, the hills, forests, villages,
and every place they go—all are blessed!
Why, Brahma was pleased merely to have made                        4
anyone who feels wholehearted love for them."[42]
The lovely tale of Ram and Lakshman's wayfaring
spread through all the pathways and forests.

And so, the sun to the lotuses of the Raghu line                   122
gave joy to the folk along the way
as he went along, observing the woodlands,
with Sumitra's son and Sita.

Ram walked ahead, Lakshman behind,                                 1
resplendent in their ascetic garb,
and between the two, Sita was as glorious
as divine maya between God and the soul.[43]

२ बहुरि कहउँ छबि जसि मन बसई ।
जनु मधु मदन मध्य रति लसई ॥
उपमा बहुरि कहउँ जियँ जोही ।
जनु बुध बिधु बिच रोहिनि सोही ॥

३ प्रभु पद रेख बीच बिच सीता ।
धरति चरन मग चलति सभीता ॥
सीय राम पद अंक बराएँ ।
लखन चलहिं मगु दाहिन लाएँ ॥

४ राम लखन सिय प्रीति सुहाई ।
बचन अगोचर किमि कहि जाई ॥
खग मृग मगन देखि छबि होहीं ।
लिए चोरि चित राम बटोहीं ॥

१२३ जिन्ह जिन्ह देखे पथिक प्रिय सिय समेत दोउ भाइ ।
भव मगु अगमु अनंदु तेइ बिनु श्रम रहे सिराइ ॥

१ अजहुँ जासु उर सपनेहुँ काऊ ।
बसहुँ लखनु सिय रामु बटाऊ ॥
राम धाम पथ पाइहि सोई ।
जो पथ पाव कबहुँ मुनि कोई ॥

२ तब रघुबीर श्रमित सिय जानी ।
देखि निकट बटु सीतल पानी ॥
तहँ बसि कंद मूल फल खाई ।
प्रात नहाइ चले रघुराई ॥

I tell again of their beauty, as it dwells in my heart:    2
like lovely Rati between her spouse and spring.[44]
And searching my mind, I offer another simile:
like Rohini shining between Mercury and the moon.[45]
Between Ram's footprints, Sita    3
set her feet watchfully, walking the path.
Protecting Sita and Ram's footsteps,
keeping them on his right, Lakshman trod the road.[46]
The beauty of Ram, Lakshman, and Sita's love    4
is beyond words—how can it be told?
Even birds and beasts were stunned to see it,
their wits stolen by Ram the wayfarer.

Whoever beheld those dear travelers—    123
Sita together with the two brothers—
blissfully and effortlessly gained
the end of rebirth's arduous road.

Even today, if one's heart just dreams    1
of sheltering those wanderers, Lakshman, Sita, and Ram,
one finds the way to Ram's abode—
a path that even sages rarely attain.
When the Raghu hero, knowing Sita was tired,    2
saw a nearby banyan and cool water,
they camped there, eating roots and wild fruits.
After sunrise ablutions, the Raghu king moved on.

३ देखत बन सर सैल सुहाए ।
बालमीकि आश्रम प्रभु आए ॥
राम दीख मुनि बासु सुहावन ।
सुंदर गिरि काननु जलु पावन ॥

४ सरनि सरोज बिटप बन फूले ।
गुंजत मंजु मधुप रस भूले ॥
खग मृग बिपुल कोलाहल करहीं ।
बिरहित बैर मुदित मन चरहीं ॥

१२४ सुचि सुंदर आश्रमु निरखि हरषे राजिवनेन ।
सुनि रघुबर आगमनु मुनि आगें आयउ लेन ॥

१ मुनि कहुँ राम दंडवत कीन्हा ।
आसिरबादु बिप्रबर दीन्हा ॥
देखि राम छबि नयन जुड़ाने ।
करि सनमानु आश्रमहिं आने ॥

२ मुनिबर अतिथि प्रानप्रिय पाए ।
कंद मूल फल मधुर मगाए ॥
सिय सौमित्रि राम फल खाए ।
तब मुनि आश्रम दिए सुहाए ॥

३ बालमीकि मन आनँदु भारी ।
मंगल मूरति नयन निहारी ॥
तब कर कमल जोरि रघुराई ।
बोले बचन श्रवन सुखदाई ॥

Seeing lovely forests, lakes, and mountains, 3
the Lord came to Valmiki's hermitage.
Ram beheld the sage's delightful abode
with its beautiful hills, woodlands, pure water,
lotus lakes, and groves of flowering trees. 4
Bees buzzed softly, drunk with nectar,
and multitudes of birds and beasts called out
as they grazed happily, without enmity.

Surveying this holy and beautiful ashram, 124
the lotus-eyed one felt delight,
and the sage, hearing of the Raghu lord's approach,
came out to receive him.

Ram prostrated fully before the sage 1
and that best of seers blessed him,
the sight of Ram's beauty comforting his eyes.
Respectfully, he led him to the retreat.
Receiving such guests, dear as his life, the great sage 2
called for sweet roots, tubers, and fruit.
When Sita, Sumitra's son, and Ram had eaten,
the sage gave them a charming place to rest.[47]
Valmiki's heart brimmed with bliss 3
as his eyes beheld the embodiment of blessing.
Then the Raghu lord, joining his lovely palms,
spoke words most pleasing to the ears.

४  तुम्ह त्रिकाल दरसी मुनिनाथा ।
   बिस्व बदर जिमि तुम्हरें हाथा ॥
   अस कहि प्रभु सब कथा बखानी ।
   जेहि जेहि भाँति दीन्ह बनु रानी ॥

१२५  तात बचन पुनि मातु हित भाइ भरत अस राउ ।
    मो कहुँ दरस तुम्हार प्रभु सबु मम पुन्य प्रभाउ ॥

१  देखि पाय मुनिराय तुम्हारे ।
   भए सुकृत सब सुफल हमारे ॥
   अब जहँ राउर आयसु होई ।
   मुनि उदबेगु न पावै कोई ॥

२  मुनि तापस जिन्ह तें दुखु लहहीं ।
   ते नरेस बिनु पावक दहहीं ॥
   मंगल मूल बिप्र परितोषू ।
   दहइ कोटि कुल भूसुर रोषू ॥

३  अस जियँ जानि कहिअ सोइ ठाऊँ ।
   सिय सौमित्रि सहित जहँ जाऊँ ॥
   तहँ रचि रुचिर परन तृन साला ।
   बासु करौं कछु काल कृपाला ॥

४  सहज सरल सुनि रघुबर बानी ।
   साधु साधु बोले मुनि ग्यानी ॥
   कस न कहहु अस रघुकुलकेतू ।
   तुम्ह पालक संतत श्रुति सेतू ॥

222

"Supreme seer of past, present, and future,    4
the cosmos is like a berry held on your palm."
Then the Lord narrated the whole tale
of how the queen had decreed his exile.

"To uphold father's word, oblige our mother,    125
let a brother like Bharat be king,
and then, to obtain sight of you, lord—
all this must result from my past merit!

Seeing your feet, king of sages,    1
is the fruition of all our good deeds.
Now command us to go to some place
where no ascetics will be disturbed.
For if he brings grief to sages and ascetics,    2
a king is burned up even without fire.
Satisfaction of seers is the root of well-being,[48]
and the wrath of these gods on earth burns countless
    generations.
Considering this, please tell me a place    3
where I may go with Sita and Sumitra's son,
and, building a shelter of leaves and grass,
may live there for a while, merciful one."
Hearing that best of Raghus' simple, sincere speech,    4
the wise seer exclaimed, "Well and nobly said!
But how else would you, banner of the Raghus, speak—
who forever guard the ramparts of revealed truth?[49]

५    श्रुति सेतु पालक राम तुम्ह
जगदीस माया जानकी ।
जो सृजति जगु पालति हरति
रुख पाइ कृपानिधान की ॥
जो सहससीसु अहीसु महिधरु
लखनु सचराचर धनी ।
सुर काज धरि नरराज तनु चले
दलन खल निसिचर अनी ॥

१२६   राम सरूप तुम्हार बचन अगोचर बुद्धिपर ।
अबिगत अकथ अपार नेति नेति नित निगम कह ॥

१    जगु पेखन तुम्ह देखनिहारे ।
बिधि हरि संभु नचावनिहारे ॥
तेउ न जानहिं मरमु तुम्हारा ।
औरु तुम्हहि को जाननिहारा ॥

२    सोइ जानइ जेहि देहु जनाई ।
जानत तुम्हहि तुम्हइ होइ जाई ॥
तुम्हरिहि कृपाँ तुम्हहि रघुनंदन ।
जानहिं भगत भगत उर चंदन ॥

३    चिदानंदमय देह तुम्हारी ।
बिगत बिकार जान अधिकारी ॥
नर तनु धरेहु संत सुर काजा ।
कहहु करहु जस प्राकृत राजा ॥

Guardian of Veda's strictures, you are Lord of creation,    5
Ram, and Janaki is your illusory power,
who brings forth, nurtures, and destroys
the cosmos at your whim, abode of mercy!
The thousand-headed serpent king who supports
the earth is Lakshman, lord of all beings.
Embodied as human princes, you go forth to do
the gods' work and to crush wicked demon hordes.

Ram, your true being transcends speech    126
and intelligence—imperceptible, unutterable,
and endless—of which the Veda constantly declares,
'No, he is neither this nor that!'

The world is a spectacle and you its viewer,    1
who sets Brahma, Hari, and Shiva to dance.
Even they do not know your secret,
so who else could ever know you?
Only one to whom you give knowledge knows you,    2
and knowing you, at once becomes you.
By your grace alone, joy of the Raghus,
your devotees know you as cooling balm for their hearts![50]
Your body, suffused with consciousness and bliss,    3
is faultless, as only initiates know, yet,[51]
taking human form for the sake of sages and gods,
you speak and act like a worldly king.

४ राम देखि सुनि चरित तुम्हारे ।
जड़ मोहहिं बुध होहिं सुखारे ॥
तुम्ह जो कहहु करहु सबु साँचा ।
जस काछिअ तस चाहिअ नाचा ॥

१२७ पूँछेहु मोहि कि रहौं कहँ मैं पूँछत सकुचाउँ ।
जहँ न होहु तहँ देहु कहि तुम्हहि देखावौं ठाउँ ॥

१ सुनि मुनि बचन प्रेम रस साने ।
सकुचि राम मन महुँ मुसुकाने ॥
बालमीकि हँसि कहहिं बहोरी ।
बानी मधुर अमिअ रस बोरी ॥

२ सुनहु राम अब कहउँ निकेता ।
जहाँ बसहु सिय लखन समेता ॥
जिन्ह के श्रवन समुद्र समाना ।
कथा तुम्हारि सुभग सरि नाना ॥

३ भरहिं निरंतर होहिं न पूरे ।
तिन्ह के हिय तुम्ह कहुँ गृह रूरे ॥
लोचन चातक जिन्ह करि राखे ।
रहहिं दरस जलधर अभिलाषे ॥

४ निदरहिं सरित सिंधु सर भारी ।
रूप बिंदु जल होहिं सुखारी ॥
तिन्ह कें हृदय सदन सुखदायक ।
बसहु बंधु सिय सह रघुनायक ॥

Seeing and hearing of your deeds, Ram,                                        4
the ignorant are deluded but the wise rejoice.
All that you say and do is true,
for as is the costume, so must be the dance![52]

You ask, 'Where should I reside?'                                      127
but hesitantly, I ask you this:
Tell me a place where you are not,
that I may point it out to you."

At the sage's speech, imbued with love's essence,          1
Ram grew shy, yet smiled inwardly.
Then Valmiki laughed and spoke again,
in words steeped in nectar's sweetness.
"Listen, Ram, as I now describe a place                   2
where you may settle down with Sita and Lakshman.
Those whose ears are like the seas,
which countless lovely rivers of your story
constantly fill, though never, ever fully—                   3
their hearts are a fitting home for you.
Those who have made their eyes into cuckoos,[53]
and live thirsting for the sight of your cloud,
scorning mighty rivers, seas, and lakes                     4
to rejoice in a single drop of your beauty—
dwell in the delightful chambers of their hearts,
Raghu king, along with your brother and Sita.

१२८ जसु तुम्हार मानस बिमल हंसिनि जीहा जासु ।
मुकताहल गुन गन चुनइ राम बसहु हियँ तासु ॥

१ प्रभु प्रसाद सुचि सुभग सुबासा ।
सादर जासु लहइ नित नासा ॥
तुम्हहि निबेदित भोजन करहीं ।
प्रभु प्रसाद पट भूषन धरहीं ॥

२ सीस नवहिं सुर गुरु द्विज देखी ।
प्रीति सहित करि बिनय बिसेषी ॥
कर नित करहिं राम पद पूजा ।
राम भरोस हृदयँ नहिं दूजा ॥

३ चरन राम तीरथ चलि जाहीं ।
राम बसहु तिन्ह के मन माहीं ॥
मंत्रराजु नित जपहिं तुम्हारा ।
पूजहिं तुम्हहि सहित परिवारा ॥

४ तरपन होम करहिं बिधि नाना ।
बिप्र जेवाँइ देहिं बहु दाना ॥
तुम्ह तें अधिक गुरहि जियँ जानी ।
सकल भायँ सेवहिं सनमानी ॥

१२९ सबु करि मागहिं एक फलु राम चरन रति होउ ।
तिन्ह कें मन मंदिर बसहु सिय रघुनंदन दोउ ॥

228

Those whose tongues are *haṃsa* geese                    128
on the clear Manas Lake of your fame,
seeking out the pearls of your countless virtues[54]—
reside in their hearts, Ram!

Those whose nostrils ever breathe                          1
the pure, fragrant offerings made to you, lord,
who eat only food consecrated to you,
wear clothes and ornaments received as your grace,
whose heads bow at the sight of god, guru, or twice-born,   2
to lovingly honor them with real humility,
whose hands constantly worship your feet,
whose hearts rely on Ram and no other,
and whose feet journey to Ram's holy places—               3
reside, Ram, in their hearts.
Those who ever repeat your supreme mantra
and worship you along with their family,
who perform diverse libations and fire rites,              4
feed seers and give them generous gifts,
who consider their guru greater even than yourself,
and wholeheartedly and reverently serve him,

and who, having done all this, ask                        129
but one reward—love for Ram's feet—
settle down in their heart's sanctuary,
you two joys of the Raghus, along with Sita.

१ काम कोह मद मान न मोहा ।
लोभ न छोभ न राग न द्रोहा ॥
जिन्ह कें कपट दंभ नहिं माया ।
तिन्ह कें हृदय बसहु रघुराया ॥

२ सब के प्रिय सब के हितकारी ।
दुख सुख सरिस प्रसंसा गारी ॥
कहहिं सत्य प्रिय बचन बिचारी ।
जागत सोवत सरन तुम्हारी ॥

३ तुम्हहि छाड़ि गति दूसरि नाहीं ।
राम बसहु तिन्ह के मन माहीं ॥
जननी सब जानहिं परनारी ।
धनु पराव बिष तें बिष भारी ॥

४ जे हरषहिं पर संपति देखी ।
दुखित होहिं पर बिपति बिसेषी ॥
जिन्हहि राम तुम्ह प्रानपिआरे ।
तिन्ह के मन सुभ सदन तुम्हारे ॥

१३० स्वामि सखा पितु मातु गुर जिन्ह के सब तुम्ह तात ।
मन मंदिर तिन्ह कें बसहु सीय सहित दोउ भ्रात ॥

१ अवगुन तजि सब के गुन गहहीं ।
बिप्र धेनु हित संकट सहहीं ॥
नीति निपुन जिन्ह कइ जग लीका ।
घर तुम्हार तिन्ह कर मनु नीका ॥

Those without lust, anger, arrogance, pride, delusion,  1
greed, excitement, passion, or hatred,
with no duplicity, hypocrisy, or artifice—
reside in their hearts, Raghu king.
Those who are dear to all, benefactors of all,  2
for whom joy and grief, praise and abuse are equal,
who speak truth, gently and on due reflection,
relying on you always, waking or sleeping,
who have no other refuge than you,  3
Ram—dwell in their hearts.
Those who consider another's wife their mother,
another's wealth more toxic than venom,
who rejoice in the prosperity of others,  4
and feel anguish at their misfortune,
who hold you, Ram, dearer than life-breath—
their hearts are an auspicious home for you.

Those for whom you are everything—  130
master, friend, father, mother, teacher—
take up your residence, you two brothers
and Sita, in the temple of their hearts.

Those who ignore others' faults, embrace their virtues,  1
endure pain for the sake of Brahmans and cows,
and make their mark in the world by moral eminence—
their minds make a fitting mansion for you.

२ गुन तुम्हार समुझइ निज दोसा ।
जेहि सब भाँति तुम्हार भरोसा ॥
राम भगत प्रिय लागहिं जेही ।
तेहि उर बसहु सहित बैदेही ॥

३ जाति पाँति धनु धरमु बड़ाई ।
प्रिय परिवार सदन सुखदाई ॥
सब तजि तुम्हहि रहइ उर लाई ।
तेहि के हृदयँ रहहु रघुराई ॥

४ सरगु नरकु अपबरगु समाना ।
जहँ तहँ देख धरें धनु बाना ॥
करम बचन मन राउर चेरा ।
राम करहु तेहि कें उर डेरा ॥

१३१ जाहि न चाहिअ कबहुँ कछु तुम्ह सन सहज सनेहु ।
बसहु निरंतर तासु मन सो राउर निज गेहु ॥

१ एहि बिधि मुनिबर भवन देखाए ।
बचन सप्रेम राम मन भाए ॥
कह मुनि सुनहु भानुकुलनायक ।
आश्रम कहउँ समय सुखदायक ॥

२ चित्रकूट गिरि करहु निवासू ।
तहँ तुम्हार सब भाँति सुपासू ॥
सैलु सुहावन कानन चारू ।
करि केहरि मृग बिहग बिहारू ॥

Those who know your goodness and their own defects,    2
who trust in you entirely,
and who cherish other Ram devotees—
dwell, with Vaidehi, in their hearts.
Caste and clan, wealth, religion, status,    3
dear family, and comfortable home—
those who leave all this to live holding you most dear,
live in their hearts, Raghu king!
Those for whom heaven, hell, and final release are equal,    4
who see you everywhere, bearing arrows and bow,
who are your servants in deed, word, and thought—
make your encampment, Ram, in their hearts!

One who never desires anything    131
and whose love for you is most natural—
in such a one's heart dwell eternally,
for it is your very own home."

So did the great sage show them an abode,    1
with loving speech that pleased Ram's heart.
Then Valmiki said, "Lord of the sun lineage,
I will tell you of a pleasant refuge for this period.
Make your home on Mount Chitrakut,    2
for everything you will need is there.
It is a delightful hill with lovely forests
frequented by elephants, lion, deer, and birds.

३ नदी पुनीत पुरान बखानी ।
अत्रिप्रिया निज तप बल आनी ॥
सुरसरि धार नाउँ मंदाकिनि ।
जो सब पातक पोतक डाकिनि ॥

४ अत्रि आदि मुनिबर बहु बसहीं ।
करहिं जोग जप तप तन कसहीं ॥
चलहु सफल श्रम सब कर करहू ।
राम देहु गौरव गिरिबरहू ॥

१३२ चित्रकूट महिमा अमित कही महामुनि गाइ ।
आइ नहाए सरित बर सिय समेत दोउ भाइ ॥

१ रघुबर कहेउ लखन भल घाटू ।
करहु कतहुँ अब ठाहर ठाटू ॥
लखन दीख पय उतर करारा ।
चहुँ दिसि फिरेउ धनुष जिमि नारा ॥

२ नदी पनच सर सम दम दाना ।
सकल कलुष कलि साउज नाना ॥
चित्रकूट जनु अचल अहेरी ।
चुकइ न घात मार मुठभेरी ॥

३ अस कहि लखन ठाउँ देखरावा ।
थलु बिलोकि रघुबर सुखु पावा ॥
रमेउ राम मनु देवन्ह जाना ।
चले सहित सुर थपति प्रधाना ॥

A holy river, famed in the *purāṇas,*                                3
was brought there by Atri's wife, through austerities—
a stream of the Ganga, called Mandakini,
a witch to devour all the infants of sin.[55]
Atri and other eminent sages reside there                            4
restraining their bodies through disciplined practices.
Go there and make all their labors fruitful,
Ram, and give that lovely mountain renown."

Thus the great sage Valmiki expounded                                132
the endless glory of Mount Chitrakut,
and the two brothers and Sita
went there and bathed in its pure river.[56]

Ram said, "This is a fine riverbank, Lakshman,                       1
so find a place to build a shelter."
Lakshman surveyed a bluff on the northern bank
surrounded by a bow-shaped ravine—
its string the river, its arrows, restraint, austerity, and          2
    charity,
and its targets, the countless sins of the dark era.
Mount Chitrakut was like a steadfast hunter
who strikes unerringly and at close range.
Reporting this, Lakshman showed the site,                            3
and the best of Raghus saw it and was glad.
The gods knew Ram's heart to be pleased
and went there with their divine architect.[57]

४    कोल किरात बेष सब आए ।
रचे परन तृन सदन सुहाए ॥
बरनि न जाहिं मंजु दुइ साला ।
एक ललित लघु एक बिसाला ॥

१३३   लखन जानकी सहित प्रभु राजत रुचिर निकेत ।
सोह मदनु मुनि बेष जनु रति रितुराज समेत ॥

१    अमर नाग किंनर दिसिपाला ।
चित्रकूट आए तेहि काला ॥
राम प्रनामु कीन्ह सब काहू ।
मुदित देव लहि लोचन लाहू ॥

२    बरषि सुमन कह देव समाजू ।
नाथ सनाथ भए हम आजू ॥
करि बिनती दुख दुसह सुनाए ।
हरषित निज निज सदन सिधाए ॥

३    चित्रकूट रघुनंदनु छाए ।
समाचार सुनि सुनि मुनि आए ॥
आवत देखि मुदित मुनिबृंदा ।
कीन्ह दंडवत रघुकुल चंदा ॥

४    मुनि रघुबरहि लाइ उर लेहीं ।
सुफल होन हित आसिष देहीं ॥
सिय सौमित्रि राम छबि देखहिं ।
साधन सकल सफल करि लेखहिं ॥

They came in the guise of tribal Kols and Kirats       4
and made lovely dwellings of leaves and grass—
two homes of indescribable beauty,
one charmingly small, one spacious.

With Lakshman and Janaki, the Lord       133
was as resplendent in this fine abode
as heart-beguiling Kama in sage's garb,
along with Rati and the springtime.

Gods, demigods, serpents, and guardians of space       1
came to Chitrakut at that time.
Ram respectfully saluted them all,
and the happy immortals claimed their eyes' reward
and showered him with blossoms, declaring,       2
"Today, master, we have found a protector."
Entreating him, they told of their suffering,[58]
and departed happily for their own abodes.
News that the Raghu prince was in Chitrakut       3
soon spread among ascetics, and they came.
When he saw the joyous band of sages approaching,
the moon of the Raghus prostrated in reverence.
The sages lifted Ram and embraced him,       4
giving their blessings for success.
Beholding the beauty of Sita, Ram, and Sumitra's son,
they knew all their spiritual practices had borne fruit.

१३४ जथाजोग सनमानि प्रभु बिदा किए मुनिबृंद ।
करहिं जोग जप जाग तप निज आश्रमन्हि सुछंद ॥

१ यह सुधि कोल किरातन्ह पाई ।
हरषे जनु नव निधि घर आई ॥
कंद मूल फल भरि भरि दोना ।
चले रंक जनु लूटन सोना ॥

२ तिन्ह महँ जिन्ह देखे दोउ भ्राता ।
अपर तिन्हहि पूँछहिं मगु जाता ॥
कहत सुनत रघुबीर निकाई ।
आइ सबन्हि देखे रघुराई ॥

३ करहिं जोहारु भेंट धरि आगे ।
प्रभुहि बिलोकहिं अति अनुरागे ॥
चित्र लिखे जनु जहँ तहँ ठाढ़े ।
पुलक सरीर नयन जल बाढ़े ॥

४ राम सनेह मगन सब जाने ।
कहि प्रिय बचन सकल सनमाने ॥
प्रभुहि जोहारि बहोरि बहोरी ।
बचन बिनीत कहहिं कर जोरी ॥

१३५ अब हम नाथ सनाथ सब भए देखि प्रभु पाय ।
भाग हमारें आगमनु राउर कोसलराय ॥

The Lord paid fitting homage to each ascetic band 134
and bade them farewell.
Engaged in yoga, prayer, sacrifice, and austerity,
they lived, free of care, in their ashrams.

When the Kols and Kirats got news of all this,[59] 1
they rejoiced as if nine treasures had come to their homes.
Bearing leaf-bowls brimming with roots and fruits
they went like paupers bent on looting gold.
Those who had already seen the two brothers 2
were questioned by others on the road.
Telling and hearing of the Raghu hero's goodness,
they all came into his regal presence.
Saluting, they set their gifts before him 3
and gazed at the Lord with intense love.
They stood stock still, as if in a painting,
their bodies flushed, eyes filled with tears.
Knowing they were stunned by love, Ram 4
spoke gentle words, showing respect to all.
Praising the Lord again and again,
they entreated him, palms joined in reverence:

"All of us have gained a guardian, master, 135
now that we have beheld your feet.
How great is our good fortune
in your coming here, king of Kosala!

१   धन्य भूमि बन पंथ पहारा ।
जहँ जहँ नाथ पाउ तुम्ह धारा ॥
धन्य बिहग मृग काननचारी ।
सफल जनम भए तुम्हहि निहारी ॥

२   हम सब धन्य सहित परिवारा ।
दीख दरसु भरि नयन तुम्हारा ॥
कीन्ह बासु भल ठाउँ बिचारी ।
इहाँ सकल रितु रहब सुखारी ॥

३   हम सब भाँति करब सेवकाई ।
करि केहरि अहि बाघ बराई ॥
बन बेहड़ गिरि कंदर खोहा ।
सब हमार प्रभु पग पग जोहा ॥

४   तहँ तहँ तुम्हहि अहेर खेलाउब ।
सर निरझर जलठाउँ देखाउब ॥
हम सेवक परिवार समेता ।
नाथ न सकुचब आयसु देता ॥

१३६   बेद बचन मुनि मन अगम ते प्रभु करुना ऐन ।
बचन किरातन्ह के सुनत जिमि पितु बालक बैन ॥

१   रामहि केवल प्रेमु पिआरा ।
जानि लेउ जो जाननिहारा ॥
राम सकल बनचर तब तोषे ।
कहि मृदु बचन प्रेम परितोषे ॥

Blessed are the earth, woods, pathways, and hills,      1
wherever you have set your feet, lord.
Blessed are the birds and beasts of the forest
whose births are fulfilled by sight of you.
And we are all blessed, together with our kin,      2
in gazing at you to our eyes' content.
You chose a fine spot to make your dwelling
and will stay at ease here in all seasons.
We will serve you in every way,      3
guarding you from elephants, lions, snakes, and tigers.
All the dense forests, hills, caves, and chasms—
we have surveyed every step of them, lord!
We will bring you to the best hunting spots      4
and show you the water sources—ponds and springs.
We and our kinfolk are your servants,
master, so do not hesitate to command us."

He who is beyond the reach of Vedic chants      136
and the meditations of sages—that most merciful Lord
listened to the speech of the tribal folk
as a father to the voices of his children.

For love alone is dear to Ram—      1
those with insight will grasp this.
Then Ram satisfied all the forest dwellers,
speaking gentle words imbued with love,

२ बिदा किए सिर नाइ सिधाए ।
प्रभु गुन कहत सुनत घर आए ॥
एहि बिधि सिय समेत दोउ भाई ।
बसहिं बिपिन सुर मुनि सुखदाई ॥

३ जब तें आइ रहे रघुनायकु ।
तब तें भयउ बनु मंगलदायकु ॥
फूलहिं फलहिं बिटप बिधि नाना ।
मंजु बलित बर बेलि बिताना ॥

४ सुरतरु सरिस सुभायँ सुहाए ।
मनहुँ बिबुध बन परिहरि आए ॥
गुंज मंजुतर मधुकर श्रेनी ।
त्रिबिध बयारि बहइ सुख देनी ॥

१३७ नीलकंठ कलकंठ सुक चातक चक्क चकोर ।
भाँति भाँति बोलहिं बिहग श्रवन सुखद चित चोर ॥

१ करि केहरि कपि कोल कुरंगा ।
बिगतबैर बिचरहिं सब संगा ॥
फिरत अहेर राम छबि देखी ।
होहिं मुदित मृग बृंद बिसेषी ॥

२ बिबुध बिपिन जहँ लगि जग माहीं ।
देखि रामबनु सकल सिहाहीं ॥
सुरसरि सरसइ दिनकर कन्या ।
मेकलसुता गोदावरि धन्या ॥

242

and bade them farewell. Bowing to him, they departed 2
and, telling and hearing of the Lord's virtues, went home.
In this manner, the two brothers and Sita
lived in the forest, delighting gods and sages.
From the moment Ram came to reside there, 3
those woods became a source of blessing.
Trees of many species flowered and bore fruit,
sheltered by a canopy of lovely vines.
As beautiful as heaven's wishing tree, 4
they seemed to have fled the gods' grove to come there.
Lines of honeybees hummed most sweetly,
and a cool, fragrant breeze blew, bringing joy.

Blue throats, nightingales, parrots, 137
cuckoos, waterfowl, and partridges—
every kind of wild bird gave its call,
delighting the ear and beguiling the mind.

Elephants, lions, monkeys, boars, and deer, 1
abandoning enmity, all ranged together.
To see Ram's beauty when he went out hunting
gave the herds of beasts special delight.[60]
All the divine groves throughout creation 2
grew envious when they saw Ram's forest.
The gods' Ganga, the Sarasvati, sun-born Yamuna,
Mekala's daughter Narmada, and blessed Godavari[61] —

243

३ सब सर सिंधु नदीं नद नाना ।
मंदाकिनि कर करहिं बखाना ॥
उदय अस्त गिरि अरु कैलासू ।
मंदर मेरु सकल सुरबासू ॥
४ सैल हिमाचल आदिक जेते ।
चित्रकूट जसु गावहिं तेते ॥
बिंधि मुदित मन सुखु न समाई ।
श्रम बिनु बिपुल बड़ाई पाई ॥

१३८ चित्रकूट के बिहग मृग बेलि बिटप तृन जाति ।
पुन्य पुंज सब धन्य अस कहहिं देव दिन राति ॥

१ नयनवंत रघुबरहि बिलोकी ।
पाइ जनम फल होहिं बिसोकी ॥
परसि चरन रज अचर सुखारी ।
भए परम पद के अधिकारी ॥
२ सो बनु सैलु सुभायँ सुहावन ।
मंगलमय अति पावन पावन ॥
महिमा कहिअ कवनि बिधि तासू ।
सुखसागर जहँ कीन्ह निवासू ॥
३ पय पयोधि तजि अवध बिहाई ।
जहँ सिय लखनु रामु रहे आई ॥
कहि न सकहिं सुषमा जसि कानन ।
जौं सत सहस होहिं सहसानन ॥

all lakes and oceans, all rivers great and small,          3
gave praise to River Mandakini.
The sunrise and sunset mountains, Kailash,
Mandar, Meru, all the abodes of the gods,
and icy Himalaya—all summits everywhere          4
sang the glory of Chitrakut Hill.
The Vindhya Range could not contain its joy
at having effortlessly acquired such renown.

"The birds and beasts of Chitrakut,          138
and all its species of vines, trees, and grasses,
are blessed treasuries of merit!"—
so the gods proclaimed day and night.

Seeing the Raghu lord, all who had eyes          1
gained their lives' reward and were freed of sorrow.
Touching the dust of his feet, the inanimate rejoiced
and became worthy of the supreme state.
That forest and hill, naturally lovely          2
and auspicious, purified even the purest.
How can one express the greatness of that place
where the sea of bliss made his home—
renouncing the milky ocean, abandoning Avadh—          3
where Sita, Lakshman, and Ram came to dwell?
The beauty of that forest could not be told
even by thousands of thousand-tongued serpents!

४ सो मैं बरनि कहौं बिधि केहीं ।
डाबर कमठ कि मंदर लेहीं ॥
सेवहिं लखनु करम मन बानी ।
जाइ न सीलु सनेहु बखानी ॥

१३९ छिनु छिनु लखि सिय राम पद जानि आपु पर नेहु ।
करत न सपनेहुँ लखनु चितु बंधु मातु पितु गेहु ॥

१ राम संग सिय रहति सुखारी ।
पुर परिजन गृह सुरति बिसारी ॥
छिनु छिनु पिय बिधु बदनु निहारी ।
प्रमुदित मनहुँ चकोर कुमारी ॥
२ नाह नेहु नित बढ़त बिलोकी ।
हरषित रहति दिवस जिमि कोकी ॥
सिय मनु राम चरन अनुरागा ।
अवध सहस सम बनु प्रिय लागा ॥
३ परनकुटी प्रिय प्रियतम संगा ।
प्रिय परिवारु कुरंग बिहंगा ॥
सासु ससुर सम मुनितिय मुनिबर ।
असनु अमिअ सम कंद मूल फर ॥
४ नाथ साथ साँथरी सुहाई ।
मयन सयन सय सम सुखदाई ॥
लोकप होहिं बिलोकत जासू ।
तेहि कि मोहि सक बिषय बिलासू ॥

How, then, shall I describe it?                                    4
Can a marsh tortoise lift Mount Mandar?
Lakshman gave service in act, thought, and speech,
his goodness and love indescribable.

His eyes forever set on Sita and Ram's feet,                      139
knowing their affection for him,
Lakshman never even dreamed to think
of his brothers, parents, and home.

In Ram's company, Sita lived happily                                1
forgetting city, family, and household.
Seeing, each moment, the moon of her husband's face,
she was as joyful as a young partridge hen.
Perceiving her lord's ever-growing love for her,                   2
she dwelt in delight, like a *kokī* in daylight.[62]
Because Sita's heart adored Ram's feet,
the forest seemed dearer than a thousand Avadhs.
A hut of leaves was lovely in her love's company,                  3
deer and birds were like her dear kin,
great sages and their wives were as in-laws,
and fare of wild roots and fruit was like nectar.
At her lord's side, simple bedding of grasses                      4
was as pleasurable as a hundred of Kama's couches.
But could one whose mere glance grants cosmic lordship[63]
ever be beguiled by sensual luxury?

१४० सुमिरत रामहि तजहिं जन तृन सम बिषय बिलासु ।
रामप्रिया जग जननि सिय कछु न आचरजु तासु ॥

१ सीय लखन जेहि बिधि सुखु लहहीं ।
सोइ रघुनाथ करहिं सोइ कहहीं ॥
कहहिं पुरातन कथा कहानी ।
सुनहिं लखनु सिय अति सुखु मानी ॥

२ जब जब रामु अवध सुधि करहीं ।
तब तब बारि बिलोचन भरहीं ॥
सुमिरि मातु पितु परिजन भाई ।
भरत सनेहु सीलु सेवकाई ॥

३ कृपासिंधु प्रभु होहिं दुखारी ।
धीरजु धरहिं कुसमउ बिचारी ॥
लखि सिय लखनु बिकल होइ जाहीं ।
जिमि पुरुषहि अनुसर परिछाहीं ॥

४ प्रिया बंधु गति लखि रघुनंदनु ।
धीर कृपाल भगत उर चंदनु ॥
लगे कहन कछु कथा पुनीता ।
सुनि सुखु लहहिं लखनु अरु सीता ॥

१४१ रामु लखन सीता सहित सोहत परन निकेत ।
जिमि बासव बस अमरपुर सची जयंत समेत ॥

When just recalling Ram makes devotees                    140
scorn mundane pleasures like withered grass,
the response of Sita, his own beloved
and the world's mother, should cause no surprise.

Whatever would please Sita and Lakshman—               1
that was what the Raghu lord did and said.
He recounted ancient stories and legends,
and Lakshman and Sita listened with delight.
But whenever Ram recalled Avadh,                          2
his eyes would fill with tears.
Remembering mother, father, kin, brothers,
and Bharat's love, goodness, and service,
the Lord, ocean of mercy, grew sorrowful,                 3
but then took courage, knowing times were bad.
Seeing this, Sita and Lakshman grieved, too,
as a person's shadow moves with him.
When Ram saw his beloved wife and brother's state,       4
he who is steadfast, merciful, and a balm to devotees'
        hearts
began recounting some holy tales.
Listening, Lakshman and Sita regained their joy.

Ram, with Lakshman and Sita in that shelter              141
of leaves, was as resplendent
as Indra abiding with Shachi and Jayant*
in the city of the immortals.

* Indra's wife and son.

१ जोगवहिं प्रभु सिय लखनहि कैसें ।
पलक बिलोचन गोलक जैसें ॥
सेवहिं लखनु सीय रघुबीरहि ।
जिमि अबिबेकी पुरुष सरीरहि ॥

२ एहि बिधि प्रभु बन बसहिं सुखारी ।
खग मृग सुर तापस हितकारी ॥
कहेउँ राम बन गवनु सुहावा ।
सुनहु सुमंत्र अवध जिमि आवा ॥

३ फिरेउ निषादु प्रभुहि पहुँचाई ।
सचिव सहित रथ देखेसि आई ॥
मंत्री बिकल बिलोकि निषादू ।
कहि न जाइ जस भयउ बिषादू ॥

४ राम राम सिय लखन पुकारी ।
परेउ धरनितल ब्याकुल भारी ॥
देखि दखिन दिसि हय हिहिनाहीं ।
जनु बिनु पंख बिहग अकुलाहीं ॥

१४२ नहिं तृन चरहिं न पिअहिं जलु मोचहिं लोचन बारि ।
ब्याकुल भए निषाद सब रघुबर बाजि निहारि ॥

१ धरि धीरजु तब कहइ निषादू ।
अब सुमंत्र परिहरहु बिषादू ॥
तुम्ह पंडित परमारथ ग्याता ।
धरहु धीर लखि बिमुख बिधाता ॥

The Lord protected Sita and Lakshman 1
as the eyelids do the eyes,
and Lakshman served Sita and the Raghu hero[64]
as an unenlightened one pampers his own body.
So the Lord dwelled contentedly in the forest— 2
the benefactor of birds, beasts, gods, and ascetics.
I have told of Ram's lovely journey to the woods—
now hear how Sumantra came back to Avadh.
When Guha* returned from escorting the Lord, 3
he saw the royal minister with the chariot,
and, beholding that courtier's grief,
the Nishad grew unutterably dejected.
Crying, "Ram, Ram! Sita! Lakshman!" 4
Sumantra fell to the ground in despair.
The horses looked southward and whinnied
like desperate birds shorn of their wings.

They would neither eat grass nor drink water, 142
and their eyes shed tears.
Observing the Raghu lord's horses,
all the tribal folk were distraught.

Then, composing himself, the Nishad spoke— 1
"Now put aside your grief, Sumantra.
You are a scholar, a knower of supreme truth.
Take courage, perceiving that fate is averse."

---

* The Nishad tribal chief.

२ बिबिध कथा कहि कहि मृदु बानी ।
रथ बैठारेउ बरबस आनी ॥
सोक सिथिल रथु सकइ न हाँकी ।
रघुबर बिरह पीर उर बाँकी ॥

३ चरफराहिं मग चलहिं न घोरे ।
बन मृग मनहुँ आनि रथ जोरे ॥
अढुकि परहिं फिरि हेरहिं पीछें ।
राम बियोगि बिकल दुख तीछें ॥

४ जो कह रामु लखनु बैदेही ।
हिंकरि हिंकरि हित हेरहिं तेही ॥
बाजि बिरह गति कहि किमि जाती ।
बिनु मनि फनिक बिकल जेहि भाँती ॥

१४३ भयउ निषादु बिषादबस देखत सचिव तुरंग ।
बोलि सुसेवक चारि तब दिए सारथी संग ॥

१ गुह सारथिहि फिरेउ पहुँचाई ।
बिरहु बिषादु बरनि नहिं जाई ॥
चले अवध लेइ रथहि निषादा ।
होहिं छनहिं छन मगन बिषादा ॥

२ सोच सुमंत्र बिकल दुख दीना ।
धिग जीवन रघुबीर बिहीना ॥
रहिहि न अंतहुँ अधम सरीरू ।
जसु न लहेउ बिछुरत रघुबीरू ॥

Recounting many consoling tales in a gentle voice,    2
he firmly led Sumantra and seated him on the chariot,
but, limp with grief, the minister could not drive it,
for pain of separation from Ram seared his heart.
The distracted horses could not keep to the road,    3
as if wild beasts had been yoked to the car.
They stumbled, then turned and looked back,
afflicted by the awful grief of Ram's absence.
If anyone spoke of Ram, Lakshman, or Vaidehi,    4
they neighed and looked at him lovingly.
But how can the horses' anguish be told?
They were as distraught as cobras bereft of their gems.

Seeing the royal minister and the horses,    143
the Nishad was overcome with grief.
He summoned four able servants
and bade them accompany the charioteer.

Guha saw the charioteer off and turned back,    1
indescribably afflicted by separation's pain.
The tribesmen brought the chariot to Avadh,
though they were continually sunk in grief.
Distracted by woe, poor Sumantra thought,    2
"Without the Raghu hero, life is useless.
In the end, this wretched body will not endure,
yet it did not earn its fame when torn from Ram![65]

३ भए अजस अघ भाजन प्राना ।
कवन हेतु नहिं करत पयाना ॥
अहह मंद मनु अवसर चूका ।
अजहुँ न हृदय होत दुइ टूका ॥

४ मीजि हाथ सिरु धुनि पछिताई ।
मनहुँ कृपन धन रासि गवाँई ॥
बिरिद बाँधि बर बीरु कहाई ।
चलेउ समर जनु सुभट पराई ॥

१४४ बिप्र बिबेकी बेदबिद संमत साधु सुजाति ।
जिमि धोखें मदपान कर सचिव सोच तेहि भाँति ॥

१ जिमि कुलीन तिय साधु सयानी ।
पतिदेवता करम मन बानी ॥
रहै करम बस परिहरि नाहू ।
सचिव हृदयँ तिमि दारुन दाहू ॥

२ लोचन सजल डीठि भइ थोरी ।
सुनइ न श्रवन बिकल मति भोरी ॥
सूखहिं अधर लागि मुँह लाटी ।
जिउ न जाइ उर अवधि कपाटी ॥

३ बिबरन भयउ न जाइ निहारी ।
मारेसि मनहुँ पिता महतारी ॥
हानि गलानि बिपुल मन ब्यापी ।
जमपुर पंथ सोच जिमि पापी ॥

These vital breaths are vessels of infamy and sin.    3
Why do they not just take their leave?
Alas! This sluggish mind lost its chance
and, even now, this heart has not broken in two."
He wrung his hands and beat his forehead,    4
like a miser who has lost his fortune,
or a self-proclaimed hero, girded for war,
who went to battle but then fled the field.

As if a high-born, discriminating Brahman,    144
proficient in the Veda and respected by the holy,
was tricked into imbibing strong drink—
such was that minister's regret.

As if a wise, virtuous woman of good family,    1
devoted to her husband in thought, word, and deed,
impelled by karma, left her lord to live apart—
such was the inferno in the minister's heart.
His eyes were damp, he could barely see,    2
his ears did not hear, his wits were distracted,
and his lips and mouth had gone dry.
Yet, barred by the exile's terms, his soul stayed.[66]
He was insufferably pale to behold,    3
like one who had murdered his parents.
His heart pervaded by the awful pain of loss,
he was like a sinner on the road to hell.

४  बचनु न आव हृदयँ पछिताई ।
अवध काह मैं देखब जाई ॥
राम रहित रथ देखिहि जोई ।
सकुचिहि मोहि बिलोकत सोई ॥

१४५  धाइ पूँछिहहिं मोहि जब बिकल नगर नर नारि ।
उतरु देब मैं सबहि तब हृदयँ बज्रु बैठारि ॥

१  पुछिहहिं दीन दुखित सब माता ।
कहब काह मैं तिन्हहि बिधाता ॥
पूछिहि जबहिं लखन महतारी ।
कहिहउँ कवन सँदेस सुखारी ॥

२  राम जननि जब आइहि धाई ।
सुमिरि बच्छु जिमि धेनु लवाई ॥
पूँछत उतरु देब मैं तेही ।
गे बनु राम लखनु बैदेही ॥

३  जोइ पूँछिहि तेहि ऊतरु देबा ।
जाइ अवध अब यहु सुखु लेबा ॥
पूँछिहि जबहिं राउ दुख दीना ।
जिवनु जासु रघुनाथ अधीना ॥

४  देहउँ उतरु कौनु मुहु लाई ।
आयउँ कुसल कुअँर पहुँचाई ॥
सुनत लखन सिय राम सँदेसू ।
तृन जिमि तनु परिहरिहि नरेसू ॥

He could not speak, but his heart lamented—  4
"When I reach Avadh, what will I see?
Whoever spies this chariot, without Ram,
will shrink from even looking at me.

And when the distraught townsmen  145
and women run to inquire of me,
I will have to answer them all,
hardening my heart like adamant.

When the poor, grieving mothers ask me—  1
God!—what will I tell them?
When Lakshman's mother inquires of me,
what cheering message will I offer?
And when Ram's birth-mother rushes in,  2
like a cow thinking of her newborn calf,
at her asking, I will reply, 'They are gone—
Ram, Lakshman, Vaidehi—to forest exile.'
To whoever asks, I will give this same answer—  3
such is the joy I will gain, going to Avadh!
And when the wretched, grief-stricken king,
whose life depends on the Raghu lord, asks me,
with what face will I answer him and say  4
that I have come back safely, having left the princes?[67]
And just hearing Lakshman, Sita, and Ram's message,
the lord of men will shed his body like a blade of straw.

१४६ हृदउ न बिदरेउ पंक जिमि बिछुरत प्रीतमु नीरु ।
जानत हौं मोहि दीन्ह बिधि यहु जातना सरीरु ॥

१ एहि बिधि करत पंथ पछितावा ।
तमसा तीर तुरत रथु आवा ॥
बिदा किए करि बिनय निषादा ।
फिरे पायँ परि बिकल बिषादा ॥

२ पैठत नगर सचिव सकुचाई ।
जनु मारेसि गुर बाँभन गाई ॥
बैठि बिटप तर दिवसु गवाँवा ।
साँझ समय तब अवसरु पावा ॥

३ अवध प्रबेसु कीन्ह अँधिआरें ।
पैठ भवन रथु राखि दुआरें ॥
जिन्ह जिन्ह समाचार सुनि पाए ।
भूप द्वार रथु देखन आए ॥

४ रथु पहिचानि बिकल लखि घोरे ।
गरहिं गात जिमि आतप ओरे ॥
नगर नारि नर ब्याकुल कैसें ।
निघटत नीर मीनगन जैसें ॥

१४७ सचिव आगमनु सुनत सबु बिकल भयउ रनिवासु ।
भवनु भयंकरु लाग तेहि मानहुँ प्रेत निवासु ॥

Since my heart's clay, deprived of the water 146
of my beloved, has not yet cracked,
I know that fate has condemned me
to a life of hellish torment."[68]

Thus lamenting the whole way, 1
he soon brought the chariot to the Tamasa's shore,
and humbly bade farewell to the Nishad guides,
who bowed to his feet and returned, sick with grief.
But the minister held back from entering the city, 2
like one who has slain a guru, Brahman, or cow.
He passed the day sitting under a tree,
and at twilight seized his opportunity.
In darkness, he went into Avadh city 3
and entered the palace, leaving the chariot at its gate.
But whoever got news of this
came to the king's portal to see the vehicle.
Recognizing it, and seeing the horses' grief, 4
their bodies grew weak as melting hailstones.
The city's women and men were as distraught
as a school of fish in a drying pond.

When they heard of the minister's arrival, 147
all the royal women grew agitated.
To him, the palace seemed frightening,
like a cremation ground full of restless spirits.

१    अति आरति सब पूँछहिं रानी ।
उतरु न आव बिकल भइ बानी ॥
सुनइ न श्रवन नयन नहिं सूझा ।
कहहु कहाँ नृपु तेहि तेहि बूझा ॥

२    दासिन्ह दीख सचिव बिकलाई ।
कौसल्या गृहँ गईं लवाई ॥
जाइ सुमंत्र दीख कस राजा ।
अमिअ रहित जनु चंदु बिराजा ॥

३    आसन सयन बिभूषन हीना ।
परेउ भूमितल निपट मलीना ॥
लेइ उसासु सोच एहि भाँती ।
सुरपुर तें जनु खँसेउ जजाती ॥

४    लेत सोच भरि छिनु छिनु छाती ।
जनु जरि पंख परेउ संपाती ॥
राम राम कह राम सनेही ।
पुनि कह राम लखन बैदेही ॥


१४८    देखि सचिवँ जय जीव कहि कीन्हेउ दंड प्रनामु ।
सुनत उठेउ ब्याकुल नृपति कहु सुमंत्र कहँ रामु ॥


१    भूप सुमंत्रु लीन्ह उर लाई ।
बूड़त कछु अधार जनु पाई ॥
सहित सनेह निकट बैठारी ।
पूँछत राउ नयन भरि बारी ॥

In great distress, all the queens questioned him,       1
but he could not answer; his speech was paralyzed.
His ears could not hear nor his eyes perceive,
and he inquired of everyone, "Where is the king?"
The maidservants saw the minister's distress       2
and brought him to Kausalya's abode.
Sumantra entered and beheld the king
looking wan as the moon bereft of nectar.[69]
Without throne, couch, or royal regalia,       3
he was sprawled on the ground, disheveled.
Gasping for breath, he lay there grieving,
like King Yayati fallen from heaven.[70]
He constantly heaved great sighs of woe,       4
like Sampati when he fell with singed wings,[71]
crying, "Ram, oh Ram, my beloved Ram,"
and then "Ram, Lakshman, Vaidehi!"

Seeing him, the minister said, "Live long,       148
be victorious," and fell prostrate.
At this, the king distractedly arose,
saying, "Tell me, Sumantra—where is Ram?"

The lord of earth pulled Sumantra to his breast       1
like a drowning one clutching at a little support.
Then, affectionately seating him close by,
his eyes filling with tears, the king asked,

२     राम कुसल कहु सखा सनेही ।
कहँ रघुनाथु लखनु बैदेही ॥
आने फेरि कि बनहिं सिधाए ।
सुनत सचिव लोचन जल छाए ॥

३     सोक बिकल पुनि पूँछ नरेसू ।
कहु सिय राम लखन संदेसू ॥
राम रूप गुन सील सुभाऊ ।
सुमिरि सुमिरि उर सोचत राऊ ॥

४     राउ सुनाइ दीन्ह बनबासू ।
सुनि मन भयउ न हरषु हराँसू ॥
सो सुत बिछुरत गए न प्राना ।
को पापी बड़ मोहि समाना ॥

१४९     सखा रामु सिय लखनु जहँ तहाँ मोहि पहुँचाउ ।
नाहिं त चाहत चलन अब प्रान कहउँ सतिभाउ ॥

१     पुनि पुनि पूँछत मंत्रिहि राऊ ।
प्रियतम सुअन सँदेस सुनाऊ ॥
करहि सखा सोइ बेगि उपाऊ ।
रामु लखनु सिय नयन देखाऊ ॥

२     सचिव धीर धरि कह मृदु बानी ।
महाराज तुम्ह पंडित ग्यानी ॥
बीर सुधीर धुरंधर देवा ।
साधु समाजु सदा तुम्ह सेवा ॥

"Dear friend, tell me, how is Ram?                    2
Where is the Raghu lord, and Lakshman, and Vaidehi?
Did you bring them back, or did they go to the woods?"
When he heard this, the minister's eyes grew moist.
Restless with grief, the king asked again,            3
"Tell me Sita, Ram, and Lakshman's message."
Recalling Ram's beauty, virtue, and noble character
time and again, the king grieved in his heart.
"I declared him king, then dealt him exile,           4
and when he heard, his mind was neither elated nor sad.
Torn from such a son, if my soul did not leave,
then who is a greater sinner than I?

Friend, take me there—to where Ram,                   149
Sita, and Lakshman are,
or else, I tell you truly, my life's breath
is now anxious to depart."

Again and again, he asked the minister,               1
"Tell me my beloved son's message,
and contrive somehow, and quickly, friend,
to bring Ram, Lakshman, and Sita before my eyes."
Taking courage, the counselor said gently,            2
"Maharaj, you are learned and wise,
a hero, first among the steadfast, a divine king,
and you constantly serve saintly ones.

३   जनम मरन सब दुख सुख भोगा ।
   हानि लाभु प्रिय मिलन बियोगा ॥
   काल करम बस होहिं गोसाईं ।
   बरबस राति दिवस की नाईं ॥

४   सुख हरषहिं जड़ दुख बिलखाहीं ।
   दोउ सम धीर धरहिं मन माहीं ॥
   धीरज धरहु बिबेकु बिचारी ।
   छाड़िअ सोच सकल हितकारी ॥

१५०   प्रथम बासु तमसा भयउ दूसर सुरसरि तीर ।
   न्हाइ रहे जलपानु करि सिय समेत दोउ बीर ॥

१   केवट कीन्हि बहुत सेवकाई ।
   सो जामिनि सिंगरौर गवाँई ॥
   होत प्रात बट छीरु मगावा ।
   जटा मुकुट निज सीस बनावा ॥

२   राम सखाँ तब नाव मगाई ।
   प्रिया चढ़ाइ चढ़े रघुराई ॥
   लखन बान धनु धरे बनाई ।
   आपु चढ़े प्रभु आयसु पाई ॥

३   बिकल बिलोकि मोहि रघुबीरा ।
   बोले मधुर बचन धरि धीरा ॥
   तात प्रनामु तात सन कहेहू ।
   बार बार पद पंकज गहेहू ॥

Birth and death, the experience of grief and joy,                    3
loss and gain, meeting and parting from dear ones,
are all in the grip of time and karma, master,
like the relentless succession of night and day.
Fools rejoice in happiness and wail in sorrow,                       4
but the resolute hold both to be equal.
Reflecting with discrimination, take courage,
benefactor of all, and abandon your grief.

Their first camp was by the Tamasa,                                  150
the second, on the holy river's shore.
Having bathed there, Sita and the two heroes
partook only of water.

Kevat the boatman rendered great service,                           1
and that night was passed in Singaraur.[72]
At dawn, they called for the sap of the banyan
and crowned their heads with matted locks.
Then Ram's friend summoned a boat,                                  2
and, placing his dear wife in it, the Raghu lord got in.
Lakshman shouldered their bows and arrows,[73]
and at the Lord's command, came aboard.
Seeing me distraught, the Raghu hero                                3
composed himself and spoke gentle words—
'Sir, convey my salutations to my father,
and again and again clasp his holy feet.

४ करबि पायँ परि बिनय बहोरी ।
तात करिअ जनि चिंता मोरी ॥
बन मग मंगल कुसल हमारें ।
कृपा अनुग्रह पुन्य तुम्हारें ॥

५ तुम्हरें अनुग्रह तात कानन
जात सब सुखु पाइहौं ।
प्रतिपालि आयसु कुसल देखन
पाय पुनि फिरि आइहौं ॥
जननीं सकल परितोषि परि परि
पायँ करि बिनती घनी ।
तुलसी करहु सोइ जतनु जेहिं
कुसली रहहिं कोसलधनी ॥

१५१ गुर सन कहब सँदेसु बार बार पद पदुम गहि ।
करब सोइ उपदेसु जेहिं न सोच मोहि अवधपति ॥

१ पुरजन परिजन सकल निहोरी ।
तात सुनाएहु बिनती मोरी ॥
सोइ सब भाँति मोर हितकारी ।
जातें रह नरनाहु सुखारी ॥

266

Then bow before him and deliver this entreaty—                4
"Father, do not worry on my account.
The forest path is blessed and easy for us
by your grace, kindness, and store of merit.

By your kindness, father, I will attain                5
all happiness in going to the forest.
Then, having fully upheld your command,
I will safely return to behold your feet."
Consoling all my mothers, bow at their feet
again and again, and entreat them—
Tulsi says—"Exert every effort so that
the king of Kosala may live happily."74

And give this message to our teacher,*                151
saluting, time and again, his lotus-like feet—
"Expound such enlightening discourses
that the lord of Avadh may not grieve over me."

Salute all the townspeople and my relations,                1
sir, and convey to them my request—
"My true well-wisher will be the one
who strives to please the ruler of men."

---

* Vasishtha, the royal guru.

२ कहब सँदेसु भरत के आएँ ।
नीति न तजिअ राजपदु पाएँ ॥
पालेहु प्रजहि करम मन बानी ।
सेएहु मातु सकल सम जानी ॥

३ ओर निबाहेहु भायप भाई ।
करि पितु मातु सुजन सेवकाई ॥
तात भाँति तेहि राखब राऊ ।
सोच मोर जेहिं करै न काऊ ॥

४ लखन कहे कछु बचन कठोरा ।
बरजि राम पुनि मोहि निहोरा ॥
बार बार निज सपथ देवाई ।
कहबि न तात लखन लरिकाई ॥

१५२ कहि प्रनामु कछु कहन लिय सिय भइ सिथिल सनेह ।
थकित बचन लोचन सजल पुलक पल्लवित देह ॥

१ तेहि अवसर रघुबर रुख पाई ।
केवट पारहि नाव चलाई ॥
रघुकुलतिलक चले एहि भाँति ।
देखउँ ठाढ़ कुलिस धरि छाती ॥

And when Bharat comes, give this message—       2
"Do not forsake ethics on gaining the throne.[75]
Guard our subjects in deed, thought, and word,
and serve our mothers, considering them all alike.
Brother, fulfill our fraternal bond       3
by serving our father, mothers, and kin,
and keep the king so contented, my dear,
that he is never anxious on my account."'
Lakshman uttered some harsh words,[76]       4
but Ram checked him, and then implored me,
making me swear repeatedly, in his name—
'Sir, do not repeat Lakshman's childish speech.'

Sita saluted me and began to say something,       152
but grew weak with feeling.
Her voice broke, her eyes filled with tears,
and her body was flushed with emotion.

Then, at a glance from that best of Raghus,       1
Kevat began to row the boat across.
So the crown jewel of the Raghus departed,
as I stood watching, laying a stone over my heart.

२ मैं आपन किमि कहौं कलेसू।
जिअत फिरेउँ लेइ राम सँदेसू॥
अस कहि सचिव बचन रहि गयऊ।
हानि गलानि सोच बस भयऊ॥

३ सूत बचन सुनतहिं नरनाहू।
परेउ धरनि उर दारुन दाहू॥
तलफत बिषम मोह मन मापा।
माजा मनहुँ मीन कहुँ ब्यापा॥

४ करि बिलाप सब रोवहिं रानी।
महा बिपति किमि जाइ बखानी॥
सुनि बिलाप दुखहू दुखु लागा।
धीरजहू कर धीरजु भागा॥

१५३ भयउ कोलाहलु अवध अति सुनि नृप राउर सोरु।
बिपुल बिहग बन परेउ निसि मानहुँ कुलिस कठोरु॥

१ प्रान कंठगत भयउ भुआलू।
मनि बिहीन जनु ब्याकुल ब्यालू॥
इंद्रीं सकल बिकल भइँ भारी।
जनु सर सरसिज बनु बिनु बारी॥

२ कौसल्याँ नृपु दीख मलाना।
रबिकुल रबि अँथयउ जियँ जाना॥
उर धरि धीर राम महतारी।
बोली बचन समय अनुसारी॥

But how can I describe my own anguish                                    2
at returning alive, bearing this message from Ram?"
Saying this, the minister could speak no more,
overwhelmed by his loss, gloom, and anxiety.
When the ruler of men heard the charioteer's words,          3
he fell to the ground, his heart burning,
and writhed there, overcome by stupefaction,
like a fish demented by the first rain's foam.[77]
Crying out in grief, the queens began to weep—               4
but how can their dreadful adversity be described?
Hearing the lamentation, even sorrow was saddened
and courage itself lost heart.

Hearing the uproar in the royal harem,                       153
Avadh erupted in dreadful commotion,
as if a bolt of lightning had struck by night
in a grove full of birds.

The king's life breath came into his throat,[78]             1
and he was as desperate as a cobra without its gem.
All his restless faculties began to fade,
like a cluster of lotuses in a drying pond.
Observing the king's despair, Kausalya knew                  2
that the sun of the solar clan was setting.
Summoning her inner resolve, Ram's mother
spoke words befitting that time of crisis.

३ नाथ समुझि मन करिअ बिचारू ।
राम बियोग पयोधि अपारू ॥
करनधार तुम्ह अवध जहाजू ।
चढ़ेउ सकल प्रिय पथिक समाजू ॥

४ धीरजु धरिअ त पाइअ पारू ।
नाहिं त बूड़िहि सबु परिवारू ॥
जौं जियँ धरिअ बिनय पिय मोरी ।
रामु लखनु सिय मिलहिं बहोरी ॥

१५४ प्रिया बचन मृदु सुनत नृपु चितयउ आँखि उघारि ।
तलफत मीन मलीन जनु सींचत सीतल बारि ॥

१ धरि धीरजु उठि बैठ भुआलू ।
कहु सुमंत्र कहँ राम कृपालू ॥
कहाँ लखनु कहँ रामु सनेही ।
कहँ प्रिय पुत्रबधू बैदेही ॥

२ बिलपत राउ बिकल बहु भाँती ।
भइ जुग सरिस सिराति न राती ॥
तापस अंध साप सुधि आई ।
कौसल्यहि सब कथा सुनाई ॥

३ भयउ बिकल बरनत इतिहासा ।
राम रहित धिग जीवन आसा ॥
सो तनु राखि करब मैं काहा ।
जेहिं न प्रेम पनु मोर निबाहा ॥

"My lord, ponder in your heart and know 3
that Ram's absence is an impassable sea
and you are helmsman of the ship of Avadh,
with all our dear ones aboard as passengers.
Be steadfast, that we may reach the far shore, 4
or else our entire clan will drown.
If you take my entreaty to heart, dear husband,
you will again meet Ram, Lakshman, and Sita."

Hearing his wife's sweet words, 154
the king opened his eyes and looked up,
like a beached and writhing fish
who is doused with cool water.

Summoning his strength, the lord of earth sat up 1
and said, "Tell me, Sumantra—where is merciful Ram?
Where is Lakshman? Oh, where is my beloved Ram?
And where is my son's dear wife, Vaidehi?"
Distraught, the king wailed and moaned 2
and the night seemed as interminable as an aeon.
He remembered the blind ascetic's curse
and told Kausalya the whole story.[79]
Relating that incident, he grew desperate 3
and said, "Hope for life, without Ram, is despicable.
What good is it to me to cling to a body
that has not fulfilled my pledge of love?

४     हा रघुनंदन प्रान पिरीते ।
तुम्ह बिनु जिअत बहुत दिन बीते ॥
हा जानकी लखन हा रघुबर ।
हा पितु हित चित चातक जलधर ॥

१५५    राम राम कहि राम कहि राम राम कहि राम ।
तनु परिहरि रघुबर बिरहँ राउ गयउ सुरधाम ॥

१     जिअन मरन फलु दसरथ पावा ।
अंड अनेक अमल जसु छावा ॥
जिअत राम बिधु बदनु निहारा ।
राम बिरह करि मरनु सँवारा ॥

२     सोक बिकल सब रोवहिं रानी ।
रूपु सीलु बलु तेजु बखानी ॥
करहिं बिलाप अनेक प्रकारा ।
परहिं भूमितल बारहिं बारा ॥

३     बिलपहिं बिकल दास अरु दासी ।
घर घर रुदनु करहिं पुरबासी ॥
अँथयउ आजु भानुकुल भानू ।
धरम अवधि गुन रूप निधानू ॥

४     गारीं सकल कैकइहि देहीं ।
नयन बिहीन कीन्ह जग जेहीं ॥
एहि बिधि बिलपत रैनि बिहानी ।
आए सकल महामुनि ग्यानी ॥

Then sage Vasishtha told numerous stories 156
befitting the occasion,
and with the light of his wisdom
dispelled everyone's grief.

# NOTES TO THE TRANSLATION

### An Enthronement Thwarted

1 The first three verses of this sub-book are a Sanskrit invocation (*maṅgalācaraṇa*); the Hindi text commences with *dohā* "0" (so numbered because it precedes rather than ends a stanza), which is among the best-known of *Mānas* verses today, as it also begins the popular prayer to Hanuman, *Hanumān cālīsā*.

2 This famous *śloka* is often sung, to a lovely melody, by devotees—either individually or congregationally—during *āratī*, or ceremonial worship in shrines to Ram.

3 With this *dohā* (numbered "0" because it precedes rather than ends a stanza) the Sanskrit invocation ends and Hindi text begins.

4 "Heir apparent," *jubarāja;* literally "young king," a designated successor who assumes kingly functions while his predecessor is still living.

5 "World-guardians," *lokapa;* deities who protect the eight cardinal directions.

6 Some commentators interpret the *dohā's* second line to mean, "Any wish of your heart, jewel of earth's rulers, can but follow its own (preordained) fulfillment." In his translation, Hill prefers not to take *mahipa mani* ("jewel of earth's rulers") as a vocative, and so renders the line, "Monarch supreme is your heart's wish, success its faithful follower" (1952: 163).

7 That is, there is no need to await an auspicious day according to the ritual calendar.

8 "Council," *pañca;* literally "the five," a reference to senior courtiers who advise on state matters.

9 "Square designs," *caukē;* auspicious geometric shapes drawn on the ground. Normally made by women with colored rice powder, those in Avadh are to be filled with precious stones.

10 "Auspicious limbs," *maṅgala aṅga;* for males, the right side of the body is considered auspicious, and for females, the left side.

11 "Welcoming drink," *aragha;* a mixture of water, milk, curds, and other auspicious substances presented to honored guests. "Sixteen courtesies" (*soraha bhānti pūji;* literally, "honored in sixteen ways")

279

refers to rituals and gifts of welcome for both guests and deities; according to commentators, these include washing of the feet, presentation of fine clothing and a seat of honor, worship with a lamp, and so forth.

12 "Obligatory restraints," *sañjama*, refers to abstinences (for example, from sexual intercourse, violent acts, and most foods; the *Mānaspīyūṣ* lists ten proscriptions) undertaken to ensure the success of an ensuing ritual.

13 "Without his brothers," *bandhu bihāi;* literally, "leaving aside brothers." This may refer both to the unfairness of singling out one brother for consecration, and also to the absence from Ayodhya of Bharat and Shatrughna, who are visiting their maternal grandfather.

14 Since Ram is beyond these karma-determined opposites, the reference is apparently to the suffering that Sharada's task will bring to others in Avadh.

15 Alternatively this may be read, "and just seeing her destroys one's own pride." Either way, it is Manthara's first invocation of Kaikeyi's chief rival for the king's favor.

16 A possible alternative reading is "Queen, ceasing to be a maid, what will I become?" (i.e., I can hardly sink any lower). This verse has become a proverb.

17 "Avadh's malefic star," *Avadha sāṛasātī;* literally, "Avadh's seven-and-a half (years of Saturn)," a reference to one of the most menacing planetary conjunctions in Indian astrology.

18 "I draw a line," *rekha khācāi;* an idiom indicating taking an oath that what one is about to state is the truth.

19 In a famous epic and puranic tale, Kadru, mother of serpents, and Vinata, mother of birds, are co-wives of the primordial sage Kashyap. Through a ruse, the former dupes the latter into becoming her slave, along with Vinata's son, the divine eagle Garuda. See *Mahābhārata* 1.13.

20 This half-*caupāī,* omitted from the Gita Press edition, is accepted by the *Mānaspīyūṣ* as "included in numerous early manuscripts" (4.116). The addition makes sense here and accords with the normal four-*caupāī* format of stanzas in this sub-book. Note, however, that the line numbering shown here consequently diverges, for this stanza, from that found in Gita Press editions.

21 Traditionally, the *left* eye is auspicious for a woman, so this confused

assertion reveals Kaikeyi's "reversed" state of mind.

22 "Sulking chamber," *kopa bhavana;* literally, "house of anger," a room in the palace to which royal women withdrew to signal their displeasure.

23 "Light of my eyes," *cakha pūtari;* literally, "the pupil of my eye," a Hindi idiom.

24 The next eight lines are in lyrical *harigītikā chand* meter.

25 "Amply endowed woman," *gajagāmini;* literally, "with the gait of an elephant"; this was a sensual compliment in traditional Indian literature.

26 "Thief's woman," *cora nārī;* although most commentators take this to mean the wife of a captured thief, who hides her grief lest she, too, be discovered, the *Mānaspīyūṣ* notes one reading as a compound referring to an adulteress (4.152).

27 This famous verse has become a proverbial saying in Hindi.

28 According to the *Mānaspīyūṣ, guñjā* refers to tiny wild seed-grains used as a counterweight by jewelers (4.156).

29 This bird, a type of ostrich or goose, is said to be separated from his mate at nightfall, and so detests the moon's rays.

30 That is, "Am I a purchased slave, and not your lawful wife?" There does not appear to be an allusion here (in the awareness of *Mānas* commentators) to the puzzling *rājya-śulka* passage in Valmiki's epic (2.99.1–10), in which Ram tells Bharat in Chitrakut that the kingdom had been promised to Kaikeyi's son as her "bride-price."

31 Some commentators interpret this line as "Give your assent, or else say no."

32 In well-known epic and puranic tales of self-sacrifice, King Shibi cut off his own flesh to equal the (ever-growing) weight of a pigeon who sought his protection when hunted by a hawk; the sage Dadhichi gave up his life so that the gods could forge a demon-slaying weapon from his bones; and the demon king Bali, who had conquered the universe, offered a dwarf Brahman (actually Vishnu in disguise) the land he could cover in three strides— magnanimously surrendering his entire dominion when the god grew to cosmic dimensions.

33 Since *asi* can be read as either "thus / in this manner" or "sword," this line could also be read as "She has pierced my soft spot with a sword," thus anticipating the imagery in succeeding lines.

34 *Phulāuba gālā:* literally, "puffing out your cheeks" (thus, holding one's breath, with lips sealed). This is an idiom also connoting displeasure, which contrasts well with uproarious laughter.

35 *Nahārū:* this obscure word has generated much commentary. Some gloss it as "lion," "tiger," or "hawk" and assume that the cow is being killed to feed one of these. Others take it to mean "without pain/regret." Neither is very satisfying in the context, but another attested meaning—a strand of sinew or gut, used for string—seems plausible. See *Mānaspīyūṣ* 4.204–206.

36 *Jāgati masānu,* "to stay awake at a cremation place," connotes a tantric ritual intended to bring a demon or ghost into one's power.

37 "To a widow pledged to burn," *sahagāminihi;* literally, "to a woman who goes with [her deceased husband]." A widow intent on self-immolation on her husband's funeral pyre would have no need of jewelry.

38 "A weed," *araṇḍu;* the castor-oil plant, which grows wild in India.

39 "Like the holy sites in sinful Magadh" (*Magahaṃ gayādika tīratha jaise,* "like Gaya, and so forth, the holy sites in Magadh"). The former kingdom of Magadh in what is today Bihar, once a bastion of Buddhism, came to be considered impure by Brahman pandits, although it contained several renowned pilgrimage places, including Gaya, where Hindus have long gone to perform life-cycle rituals.

40 Literally "my body became cool."

41 "Army of pitiful sentiment," *karuna rasa kaṭakaī;* the aesthetic mood of pity or compassion is here strikingly juxtaposed with the martial image of an army besieging the city.

42 "Scaffold," *ṭhāṭā;* a framework or skeleton temporarily set up to support a thatched or canopied structure, as for a festival.

43 Some interpret this line to mean that the king has become, through Kaikeyi's obstinacy, a vessel or source of all woe. The relative pronoun *jo* ("who/which") allows either reading.

44 Legendary kings who endured great suffering in order to keep their word; see note 32.

45 Alternatively, "so Avadh will be without Tulsidas's lord."

46 Literally, Tulsidas says that Ram's enthusiasm was "fourfold" (*cauguna*). Commentators provide varying lists of four reasons for his excitement (see *Mānaspīyūṣ* 4.270–272), and several interpret the following half line to refer to Ram's worry at being

chosen over his brothers for the post of *yuvrāj* (see 2.10.4–5), of which he is now relieved by his conviction that the king will not hold him back.

47 "Harsh fetter," *alān;* according to commentators, this refers to a wooden shackle lined with iron teeth that was placed around the ankles of newly caught elephants to restrict their movement.

48 As usual, Tulsidas ventures a simile for what he has just declared "cannot be said." Here, Kaushalya's condition is likened to that of a poor man suddenly given the "post" (*padabī*) of "giver of wealth" (*dhanada*), an epithet of Kuber, the god of riches.

49 The *cātaka* bird and his mate are said to drink only raindrops that fall during the lunar asterism of *svāti* in the monsoon month of Sharad.

50 In her excited speech, Kaushalya thrice uses an expression meaning "I sacrifice myself" (*balihārī*), a conventional idiom, difficult to convey in English, of heartfelt avowal and (especially) maternal protection, indicating willingness to take on any misfortune that a child might have to suffer. I have rendered this "By my life," "I avow," and "by your mother's life."

51 The *javāsā* (*javāsa* in the dialect of the poem) is a prickly, medicinal plant that sheds its leaves at the start of the rainy season.

52 The foamy bubbles (*māñjā*) produced on ponds and rivers by the first monsoon downpours were believed to cause dementia in certain species of fish.

53 Rahu is the demon who swallows the moon (here called *sudhākara,* "giver of nectar") and the sun, causing eclipses.

54 "Mole," *chuchundara;* a kind of odious mole or muskrat. According to the *Mānaspīyūṣ,* when a snake catches one in its mouth, it faces a dilemma: if it swallows the creature (believed to be poisonous), it will die, but if it disgorges it, the rodent will blind the snake (4.284). This is a common northern Indian idiom, equivalent to the English "between a rock and a hard place."

55 Commentators are divided as to whether *gosāĩ* ("lord," "master") should be taken as a vocative, since some feel that Kaushalya would not address Ram in that manner. Alternatively, some read it as a reference to the supreme God ("May all gods, ancestors, and the Master..."). Syntactically, the vocative meaning seems preferable.

56 The *Mānaspīyūṣ* comments: "To draw on the ground with one's toenails, to leave a mark there, is a gesture of anxiety. A person

who sits worrying begins spontaneously doing this, and this habit is found especially among women" (4.297).

57 The reference is to epic and puranic tales concerning the dangers of obstinacy. Galav, a pupil of Vishvamitra, insisted on giving his teacher a guru-gift even when the sage said he wanted none. As a result, he was assigned the impossible task of procuring 800 stallions with black-tipped ears. The once-virtuous King Nahush, temporarily appointed to the role of Indra, became deluded by pride and forced the divine sages to bear his palanquin. As a result he was cursed by Agastya to incarnate as a boa constrictor for ten thousand years.

58 "With your swaying gait," *haṃsgavani;* a conventional designation for an ample-hipped woman, who waddles like a *haṃsa,* or wild goose.

59 The *cakvī* (the female ruddy shelduck or "ruddy goose," also known as *cakravāka*) was believed to be united with her mate only by day.

60 Yama, god of retribution, presides over a subterranean hell in which sinners are tortured after death.

61 "Inner knower," a literal translation of *antarajāmī,* a common epithet of God.

62 A possible alternative reading is "lest your hard-hearted mother forget you"—implying that, if a mother (*jananī,* "birth-giver") is unfeeling enough to live through such separation, she might even forget her son.

63 Literally, "breaking a blade of grass [*tṛnu tore*] toward body, home, and all." According to the *Mānaspīyūṣ,* the idiom refers to a moment in Kshatriya funeral rites when mourners break a blade of grass, signifying the end of all ties with the deceased (4.337).

64 The verb used (*byānā*) normally refers only to the birthing of animals.

65 Old manuscripts show variation in this line, which opens a lyrical stanza in *chand* meter, with the Gita Press edition favoring a vocative (*tāt,* "son") and the *Mānaspīyūṣ,* a present participle (*jāt,* "going"). I prefer the latter. This affects how the following word (*tumhare*), seemingly a contracted postposition, is read: either as "because of you," or "with you."

66 Lakshman is referred to here as "the lord" (*prabhu*), a reminder of his divine status as partial avatar.

67    Presumably Lakshman remains wary (*saṅkita*) lest some hindrance yet arise to prevent him from accompanying Ram and Sita.

68    See note 59.

69    "Provisions," *barṣāsana;* although this literally means "food for a year," commentators assume that Ram arranged sustenance for the Brahmans for the full term of his exile.

### Journey to the Forest

1    That is, the gods were happy because Ram would soon come into conflict with Ravan, and sad because of the pain being inflicted on his family and subjects.

2    "Savage huntress," *kirātini;* a woman of the forest-dwelling Kirat tribe.

3    This may also be read: "Leaving home, all the people, even children and the elderly, went with the exiles." However, commentators observe that the very old and very young would not have been able to keep up with them.

4    Literally, "praising fish" (who are thought to be unable to close their eyes).

5    "Profound fatigue," *śrama bhārū;* according to commentators, this refers to the weariness of innumerable births and deaths.

6    "Root source," *kanda;* this word can also be translated "cloud."

7    The Nishad *(niṣād)* were forest-dwelling hunter-gatherers, considered impure and outside the fourfold social order of Arya society. But, living in proximity to Avadh, Guha's people show loyalty to its rulers, and Guha seems to have a preexisting friendship with Ram.

8    "Rosewood tree," *sinsupā;* according to some commentators, this refers to the evergreen shisham tree or Indian rosewood, though others favor the ashoka or the custard apple.

9    "To set out, with his own hand," *rākhesi pānī.* Since the word *pānī* may be read as either "hand" (Sanskrit, *pāṇī*) or "water," some commentators favor the reading "he set out in brimful leaf cups, with water." Some manuscripts substitute *ānī* ("having brought") for *pānī,* and the *Mānaspīyūṣ* speculates that this may be because "orthodox pandits thought that water and other things brought by the hand of an untouchable should never be accepted." However, it adds that Ram did not observe such

taboos, because "Where there is love, rules do not apply" (4.401, footnote).

10  Literally, "he sat in warrior posture" (*baiṭhi bīrāsana*).

11  The next two stanzas, a discourse of great poetic beauty (and a surprisingly philosophical intervention by the often fiery Lakshman), are popularly known as the "Lakshman Gita" for their resemblance to Krishna's battlefield instruction to Arjuna.

12  As the *Mānaspīyūṣ* notes, the absence of postpositions permits the line to equally be read: "As when a beggar, in a dream, becomes a king, or the lord of heaven [Indra], a pauper" (4.413).

13  "Delights," *sukhadārā;* Tulsidas uses an unusual compound here, the second element of which is a feminine noun connoting a wife. The meaning seems to be "one who gives pleasure."

14  The sticky white sap of the sacred banyan tree (in Hindi, *vaṭ, bargad*) is used by many sadhus to mat their hair into dense, tangled masses (*jaṭā*), signaling their indifference to worldly grooming.

15  On Shibi, Dadhichi, and Bali, see n. 32 to the first section, "An Enthronement Thwarted." King Harishchandra surrendered his kingdom, together with his family and himself as slaves, to the sage Vishvamitra in fulfillment of an oath. In another famous puranic story, King Rantidev, who had sworn to give anything to guests, was sorely tested by the gods who, when he and his family were on the verge of starvation, presented themselves as hungry visitors of various social classes; when the king compassionately gave their last sip of drinking water to an untouchable, the gods were satisfied and blessed him and his family.

16  In Valmiki's version, the speech, displaying great anger toward the king, is indeed reported to Dasarath by the minister (though it is curiously absent from the scene of his last dialogue with the exiles). See *Rāmāyaṇa* 2.52.18–22.

17  "Brother-in-law," *devara;* a culturally weighted word for a husband's younger brother, connoting a relationship that is ideally cherishing and protective.

18  "Boatman," *kevaṭa;* an occupational term for boatmen and fishermen; "Kevat" is commonly used in Hindi as the name of this beloved character.

19  See the Ahalya episode, 1.210–211.

20  The term *aṭapaṭe* can connote "confounding," "stammering," "enigmatic," "unintelligible," or "twisted," but also (according

to the *Mānaspīyūṣ*) "rustic," "clumsy," "rough" (4.446). It points to Kevat's ingenious concealment of his devotion behind a "pragmatic" concern that simultaneously displays his awareness of Ram's divinity.

21 This order, too, is sweetly "devious," for the original (*utārahi pārū*) lacks an object. Seemingly, it means "Take [me/us] across!" but it can also refer to Kevat's conveying himself and his lineage over the sea of rebirth by washing Ram's feet, a theme that the next *dohā* reinforces.

22 In Vaishnava myth, the Ganga originates from Vishnu's toenails. The previous *caupāī* alludes to Vishnu's three world-conquering steps when in the guise of his dwarf avatar. In keeping with the playful yet theologically charged mood of this passage, the phrase I have rendered as "became entranced" *(moha mati karaṣī)* is ambiguous: it may refer to Ganga herself, or to all who witnessed this event (e.g., the gods, who will appear in the next verse) having their intellect "drawn toward" loving infatuation *(moha).*

23 "Ferrying his ancestors to salvation," *pitara pāru kari.* More literally, this means simply "bringing [his] fathers across," though *pitara* can refer to forebears of both genders, and a crossing of the proverbial sea of rebirth is implied.

24 Literally, "having worshiped *pārthiva.*" *Pārthiva* means "made of earth" and is assumed by commentators to refer to a temporary lingam of clay or sand on a riverbank. Hence, Ram is understood to propitiate Shiva for success on his journey into exile.

25 Literally, Ganga declares that Sita's glance confers "[the state of being a] *lokapāla*"—one of the deities who preside over the quadrants of space.

26 "Reassured them," *kari paritoṣu;* literally, "having satisfied them." Presumably he explained his need to accompany Ram and that he would be gone for only a short time.

27 "The king of pilgrimage places," *tīratharāja;* this is Prayag (in modern Allahabad), the confluence of the Ganga, Yamuna, and (invisible) Sarasvati rivers. Tulsidas has already fulsomely praised this holy place in a passage in *Bālkāṇḍ* in which it is likened to the companionship of saintly people (1.2.3–3.1). Here, in an extended simile that makes up the rest of the stanza, the features of the site are likened to the entourage and accouterments of a king.

28 This deity, a form of Vishnu (identified simply as "Madhav" by the poet), is enshrined near the confluence at Prayag.

29 Among the trappings of a king are fly whisks, traditionally made of yak tail and with a silver handle, that are used to agitate the air around him. Since the hairs may be white or black, the allusion to the dark- and light-colored water of (respectively) Yamuna and Ganga is apt.

30 "Triple confluence," *benī* (an abbreviation of *trivenī*, or "three strands"); the spot where the Yamuna and Ganga meet and are believed to be joined by the subterranean River Sarasvati.

31 Literally, they felt "with-master/protector" (*sanātha*), a term also used to connote a child or woman whose father/husband is alive and able to provide care and protection.

32 This half verse begins a puzzling passage (of four *caupāīs* and a *dohā*—the standard length of an *Ayodhyākānd* stanza) that appears to have been inserted into the narrative, for the villagers' criticism of Ram's parents resumes abruptly two lines before *dohā* 2.111. Though it seems to be an interpolation, its reported presence in the oldest manuscripts has led most commentators to accept it as an addition by Tulsi himself. They offer theories about the identity of the mysterious young ascetic: that he is Hanuman or the fire god Agni in disguise, or the poet himself, entering the narrative through a meditative vision. The most enigmatic phrase in the passage, and perhaps the key to its interpretation, is *kavi alakhita gati* (literally "poet-invisible-state," translated as "poet yet unknown"). This may mean that the identity of the visitor is unknown to the poet (hence, a deity in disguise) or, alternatively, that he is a "poet yet unknown" (that is, Tulsidas himself, as a young sadhu). Although the Kashiraj edition retains the passage, it gives no number to its *dohā*, yielding an *Ayodhyākānd* of 325 stanzas; the Gita Press and other popular editions do not follow this practice. For extended discussion of the manuscript evidence and all theories, see *Mānaspīyūṣ* 4.482–490.

33 This may equally be read: "considering her his mother, and she blessed her child."

34 This half line abruptly returns to the villagers' comments, which were interrupted after 2.110.3 by the mysterious ascetic's arrival. The vocative *sakhi*, referring to a woman's

female friend, implies that women are speaking.

35  Yamuna, along with her twin brother Yama (god of death), are considered the children of the sun.

36  That is, astrological texts must wrongly identify the marks of royal destiny, which would preclude such a humble mode of travel.

37  "Wishing stones," *suramani;* literally, "god-stones." The allusion is to the legendary stone, also called *cintāmaṇi,* that is believed to grant any desire.

38  "Bay leaf tree," *tamāla;* a type of evergreen laurel. Its dark green leaves, aromatic and flavorful, are used in both traditional medicine and food preparation.

39  Commentators interpret this to mean that she did not want to slight the village women by avoiding their innocent question, yet felt too shy to answer it (by convention, noble women did not forthrightly identify or speak of their husbands). According to the nineteenth-century commentator known as Punjabiji, by looking at the earth (from which she was born), Sita felt the embarrassment of speaking of her husband in her mother's presence (*Mānaspīyuṣ* 4.505). "Fair" translates *barabaranī*—literally, "of excellent color"—which traditionally connotes a light complexion.

40  The divine cobra, Shesh, supports the earth on his upraised hood.

41  The male and female of the "ruddy goose" species (*cakvā, cakvī*) were believed to mate only during the day and be separated at nightfall.

42  This apparently refers to 2.120.1–3, in which it is stated that the divine trio cannot have been made by Brahma, the creator. Being unable to duplicate their beauty, he consigned them to the forest.

43  This simile (along with the two that follow it) has rightly occas-ioned much commentary. Tulsidas likens Sita to *māyā,* a feminine word that is often translated "illusion" and some-times personified as a goddess. Connoting the divine power to create form and appearance, it can have negative connotations in some philosophical systems (notably for the nondualist or Advaita school). Vaishnavas, however, generally regard it as an aspect of God's creative play, and Tulsi, highlighting Sita's luminous beauty and mediatory status, seems to favor this understanding. For numerous interpretations, see *Mānaspīyūṣ* 4.518–522.

44 Rati is the wife of Kama, god of love, whose inseparable companion is springtime.

45 The asterism Rohini is considered the moon god's wife and Mercury (*budh*), his son.

46 The poet's remark that Sita walked "watchfully" or "fearfully" (*sabhītā*) is interpreted by commentators to mean that she did not want to place her feet in her husband's footprints and thereby efface them. Lakshman's manner of walking reflects the custom of honoring a deity or sacred object by keeping it to one's right (e.g., when circumambulating it).

47 "Gave them a charming place to rest," *āśrama diye suhāe.* Some old manuscripts offer *āsana* for *āśrama,* yielding "gave them a charming place to sit."

48 The word I have translated as "seer" is *vipra,* literally "trembler," which may once have alluded to ancient seers who recited the Vedic hymns in a trance-like state. Like *bhūsura* ("gods of the earth") in the next half line, it is conventionally glossed as "Brahman," though in the context it clearly refers to forest-dwelling ascetics.

49 "Ramparts," *setu;* this word connotes a restraining barrier, such as a wall, dam, causeway, or border. Valmiki calls Ram the protector of the *setu* of *śruti,* Vedic revelation. The eight-line verse that follows, expanding on this, is in lyrical *chand* meter.

50 "Cooling balm," *candana;* literally "sandalwood," but here understood to be the fragrant, cooling paste made by mixing ground sandalwood dust with water.

51 "Initiates," *adhikārī;* those who possess the authority to have certain knowledge.

52 According to the *Mānaspīyūṣ* (4.538), Tulsidas alludes to a popular folk saying.

53 The *cātak* is a kind of cuckoo that is believed to drink only raindrops.

54 The wild Himalayan goose (*haṃsa,* though here the female of the species, *haṃsinī,* is invoked, to accord with the gender of "tongue" in Hindi) is said to feed on pearls in Lake Manasarovar.

55 Tulsidas alludes to the puranic tale of how this devoted wife, Anasuya, brought a stream of the Ganga to provide water to her husband, the sage Atri, during a long drought. Anasuya herself will appear in *Araṇyakāṇḍ* (3.5). He then puns on the apparent occurrence within the river's name (which is generally understood

to mean "having a gentle current") of the word *ḍākinī,* denoting a type of witch believed to cause miscarriages and to eat the young of human beings and animals.

56 Since the hill of Chitrakut, today identified with a pilgrimage place on the border of Uttar Pradesh and Madhya Pradesh states, is thought to have been located close to Valmiki's ashram, Ram's journey to it does not require further description.

57 This is presumably Vishvakarma, builder and craftsman of the gods.

58 That is, the gods described their suffering owing to Ravan's depredations.

59 These names (here presumably referencing mundane people and not gods in disguise as in the previous stanza) identify hunter-gatherer communities traditionally considered violent and impure by upper-caste standards. Ram's kindness to them, and their loving response to him, must be understood in this context.

60 The nonvegetarian diet and hunting regimen of Valmiki's Raghu brothers is barely hinted at here, in the participial phrase *phirata ahera* ("roaming on the hunt"), which the *Mānaspīyūṣ* obliquely glosses as "bearing a hunting bow" (4.587). Instead, the game animals, like everyone else, delight in the vision of Ram's beauty.

61 Mekala identifies a section of the Vindhya Range in which rise the headwaters of the great Narmada River.

62 The female of a type of waterfowl, the ruddy shelduck or Brahminy duck, also called *cakvī,* believed to suffer separation from its mate by night.

63 "Grants cosmic lordship," *lokapa hohī;* literally, "makes one a world-guardian," one of the deities who preside over the quadrants of space.

64 This half line may also be read, "and Lakshman and Sita served the Raghu hero."

65 That is, it did not become praiseworthy by dying.

66 The symptoms described in the preceding lines are all said to be signs of imminent death. However, Sumantra's soul lingers on in the hope of seeing Ram again in fourteen years.

67 "Safely," *kusala;* this word, connoting a state of well-being, may be read here as referring either to the minister's return or to his safe delivery of the princes into exile. Either way, it is used sarcastically

to suggest his own disgust at what he must report.

68 "A life of hellish torment," *jātanā sarīru;* literally a "torture-body," supposedly acquired by a sinner who must undergo punishment in Yama's subterranean realm.

69 The moon is considered the repository of the nectar of immortality (*amṛta*).

70 In a famous Mahabharata tale, King Yayati falls from heaven as a result of his excessive pride. See *Mahābhārata* 1.81–88.

71 This legendary vulture, whose wings were burned when he flew too close to the sun, will later be encountered by Ram's monkey allies (4.28).

72 In Sanskrit, Shringaverapura, the name of the Nishad settlement.

73 Some commentators interpret this half line as, "Lakshman carried their weapons and placed them on board."

74 This quatrain is in the lyrical *harigītikā chand* meter. Though it expands on Ram's speech as reported to the king by Sumantra, Tulsi adds his own poetic signature in the final line.

75 An alternative interpretation of this half line yields, "It is prudent not to abandon a throne, once gained."

76 This is an allusion to a passage in Valmiki's text in which Sumantra reports that Lakshman gave a stinging rebuke to the king, including the statement that he would no longer regard him as his father (*Rāmāyaṇa* 2.52.18–22).

77 See note 52 to the first section, "An Enthronement Thwarted."

78 That is, in preparation for leaving the body.

79 The reference is to Valmiki's account of an ascetic whom the youthful Dasarath accidentally killed while hunting; the ascetic's old, blind father, just before dying, cursed the king that he would similarly expire from grief over the loss of a son. See *Rāmāyaṇa* 2.56–58.

80 That is, the king is as valued among people as eyesight is among bodily faculties.

# GLOSSARY

AVADH (*avadha;* unconquerable)
the kingdom and city of Ayodhya

BHARADVAJ a Vedic sage
residing at Prayag and one of the
narrators of the *Mānas*

*cakor* the chukar partridge that,
according to legend, forever
craves the sight of the moon
and feeds on its beams (and
occasionally on fire); a poetic
trope for fervent lovers and
devotees

*cātaka* a type of cuckoo, believed
to drink only raindrops that fall
during a particular period in the
monsoon season

GAURI (*gaurī;* fair, light-
complexioned) Parvati

*haṃsa* mythical bird that lives in
the Himalayas, feeds on pearls,
and has the ability to separate
milk from water; a literary trope
for the enlightened soul, it is
often depicted by Tulsidas flying
above or floating on Lake Manas;
sometimes identified with the
bar-headed goose that breeds in
Central Asia and winters in India,
crossing the Himalayas in its
annual migrations

*kok* a type of ostrich or goose, said
to suffer separation from its mate
at each nightfall

MANU primordial king and
lawgiver, to whom a famous

treatise on dharma is attributed

MAYA (*māyā;* fabrication,
semblance) the illusory power
of the gods, often personified as
a goddess

MITHILA Sita's parents' kingdom
and an epithet for its king

RAMCHANDRA (*rāmacandra;*
Ram, the moon) epithet of Ram,
highlighting his beauty

RATI (*rati;* passion) the wife of
Kama, god of love

SHANKAR (*śaṅkara;* auspicious,
benevolent) Shiva

VAIDEHI (*vaidehī;* daughter of
Videha) epithet of Sita

# BIBLIOGRAPHY

*Editions and Translations*

*Kalyāṇ Mānasāṅk.* 1938. Edited by Hanuman Prasad Poddar. Commentary by Chinmanlal Gosvami and Nanddulare Vajpeyi. Gorakhpur: Gita Press.

*Mānaspīyūṣ.* 1950. Edited by Anjaninandansharan. 7 vols. Gorakhpur: Gita Press.

*Rāmcaritmānas.* 1962. Edited by Vishvanath Prasad Mishra. Ramnagar, Varanasi: All-India Kashiraj Trust.

*Tulsī granthāvalī, pratham khaṇḍ,* vol. 1: *Rāmcaritmānas.* 1973. Edited by Ramchandra Shukla et al. Varanasi: Nāgarīpracāriṇī Sabhā.

Atkins, A. G., trans. 1954. *The Ramayana of Tulsidas.* 2 vols. New Delhi: Birla Academy of Art and Culture.

Bahadur, Satya Prakash, trans. 1978. *Rāmcaritmānas.* Varanasi: Prācya Prakāśan.

Dev, Satya, trans. 2010. *Tulsi Ramayan in English Verse.* New Delhi: Vitasta Publishing.

Dhody, Chandan Lal, trans. 1987. *The Gospel of Love: An English Rendering of Tulasi's Shri Rama Charita Manasa.* New Delhi: Siddharth Publications.

Goswami, Chimanlal, trans. 1949. *Śrīrāmacaritamānasa.* Gorakhpur: Gita Press.

Growse, Frederic Salmon, trans. 1978. *The Rāmāyaṇa of Tulasīdāsa.* New Delhi: Motilal Banarsidass. Original edition, Kanpur: E. Samuel, 1891.

Hill, W. Douglas P., trans. 1952. *The Holy Lake of the Acts of Rāma.* London: Oxford University Press.

Lutgendorf, Philip, trans. 2016. *The Epic of Ram.* Vols. 1 and 2. Cambridge, Mass.: Harvard University Press.

Nagar, Shanti Lal, trans. 2014. *Shri Ramcharitmanas.* 3 vols. Delhi: Parimal Publications.

Prasad, R. C., trans. 1988. *Tulasidasa's Shriramacharitamanasa* (The Holy Lake of the Acts of Rama). Delhi: Motilal Banarsidass.

*Other Sources*

Gandhi, Mohandas K. 1968. *An Autobiography, or, The Story of My*

*Experiments with Truth.* Translated by Mahadev Desai. Ahmedabad: Navjivan Publishing House. Original edition, 1927–1929.

Grierson, George. 1977. "Tulasīdāsa, the Great Poet of Medieval India." In *Tulasidasa: His Mind and Art,* ed. Nagendra. New Delhi: National Publishing House, pp. 1–6.

Lutgendorf, Philip. 1991. *The Life of a Text: Performing the* Rāmcaritmānas *of Tulsidas.* Berkeley: University of California Press.

———, trans. 1994. "Sundarkand." *Journal of Vaishnava Studies* 2, 4: 91–127.

———, trans. 1995. "*Ramcaritmanas:* From Book Five, The Beautiful Book." In *The Norton Anthology of World Masterpieces,* expanded edition, ed. Maynard Mack. New York: W. W. Norton, 1: 2316–2332.

———, trans. 2001. "From the Ramcaritmanas of Tulsidas, Book Five: Sundar Kand." *Indian Literature* 45, 3 (203): 143–181.

Macfie, John Mandeville. 1930. *The Ramayan of Tulsidas, or the Bible of Northern India.* Edinburgh: T. & T. Clark.

*Mahābhārata.* 1933–1959. Critically edited in 19 volumes. General editor, Vishnu Sitaram Sukthankar. Poona: Bhandarkar Oriental Research Institute.

McGregor, Stuart. 2003. "The Progress of Hindi, Part 1." In *Literary Cultures in History: Reconstructions from South Asia,* ed. Sheldon Pollock. Berkeley: University of California Press, pp. 912–957.

Orsini, Francesca. 1998. "Tulsī Dās as a Classic." In *Classics of Modern South Asian Literature,* ed. Rupert Snell and I. M. P. Raeside. Wiesbaden: Harrassowitz, pp. 119–141.

*Rāmāyaṇa.* 1960–1975. *The Vālmīki-Rāmāyaṇa.* Critically edited in 7 volumes. General editors, Govindlal Hargovind Bhatt and Umakant Premanand Shah. Baroda: Oriental Institute.

Stasik, Danuta. 2009. "Perso-Arabic Lexis in the *Rāmcaritmānas* of Tulsīdās." *Cracow Indological Studies* 11: 67–86.

# INDEX

297

# ABOUT THE BOOK

Murty Classical Library of India volumes are designed by Rathna Ramanathan and Guglielmo Rossi. Informed by the history of the Indic book and drawing inspiration from polyphonic classical music, the series design is based on the idea of "unity in diversity," celebrating the individuality of each language while bringing them together within a cohesive visual identity.

The Hindi text of this book is set in the Murty Hindi typeface, commissioned by Harvard University Press and designed by John Hudson and Fiona Ross. The proportions and styling of the characters are in keeping with the typographic tradition established by the renowned Nirnaya Sagar Press, with a deliberate reduction of the typically high degree of stroke modulation. The result is a robust, modern design.

The English text is set in Antwerp, designed by Henrik Kubel from A2-TYPE and chosen for its versatility and balance with the Indic typography. The design is a free-spirited amalgamation and interpretation of the archives of type at the Museum Plantin-Moretus in Antwerp.

All the fonts commissioned for the Murty Classical Library of India will be made available, free of charge, for non-commercial use. For more information about the typography and design of the series, please visit *http://www.hup.harvard.edu/mcli*.

Printed on acid-free paper by Maple Press, York, Pennsylvania.

Joy of the Raghus, dearer than breath!       4
Too many days have passed, living without you.
Oh Janaki, Lakshman! And oh, best of Raghus—
bounteous cloud to the rainbird of your father's soul!"

Saying "Ram, Ram," and "Ram," again and again,     155
and then yet again saying "Ram, Ram, Ram!"
the king left his body in separation's anguish
and went to the realm of the gods.

In living and dying, Dasarath won fulfillment,    1
and his pure fame spread through countless worlds.
Living, he beheld the moon of Ram's face;
parted from Ram, he preferred to die.
All the queens wept, distraught with grief.    2
Recounting his beauty, nobility, strength, and glory,
they gave vent to every kind of lamentation
and fell to the ground again and again.
Male and female servants grieved sorely, too,    3
and weeping spread to every home in the city.
"Today, the sun of the solar clan has set—
the apex of dharma, treasury of virtue and beauty!"
Everyone heaped abuse on Kaikeyi,    4
who had deprived the whole world of its eyes.[80]
So the night passed in lamentation,
until all the eminent seers arrived.

१५६ तब बसिष्ट मुनि समय सम कहि अनेक इतिहास ।
सोक नेवारेउ सबहि कर निज बिग्यान प्रकास ॥